D0968738

WILLIAM ARCHER

PUBLISHED ON THE FOUNDATION
ESTABLISHED IN MEMORY OF
OLIVER BATY CUNNINGHAM
OF THE CLASS OF 1917, YALE COLLEGE

Photo by] [*J. Russell & Sons*

WILLIAM ARCHER

WILLIAM ARCHER

LIFE · WORK
AND FRIENDSHIPS

by

LIEUT.-COLONEL C. ARCHER

NEW HAVEN
YALE UNIVERSITY PRESS
1931

THE OLIVER BATY CUNNINGHAM MEMORIAL PUBLICATION FUND

The present volume is the eleventh work published by the Yale University Press on the Oliver Baty Cunningham Memorial Publication Fund. This Foundation was established May 8, 1920, by a gift from Frank S. Cunningham, Esq., of Chicago, to Yale University, in memory of his son, Captain Oliver Baty Cunningham, 15th United States Field Artillery, who was born in Chicago September 17, 1894, and was graduated from Yale College in the Class of 1917. As an undergraduate he was distinguished alike for high scholarship and for proved capacity in leadership among his fellows, as evidenced by his selection as Gordon Brown Prize Man from his class. He received his commission as Second-Lieutenant, United States Field Artillery, at the First Officers' Training Camp at Fort Sheridan, and in December, 1917, was detailed abroad for service, receiving subsequently the Distinguished Service Medal. He was killed while on active duty near Thiaucourt, France, on September 17, 1918, the twenty-fourth anniversary of his birth.

PRINTED IN GREAT BRITAIN BY
UNWIN BROTHERS LTD., WOKING

TO THE MEMORY OF

FRANCES ELIZABETH ARCHER

A YOUNGER SISTER OF "THE LADY WITH THE LAMP"

De tout temps, elle fut la personne qui demanda le moins à son voisin ce qu'il fallait penser.

SAINTE-BEUVE (*of Mme du Deffand*)

Criticism should not be querulous and wasting, all knife and root-puller, but guiding, instructive, inspiring; a south wind, not an east wind.

EMERSON

The great, dominant, all-controlling fact of this life is the innate bias of the human spirit, not towards evil, as the theologians tell us, but towards good.

WILLIAM ARCHER (*Knowledge and Character*)

PREFACE

In glancing through the pages of this book, I have been struck by its incompleteness as a record of William Archer's friendships. The names of many men with whom, at one period or another, he was closely allied, and with whom he was in cordial relations to the end—such men as George Moore and Graham Wallas in England, George Pierce Baker and William Lyon Phelps in America, Albert Feuillerat in France, Leon Kellner in Austria, Otto Jespersen in Denmark, Christen Collin in Norway—appear, if they appear at all, only in a passing mention. The fates that govern the survival and the subject-matter of letters are mainly responsible for this defect; for, to have any interest at all for the general reader, a friendship must, as it were, be shown in action.

To all who have contributed letters written by William Archer, or have aided me with reminiscences of him, my grateful acknowledgements are due. Most of the letters reproduced are from the large Granville-Barker, Murray, Robertson, and Shaw collections. But many other letters, even when not quoted, have furnished valuable data. I must not omit to thank Mrs. John Corbin for Archer's spirited account of his experiences at an American health-resort.

For recollections I have, in particular, to thank Mr. Edward Rimbault Dibdin, Mr. J. T. Grein, Mr. Alexander Philip, Sir Arthur Pinero, and Miss Elizabeth Robins. And I deeply regret that, while this book was in the making, Sir Hector Mackenzie, Archer's oldest friend and one of his dearest, has passed beyond the reach of thanks.

For their kindness in sanctioning the publication of letters to William Archer I am indebted to Mr. Winthrop Ames, Sir James Barrie, Viscountess Bryce,

Mr. Harley Granville-Barker, Mrs. Thomas Hardy, Miss Mildred Howells, the late Statsminister Sigurd Ibsen, Professor Gilbert Murray, Mr. Lloyd Osbourne (representing Robert Louis Stevenson and Mrs. Stevenson), Sir Arthur Pinero, the Right Hon. J. M. Robertson, Mrs. Theodore Roosevelt, Mme Edmond Rostand, Mr. George Bernard Shaw, Sir William Watson, and the late Mr. Charles Whibley (representing William Ernest Henley); as well as to the representatives of Sir Edmund Gosse, Henry James, Brander Matthews, and Francis Thompson.

The authorities of the British Drama League have been most courteous in facilitating my use of material from the collection of theatrical books and mementoes bequeathed by William Archer to their Library—where (in the room where Thomas Hardy served his apprenticeship as an architect) the critic's bust looks down on the students and lovers of the stage who frequent the place. And, for leave to reproduce the illustrations at pp. 72 and 256, I have to thank Mrs. George Halkett and Mr. Max Beerbohm.

Finally, both I and any readers this book may have are deeply indebted to Mr. Harley Granville-Barker for his valuable criticism and advice.

The numerous Norwegian words and phrases occurring in William Archer's letters to me have been translated (except in cases where the meaning seemed plain), the English equivalents being placed in square brackets. Nearly all quotations, where the contrary is not obvious, are from Archer's own writings.

C. ARCHER

WORPLESDON,
16th March, 1931

CONTENTS

ILLUSTRATIONS

WILLIAM ARCHER

I

PARENTAGE

On Sunday, May 25, 1924, seven months before his death, William Archer noted, in the concise diary which, in the comparative leisure of his last years, he had begun to keep:

"Went solitary walk, and reflected how astonishingly fortunate my life had been in many respects."

Character and intellectual force being chief factors in shaping a man's fortunes, we, who are in a better position to estimate those factors in his case, need feel no astonishment at the measure of success that his life attained. Yet in some respects the Fates undoubtedly stood his friend, and not least in respect of his immediate ancestry on both sides, in which we can clearly trace the building up of the intellect and character which, in a wider sense than that generally given to words, were to "make his fortune".

The founder of the Archer family of Perth is reported by irreverent family tradition to have "come to Scotland with Cromwell and set up a public-house". However that may be, the family makes its first appearance in written record when, in 1672, John Archer, "son to Andrew Archer, maltman-burgess," was apprenticed to the mystery of the ancient Incorporation of Glovers, well known to readers of *The Fair Maid of Perth.* John became a freeman-glover in 1684, and the records of the Incorporation show that one or more of his descendants in each generation availed themselves of their hereditary right to join the Guild and enjoy its privileges, even after the family had long ceased to practise the glover's trade.

In the early years of the nineteenth century we find Charles Archer, fourth in descent from John, the senior member of Charles Archer and Son, a firm of timber merchants doing a considerable trade with Norway and Sweden. Things seem to have gone badly with the firm in the years of business depression following the long war, and in 1825 William Archer, the son and junior partner, attracted by an opening in the lobster trade and by the cheapness of living in Norway, determined to try his fortunes in that country. During a business journey in Norway, six years before, he had fallen deeply in love with the little town of Larvik, on a beautiful bay of the southern coast; for he was a devoted lover of the "romantic" in scenery (so his diary always terms it), and became in later years a notable landscape gardener. Buying and fitting out the schooner *Pomona* at Greenock, he embarked in her with his wife (born Julia Walker) and their already numerous children, and, passing through the Forth and Clyde Canal, set sail from Grangemouth, and landed at Larvik in the autumn of 1825. Next year the family found a permanent abode in an old timber house, standing alone on a promontory of tumbled rocks and garden ground that juts from the north-eastern curve of the bay near the Custom House. Tolderodden (so the property was called—as who should say, "Gauger's Point")[1] was acquired in exchange for the *Pomona* and a small payment in cash. Here the couple lived (Julia Archer never saw Scotland again) till their deaths at a ripe old age; here they brought up their large family in plain living and straight

[1] Or, according to some, "Toller's Point", from the name of a previous owner.

thinking; and from here they sent out many tall sons to seek their fortunes in the world, chiefly in Australia, where several members of the mother's clan were already, in the thirties, prosperously established.

The upbringing of the sons and daughters was, in the beginning, Spartan enough, for means were very narrow and the family continued to grow. But the place was a paradise for boys, where, in the words of one of them, they had their fill of "boating, swimming, skating, running on ski, scrambling among the rocks, and tumbling into the fjord which bounded the property on three sides". And in the course of years the house was extended, and the garden ground, at first something of a wilderness, was converted, by the industry and taste of the father of the family, into one of the beauty-spots of the south Norwegian coast.

As the elder sons began to prosper in the world (with a modest prosperity, for the family had a curious talent for evading great wealth), life became easier in the old house. In the eyes of those who had passed their boyhood there, nothing was too good for "Odden"; and the place drew them back with a magnetism which time rather increased than lessened. The unmarried sons came home there, one by one, to set up their nest; the married came as often, and with as many of their children, as they could. By the third quarter of the century the place had come to be looked on, by a great tribe in Norway, England, and Australia, as the Mecca of their race. The old house overflowed all through the short, bright summers with holiday-makers of all ages—for the younger generation, indeed, holidays hardly counted as holidays unless they were spent at Tolderodden.

The sixth son, Thomas Archer, born at Glasgow in

1823, went out into the world at an even earlier age than his elders. In 1837, when he had but just turned fourteen and had enjoyed some four years' schooling, an opportunity offered for sending him to Australia under an elder brother's escort; and, encouraged by the opinion of a discerning English friend that "Tom was a fellow who would educate himself", the parents decided to let him go. The friend's prophecy was in some measure fulfilled, for, in the course of twelve years' strenuous work in Australia, as apprentice on his grand-uncle's run, and later as shepherd, drover, explorer, and finally squatter, we have glimpses of him: praying for rain to detain him at a station where there happened to be a small library; reading and re-reading Snorre Sturlesön's *Sagas of the Kings* and any other books he can lay hands on; and, when thrown on his own resources with no companion but a black boy or two, solacing his loneliness by singing or reciting Scottish and Norwegian ballads, or by inditing burlesque epistles in English or Norwegian verse to his brothers or his friends in Norway.

In 1849 came the Californian gold-rush, and, moved partly by the usual hopes of the gold-seeker and partly by homesickness (for "California was more than half way home"), Thomas Archer set out for San Francisco, leaving his Australian interests in the hands of his brother and partner. After three years, two of them disastrous, of the hardest manual labour at the diggings, varied with a little Indian fighting, the adventurer at last accumulated a small pile of gold dust—small, but sufficient to enable him to set his face homeward with an easy mind. But a happy fate lay in wait for him by the way. At Perth, where he had gone, in passing, to visit relations and see a younger brother, he became acquainted with the family of his brother's employer, James Morison, and straightway fell in love with the second daughter, Grace Lindsay Morison. The natural misgivings of a home-keeping family were, with some difficulty, overcome; the young couple were soon formally engaged, and their marriage followed in 1853.

Writing in 1879 to a friend on "the insight fiction gives us into the characters of others", William Archer illustrated his thesis by the remark: "I could not have appreciated my father's character as I do, had I not studied Colonel Newcome." Thomas Archer might, indeed, not unaptly have been likened to a Thomas Newcome safeguarded by a more developed sense of humour and by a fortunate marriage.

His wife came of a family, believed to be remotely of Norwegian extraction, which had been settled in Perth for at least two hundred years, and for three generations had furnished the Fair City with burghers of some note. From a very early date the Morisons seem to have been engaged in one branch or another of the book-trade. Robert Morison (1722–91)—who, when quite a young man, had been appointed Postmaster[1] of Perth, and who held that office for many years—had become by 1753 a stationer and bookseller, and a few years later we find that he has set up a publishing business. Under his son James and his grandson David the business was greatly extended, and the Morison Press became an institution on which the city might reasonably plume itself, turning out annually from 20,000 to 30,000 volumes of standard literature, including such works as *The*

[1] Tradition has it that when the Highland army was round the city in "the '45", he was waylaid one dark night when carrying the Royal mails. Spurring his horse and laying about him with his hanger, he broke through and escaped, and, on reaching his destination, found a man's severed hand still gripping his bridle-rein.

Scottish Poets, Thomson's *Seasons, The Poems of Ossian,* Cook's *Voyages,* and the *Encyclopædia Perthensis,* an ambitious work in twenty-three volumes, highly esteemed in its day. Both James and his son David were reputed notable linguists and Hebrew scholars; both produced volumes of Biblical exegesis; and David (who was "the well-known antiquary, Mr. Morison of Perth", so freely quoted by Sir Walter Scott in the notes to *The Fair Maid of Perth*) was, in addition, artist-lithographer, chemist, and inventor. He was perhaps the most remarkable member of a family which was, a local historian says, "for many generations the literary salt of the town".

David's younger brother, James Morison the second, the father of Thomas Archer's bride, had a full share of the family love of literature, and was, besides, a man of much general ability and force of character; qualities which, by the middle of the century, had enabled him to build up a flourishing business as actuary and accountant, and had made him a leading elder in the Perth congregation of the Glasite or Sandemanian Church, to which many members of the family belonged.

The principles of this body, which modelled itself on the Primitive Christian congregations, while extremely strict in matters of doctrine and morals, were much more indulgent in things indifferent than those held at the time by other Scottish sects. The Sabbath, it is true, was most strictly observed. But harmless gaieties, such as dancing, amateur acting, etc., were allowed and even encouraged amongst the young folk on all fitting occasions; literature, as we have seen, was held in high esteem in some families of the connection; and the theatre was by no means banned. Moreover, while the study of the Bible and attendance on the prescribed religious exercises were an obligatory and all-important part of the nurture of the younger generation, no pressure or persuasion might lawfully be employed to induce them to become members of the Church.

James Morison's stern religious doctrines, and his sense of the responsibilities attaching to his position in the Glasite communion, gave a certain austerity to his walk and conversation, which inspired not a little awe in his own family circle, and even beyond it. But the impression produced by this severity was softened by his engaging simplicity of character and his overflowing sense of humour. He had an endless fund of good stories, which he told with irresistible gusto. It was, indeed, a pleasant thing to see the old gentleman in later days, over the light but excellent late supper which always closed the Sunday evening, relaxing after the strain of the day-long religious exercises, setting the table in a roar with one tale after another in the broadest Scotch, and laughing at them himself till the tears ran down. His devotion to the grave studies of theology did not interfere with his keen relish for the best in profane literature; he has even been known to quote Shakespeare[1] in the pulpit, not, of course, by name, but as "one who, humanly speaking, had the deepest knowledge of the heart of man"; and his nearest approach to an imprecation, uttered when he missed an easy stroke at croquet or parlour billiards, was: "Villainous saltpetre!" In his old age he was a great reader of novels. "Most of them", wrote his grandson many years later, "he professed to despise, and did, in a sense; but I can see him now, pacing up and down his study, eagerly narrating the plot of the story he had just been reading, and chuckling over tit-bits of character in it. . . . I have since learnt that one of the books he

[1] Dogberry's boast of being "a fellow that hath had losses".

read and was far from despising was *Evan Harrington* —at a time when the name of Meredith meant nothing to the ordinary novel-reader."

Many members of James Morison's family had inherited a love of books, and, severe as was the discipline enforced in the household, it did not stand in the way of their indulging this love. In this, as in many other Scottish families, the name of "Sir Walter" was held in reverence, and the children were turned loose at an early age into the fair domain of the Waverley Novels, as into a garden where no poisonous plants were to be feared. Dickens and Thackeray's books, too, as they appeared, were eagerly devoured. In the daughter who became the wife of Thomas Archer a strong and discriminating taste for reading was clearly marked, while she had inherited besides much of her father's practical ability and force of will.

The pair had planned to live their life in Australia. But the climate, in the rough conditions then prevailing, proved unfavourable to the young wife's health, and they lost their first child soon after its birth. Reluctantly, in 1855, they turned their backs for the time on the Colony, and, after a stormy and perilous voyage round the Horn, reached Scotland again, and settled at first in Perth. Here, on September 23, 1856, William Archer was born, the eldest of a family which numbered in the end five sons and four daughters.

II

1856–1876

BOYHOOD AND YOUTH

THE story of William Archer's first fourteen years is punctuated by repeated changes of scene. Thomas Archer had no settled occupation, for his occasional essays in farming invariably proved too costly to be pursued. Want of settled employment inclines to wandering; the family moved from hired house to hired house; and the children grew up without finding any local home to divide their affection with the earthly paradise in Norway, which they saw only at intervals.

In 1857–58, when the eldest son was an infant, and again in 1860, when he was four years old, Thomas and Grace Archer lived for a time in Larvik, close by the old house at Tolderodden—"the first place I can remember", William Archer wrote long after, "and the last that I shall forget." By the time the second visit ended the boy had lost nearly all his English, and spoke nothing but Norwegian. This, again, he forgot completely after the return to Scotland; but it is perhaps not too fanciful to suppose that the spirit of the language had entered into his blood, rendering it easier for him to master it in later years.

There followed sojourns, each of a few years, at Arndean in Clackmannanshire, near the little town of Dollar, where the eldest son had his first formal schooling; at Scone, near Perth, where he attended the Academy, and, among other notable schoolfellows, had Patrick Geddes for a playmate; and at a small manor near Lymington, on the Solent. At

Lymington the twelve-year-old boy had his memorable first experience of "a real theatre", thus described[1] by him in later days:

"I was a country-bred child, and none of my family had any connection with the stage, or any particular interest in it; yet I cannot remember the time when the word 'theatre' had not a strange fascination for me. I did not in the least know what a theatre was, but I knew it was one of the things I most wanted to know. 'Pepper's Ghost', with a dumb-show representation of the story of Faust and Marguerite, was the first theatrical entertainment I ever saw, and it made an epoch in my experience. . . . Thenceforward, for years, my great ambition was to possess a toy theatre. The ambition was never realized, for I could no more have bought one than I could have bought Drury Lane, and my mechanical genius was quite inadequate to constructing one. I got the length, however, of tracing the costume-plates in Knight's *Pictorial Shakespeare,* pasting them on cardboard, colouring them, and cutting them out; but, alas! the cardboard invariably curled up, so that not only Richard the Third, but my whole dramatic company, seemed afflicted with incurable spinal curvature. I must have been twelve or thirteen before I saw the inside—or for that matter the outside—of a real theatre. My father had promised to take me for a short yachting cruise in the Solent. We were to lie for some days in Portsmouth Harbour, to visit the 'Victory' and the 'Duke of Wellington', to see a volunteer review, and, in short, to partake in all manner of delights. The whole experience—the sailing, the living on board ship, and everything—was heaven[2]

[1] Epistle Dedicatory to R. W. Lowe, *The Theatrical "World" of 1893.*

[2] The weather must have been unusually propitious; for William Archer was one of the worst of sailors, and suffered severely, some-

itself to me; but I knew there was a theatre at Portsmouth, and what I had chiefly set my heart on from the moment the trip was mentioned was to persuade my father to take me to it. He did; we saw Wallace's *Maritana*; and the daring and wit of Don César de Bazan seemed to me incomparable—almost superhuman."

Already the boy was a voracious reader, and forward for his years, and it must soon have been evident that he had outgrown the resources of the Lymington school, and that more continuous and systematic education was called for. The next move of the family then, made early in 1870, was to Duloch, a large house near Inverkeithing in Fife, within easy reach of Edinburgh; and in September 1870 the youth was entered at the newly established "George Watson's College", and was sent from home for the first time to board in the family of a master.

Looking back on his school and college days, William Archer more than once spoke of the education he received with some severity. "The Scottish school and college course in my day", he says,[1] "was carefully devised so as to prevent even a moderately intelligent boy from coming into anything like vital relation with classical literature"; and he proceeds to give a summary of the modest results, in knowledge and appreciation, of his first-hand "communion with the poets of antiquity".

But it was not only, not even chiefly, for its defects on the classical side that he was disposed to blame the education of his youth. Its chief sin in his eyes was one of which the English system of that day, and

times alarmingly, on his many voyages, till, late in life, he discovered a specific which, to his faith, was the sovereign'st thing on earth against sea-sickness.

[1] Introduction to *Poets of the Younger Generation*, 1901.

of later days, was at least equally guilty. "What is the fundamental task of a liberal education?" he asks.[1] "What should be its constant endeavour? Surely to awaken and keep ever alert the faculty of *wonder* in the human soul. To take life as a matter of course—whether painful or pleasurable—that is the true spiritual death. From the body of that death it is the task of education to deliver us." It was the failure of his education to fulfil this task that was the chief count in his indictment. "Tardy self-education", he says later on, "has taught me to lament my unseeing eye and uncomprehending mind. . . . Too late I have come to life a little. A tree awakens in me a vague reverence, a flower a shamefaced worship; and by these feelings the intensity of life is indefinitely enhanced for me. Was I, forty years ago, such a young dolt as to be quite inaccessible to them? I doubt whether my educators, on the Day of Wrath, will be able to plead that justification."

It may be that there is a tinge of injustice in this indictment. Certainly both English and Scotch systems were far enough from the ideal of a liberal education set forth in *Let Youth But Know*. But we may see reason to think that the failure of the Scotch course to bring him in the best way into touch with "the breath and finer spirit" of history, the humanities, may have been due, in part at least, to the prepossession of his mind with other interests—with contemporary literature and the stage. Again, the mathematical course may well have offered him one of the keys to what he calls "Aladdin's Palace" (the phenomena of Nature); but this key was of little use to him, for, as will be seen, he was strangely incapable of even the elementary branches of mathematics. And it may at least be said for his education

[1] *Let Youth But Know*, 1905, chap. ii.

that, if in a sense a misfit, it at all events gave him more room to grow than he would have found amid the conventions and conformities of an English public school.

Of his Edinburgh school life we have accounts from several of his contemporaries. All agree that he already showed a strong bent towards literature and criticism. As to his social qualities, there is already the same difference of opinion which persisted throughout his life. One account, by a school-fellow a year junior to him, speaks of his going his own way, choosing his own line, and, though friendly enough, not forming any close intimacies. On the other hand, it is certain that he formed one close and warm friendship, which lasted unbroken and undimmed till death; and this friend, speaking no doubt of his Edinburgh career in general, writes: "He made many friends, and retained their friendship for life."

"W. A. was not keen on games", Sir Hector Mackenzie goes on. "His favourite exercise was walking, and we had many walks together. He was an omnivorous reader, and surprised me with his knowledge of Dickens and Thackeray, and of the *Ingoldsby Legends*. He took a good place in his classes, except in mathematics, for which he never showed any aptitude.

"In 1872 an examination was held to award four bursaries of £25 a year, tenable at Edinburgh University for four years, and one of these was awarded to W. A. and another was awarded to me. In November 1872 we matriculated together at Edinburgh University."

Another class-mate[1] says: "He was a tall, big-boned, erect boy, with a frank, open countenance . . . of a peaceable disposition and a very even temper . . .

[1] Mr. Alexander Philip.

C

pleasant to talk to; not very communicative; with a good deal of self-confidence and a touch of genial irony. . . . He was quick-witted and clever, and was able, without, I should think, much burning of the midnight oil, to take a creditable position in his class. He did not seem to have any special ambition to gain medals or prizes. . . . He always carried his school-books in a knapsack suspended on his shoulders; and I think I see him yet, marching off with manly stride, knapsack on his back, at the close of the day. . . . He was a bit of a mystery to us, I think. We understood he was a native of Perth, and also that he had frequently visited Norway and was *au fait* with things Scandinavian; but why or how I fancy we hardly knew." To complete the picture, it may be added that he had a notably hearty appetite, an almost insatiable thirst for cold water, and (though he was never a teetotaller) none, then or afterwards, for alcohol.

In March 1872, having seen their eldest son safely launched in Edinburgh, William Archer's parents set sail, with the rest of their children, for Australia; and here, at Gracemere in Central Queensland, the head-quarters of the firm of squatters in which Thomas Archer was a partner, the family lived for the next eight years.

The withdrawal of his family to the other side of the globe during eight formative years of his life had a marked influence on William Archer's development. Its importance was twofold. On the one hand it favoured his natural bent toward independence and self-reliance, by leaving him far freer from the supervision and control of his elders than the average youth of his age and of his time. His Perth relations, it is true, kept an eye on him from a distance. But the boy was doing well in his classes; he was notably steady in conduct and affectionate in disposition; he was moderately regular in his attendance at the Glasite meeting-house; and the principles and traditions of his mother's family were against too curious inquiry into the deeper things of the mind.

Again—a matter of almost equal importance—the change led to greater intimacy with Norway and things Norwegian. "Grandpapa in Norway" was now dead; but the brave old Scotch lady, his wife, with her two unmarried daughters (one, the admired and beloved autocrat of the household; the other, of a nature as sweet as the music that flowed from her cherished Bechstein) and the sons who from time to time were at home, still, all through the summer, kept open house for the clan. A younger son, Colin Archer,[1] had returned from Australia, married in Norway, and built himself a house hard by; and the families of elder daughters married to Norwegians were settled in the town. Thus "Odden" in the summer-time was more populous and more attractive than ever. Hitherto William Archer's holiday visits there had been much-coveted occasional treats; now that he had no home in Scotland they became regular annual events.

He was something of a strange bird in a flock of young folks whose joy of youthful sports was sailing, from which the infirmity of his sea-legs debarred him, or fishing, which he contemned; and who had no time to spare from the chief delights of his life, books and reading. This separateness, and also his serene satisfaction with it, come out characteristically in a brief sketch, written much later, of the events of his mental life.

[1] Later the eminent naval architect, builder of the *Fram*, and designer of the unsinkable sailing "Rescue Boats" which saved many scores of fishermen's lives.

"Once, when I was a little boy, on a summer visit in Norway, I heard an aunt of mine reproving her son, a boy of my own age, for some 'disorder in the dress' for which she had not Herrick's appreciation. He pointed out that I was in the same plight; whereupon my aunt replied in Norwegian, a tongue I was supposed not to understand: 'Oh, but he's only a bookworm'. I knew more Norwegian than they thought; at any rate I understood that phrase; and I have treasured it ever since, as the first, and perhaps the most gratifying compliment ever paid me."

Already in 1871, no longer satisfied with the smattering of the colloquial tongue which he had picked up from listening to the bi-lingual talk around him, he had made the plunge into Norwegian literature which was to mean so much in his life. "I rather 'bowled him out'", wrote his father, describing the Christmas holidays of that year, "reading *Peder Paars*[1] in bed in the morning with two lamps—but I didn't 'split' on him, as it was holiday time—at any other time I would, of course, have felt it my duty to call him over the coals severely! He is not keeping his places at school this quarter so well as he did last session—but his masters say he is attentive and does his best, and so I am quite satisfied, though I suspect that being strongly addicted to the study of Norsk has something to do with it—but I am thankful if he has no worse vice than that. . . ."

It was the contemporary literature of Norway, however, that chiefly captured the boy's imagination, and it was not long before the star of Ibsen had risen above his horizon. "I used to see in the Norwegian shop-windows books by one Henrik Ibsen, but my interest in him was not excited until one day I chanced to hear a lady express the opinion that

[1] Holberg's mock epic.

Love's Comedy was *glimrende vittig*—brilliantly witty. 'Hullo!' thought I, 'if there is anything brilliantly witty in Norwegian I must read it', and I bought the paper-covered book; little thinking how much that series of paper-covered books was to mean for me. From *Love's Comedy* I went on to *The League of Youth, Brand, Peer Gynt, The Vikings, The Pretenders* —all that the poet had yet published." "*Emperor and Galilean*", he says elsewhere, "was then his latest work. When the 'World-Historic Drama' came into my hands, I remember locking myself up in a little bare hutch of a bathing-house by the fjord, in order to devour its ten acts in the luxury of unbroken solitude. By the connivance of my grandmother's housekeeper (an old ally of mine), I laid in provisions to enable me, if necessary, to stand a siege. Even in those early days, you see, Ibsenite and Ishmaelite meant much the same thing. But how I should have stared had I foreseen that such a word as 'Ibsenite' would ever be added to the English language!"

In these years, too, the foundations were laid of his practical knowledge of Northern theatrical art. Playbills of November 1869 (apparently the first of his large collection) show that already in that year he was in Copenhagen, and saw at the Royal Theatre one of Bournonville's ballets (a special feature of that great theatre) and an adaptation of a vaudeville of Scribe's. Three years later we find him again in the old Northern city, staying with Danish friends; and a letter describing the visit, to Mr. Ernest Cheesman, a friend who was a sort of good genie to his boyhood, ends with a passage "significant of much": "Out of the nine days I have been here I have been eight times to the theatre (and a splendid one the Royal Theatre is). Tomorrow I go on to Hamburg and then home. By the by, this is my sixteenth birthday." Needless to add that he collected a Hamburg playbill (*Czaar und Zimmerman*) on his way home.

Among the pieces seen at the Royal Theatre were *Lohengrin*, Holberg's *Mascarade*, and *Les Fourberies de Scapin*—the last two brilliantly cast. There can be no doubt that these early experiences in the "House of Holberg" sowed the seeds of the conviction that inspired his persistent, life-long efforts for the establishment of a National, or at the least an Endowed, theatre in England.

Fresh from these experiences, the sixteen-year-old youth returned to Edinburgh for the opening of the first session of his University career, and it is not surprising that that career proved to be of an unconventional cast. The story of his strictly academic activities is summarized by Sir Hector Mackenzie, his fellow-bursar from George Watson's College:

"We were both fairly diligent students", he writes. "W. A. was distinguished in the Greek class principally by the English verses which he wrote for Professor John Stuart Blackie; and in the class of English Literature by the essays and verses which he wrote for Professor David Masson, who thought highly of his efforts. He did not shine in the classes of Philosophy. He had, as I have said, no aptitude for Mathematics. I remember meeting him coming out from a written examination paper in the Mathematical class. There were twelve questions, and I asked him how he had got on. He said he had answered half a question: but on his telling me how he had answered it, I told him his answer was wrong. To this day I don't know how he managed to satisfy the examiners in the final examination for the M.A. degree; but I gave him some coaching and I suppose helped him through in some degree." Archer's own explanation of this apparent miracle was a simple one. His friend (then as distinguished in mathematics as he was afterwards to be in medicine) divined beforehand, he declared, a number of the questions that were likely to be set in the mathematical papers, and made him learn the answers by heart. His gift of clear and logical exposition, too, may have stood him in good stead even in this ordeal, as it did on other similar occasions.

Of his college exercises one of the most important in his own eyes seems to have been the writing of an essay on Wordsworth for a prize competition, soon after he had emerged from "the normal attack of Byronism". "It was from Wordsworth", he says, "whom I read for a college essay, that I learnt the true meaning of the word poetry. I did not win the prize, but I won what was more valuable—a perception, as yet vague and uncertain enough, of the difference between style and fustian."[1]

But his college studies were only a part, and perhaps not the most important part, of his activities during these years. A "Reading Diary" shows that, outside the prescribed course of study, or only partially in connection with it, he got through an amount of miscellaneous reading formidable in mass and bewildering in variety. And very few books of importance are passed over without a line or two of pithy comment, often crude and hasty, but always his own.

One of the first entries ("Finished John Stuart Mill's *Autobiography*; one of the most entrancing books I ever read") marks a stage in his spiritual life. "The year '73", he says—"my seventeenth year—was one of marked importance to me. It brought

[1] The Records of the Philomathic—the Students' Debating Society—show him reading addresses on Wordsworth, *King Lear*, Dickens, and Björnson, and "stoutly maintaining the affirmative on the question: 'Is the influence of the theatre beneficial?' "

three new characters upon the stage of my thoughts—John Stuart Mill, George Eliot, and Henrik Ibsen. Reading Mill's *Autobiography* immediately on its appearance, I learned that other people, and men of credit and renown in the intellectual world, had been thinking on the very lines along which my own thoughts had for years been stumbling and groping. The effect of this discovery upon a boy who had had no opportunity and small inclination to make any intellectual confidants was naturally very great. Somewhat similar was the effect produced on my mind a year or two later, when, in the course of my college studies in philosophy, I found brilliantly formulated by Bishop Berkeley an idealistic criticism of the external universe which had been darkly germinating in my mind ever since childhood. Does one ever, I wonder, carry away from a metaphysical treatise anything that one has not brought to it, at any rate in germ? It seems to me doubtful.

"For ten years onwards from 1873", he goes on, "George Eliot was probably the paramount influence in my mind." . . . We have already seen how he came acquainted with Henrik Ibsen, and shall have ample opportunity to follow the results of the acquaintanceship.

We must conceive him from the very beginning of his college days as spending much of his time, both in Edinburgh and on holiday visits to London, in theatre-going, though he seems to have neglected at first what soon became almost a sacred duty—the preservation and hoarding of his playbills. Those were the last days of the stock companies, which were rapidly being discontinued in favour of the touring system; but at every novelty, whether given by the theatre's own troupe or by a touring company, he was sure to be present; and it is clear that, stock or

TOLDERODDEN, THE ARCHERS' HOME IN NORWAY
(*about* 1890)

touring company, performance good, bad, or indifferent, he rarely failed to draw amusement and profit from the entertainment. "Oh! what deliciously bad acting we have seen in our time", he breaks out. "Not the colourless incompetence of to-day, but the elaborate, the strenuous, the exquisite execrableness of the third-rate stock-company actor. It is the mark of your true devotee of the drama that he takes almost as much pleasure in characteristically bad as in good acting, and that the vilest performance of the wretchedest play will sometimes afford him rare entertainment, simply as a quaint scene from the human comedy."

The fellow-devotee to whom these words were addressed (in the delightful Epistle Dedicatory to *The Theatrical "World" for 1893*) now comes upon the scene in the person of Robert W. Lowe, a man some years older than Archer, already engaged in the business of insurance, which was to be his bread-winning employment throughout life, but with leisure enough to indulge to the full the love of the theatre which he shared with the young undergraduate. An excellent mimic and amateur actor and a man of endearing geniality and humour, he was to be the young man's comrade on many hundreds of theatre days and nights, his collaborator in his first critical razzia, and later in more sober work in theatrical history. His death, in 1902, was the first heavy personal loss that befell his younger friend.

The insurance business in Edinburgh at this time would seem to have had some natural affinity with the drama and its allied arts, for the same or a neighbouring office produced two kindred spirits and allies in George R. Halkett, a draughtsman and caricaturist of notable talent, later Art Editor of the *Pall Mall Magazine*, and Edward Rimbault Vere

Dibdin, a great-grandson of the sweet singer of "Tom Bowling", who had inherited a share of his ancestor's facility and charm in verse and music, and was to develop considerable gifts as a critic of art. The four young men were thus armed at all points for the assault on the fortress of art, and their alliance, throughout the next three years, was fertile in all manner of literary, artistic, and dramatic projects. It was held together, the records of the time make clear, not only by community of tastes, but also by the common affection of the other three members for the young undergraduate, and their belief in his star.

Eighteen hundred and seventy-five was a year of great events. On February 6th the Theatre Royal went up in flames (mourned by the young devotee in a melodious *In Memoriam* poem), and the venue of the theatre nights was changed to "the tawdry and grimy little Princess's in Nicolson Street", where, in that and the succeeding years, the young critic and his friend gained the "tolerably liberal education" in the classical drama described in the Epistle Dedicatory. One important factor in that education was furnished by the starring visits of Miss Ellen Wallis, one of the last, and not the least worthy, of the older school of Shakespearean actresses. "To this lady", he says,[1] "in whom survived a good deal of the Macready tradition, transmitted to her by her teacher, John Ryder, I owe the best part of my Shakespearean education. Looking back, I can recognize the limitations, beyond her own control, which prevented her from taking a leading position on the London stage, or rivalling the lovely Adelaide Neilson in popular favour. But in intelligence—in thorough understanding of the dramatic opportunities of her characters—

[1] "Edinburgh Theatres Twenty-five Years Ago", the *Student*, January 1901.

she was far and away ahead of Miss Neilson. The Americans draw a distinction between the 'reading' and the 'acting' of a part—meaning by the 'reading', as I understand it, all that concerns diction, accentuation, pauses, the bringing out of those effects which reside in the words themselves. Well, in the 'reading' of Rosalind, Juliet, Imogen, I still believe Miss Wallis to have been superior to any other actress I have seen in the parts; and there were splendid moments in her Cleopatra. Her Isabella, in *Measure for Measure*, I never saw."

In journalism the young undergraduate had made his début as early as 1873, when his seventeenth year was not yet out. A visit to the Vienna Exhibition of that year was the occasion. Five articles in the *Alloa Advertiser*, entitled "Notes of Travel", record his impressions of Vienna and its Exhibition, and of Prague, Dresden, and Berlin. Boyish and immature in parts, the letters are yet lively and amusing, and contain characteristic passages that curiously foreshadow endeavours and events yet far in the future. The British Section[1] at the Exhibition strikes him as making a very poor show, though he hopes, without much assurance, that it makes up in solid value what it lacks in showiness; his theatrical experiences in Vienna and Dresden inspire an outburst on the necessity for a State Theatre in England ("When shall we in England have a National Theatre? etc."); and, finding Prussia swamped with soldiers, and the *pickelhaube* one of the most prominent features of the North German scene, he is moved to declare that: "Whatever be our opinion of the

[1] The English Art Exhibit he considers "glaringly inferior". It is curious to find Henrik Ibsen, who was also a visitor to Vienna in that month of August 1873, speaking of the same exhibit as "composed almost entirely of masterpieces". (*The Correspondence of Henrik Ibsen*, pp. 260–261.)

advantages or disadvantages of compulsory service, it is evident that we must have it if we are ever to cope, on Continental ground, with a nation like this", in which "every seventh man is a soldier in time of peace, and every second man would become one in time of war".

Less than two years later (April 1875) he has become a salaried journalist. "One day, while still a student of the Edinburgh University", he writes, "I sent an article at random to the recently started 'Evening News' of that city. The subject I forget—probably one of the ecclesiastical controversies which used to shake Scotland (partly with laughter) in those days. To my surprise, the editor, Mr. Hugh Wilson, sent for me, and asked me if I would like to do a daily editorial for the paper. For two years" [as we shall see, the two years were separated by a year's interval] "I wrote a daily column of leading matter for the 'Evening News', and am glad of this opportunity to express my sense of obligation to the Wilson Brothers, my liberal and kindly employers. It appals me to think of the terrible stuff I must often have turned out, for my ignorance of politics, and of most other subjects, was stupendous. Fortunately the paper was by way of being independent, so that I was not forced to work up the unreal enthusiasm and indignation of the partisan hack. My crudities and puerilities were at least sincere."

His bondage to his desk at the *Evening News* office cannot have been very strict, for at the end of May 1875 we find him in Paris, with Lowe for companion, on the memorable visit thus celebrated in the Epistle Dedicatory: "Shall we ever forget that evening in the parterre of the Français, when Bornier's *La Fille de Roland* was the novelty of the hour? It was our first visit to Paris, and we knew nothing of the French stage; so when Roland's daughter glided upon the scene, a snow-white, willowy figure with lustrous eyes, we looked at our programme with a sudden access of curiosity, and read for the first time the name of Sarah Bernhardt."

Apart from these more important occupations, the half-serious diversions carried on during these years, either alone or in collaboration with one or more of his friends, were so numerous as to embarrass the historian. "How he found time for all he did", says the friend already quoted, "and at the same time attended the classes at the University and took his degree at the appointed time, passes all comprehension." Attempts — inevitably fruitless — to regenerate local comic papers; mock-heroic poems on stirring University events (which found considerable favour with the undergraduate public and with the learned and eccentric Professor of Greek, John Stuart Blackie); election squibs; a novel in the manner of Scott—*The Doom of the Destroyed: or Edinburgh in the Eighteenth Century*—which ran its course in the weekly *North Briton*; a farce—*Mesmerism: or Quits*—performed by a local Literary Association, in which, as the Secretary of the Association wrote sadly to the author, "the characters strove to outdo each other in rascality, and the minister, who might have been expected to represent morality, was the worst of the lot"—these are only a few of the most prominent items in a list of the "ploys" which must have filled up every spare moment of his time and doubtless served as a valuable safety-valve for youthful high spirits and the joy of life.

These happy days of strenuous work and play came to an end in April 1876, when his name appeared in the final pass-lists and he received the degree of Master of Arts. The Merits Lists show that he had to be content with an Honourable Mention in the Class of Junior Humanity, and with the fifth place in the Class of English; but that, in the Class of Senior Greek, he achieved what must surely have been, in that Class, a rare distinction—a Prize for Original English Poetry.

There followed a short visit to the North, in the course of which he saw Björnson's drama, *A Bankruptcy,* in Copenhagen, and, at Christiania, Ibsen's *Peer Gynt*. Then, towards the end of June, he set sail from Plymouth for Australia.

III

1876–1877

ROUND THE WORLD

"VOYAGES, like kingdoms", says Archer, in a manuscript account[1] of this year of travel, "are happiest when they have no history, and ours was as destitute of history as a nation yet unborn." But, though barren in external events, this voyage was fertile in spiritual adventures. "The books he bores into", he said in later years, "are the events of a book-worm's life"; and no two months of this bookworm's life were to be richer in that class of event. "I read more on the way out", he writes to his friend Mackenzie, "than I ever did in my life before. From nine in the morning till twelve at night I read without ceasing, leaving only short intervals for meals. Among other things I got through two-thirds of Thiers' *French Revolution*, the whole of Carlyle's ditto, 4 other volumes of Carlyle, 3 novels of Thackeray, 2 plays of Schiller, 2 plays of Goethe, a novel of Victor Hugo, and a large volume of Scandinavian mythology, besides a lot of miscellaneous Norwegian. If ever I want to learn the differential calculus, I'll take a trip round the world with only the works of Kelland and Tait to amuse me."

The portion of *A Ramble Round* devoted to the Australian visit, with its pictures of Melbourne and Sydney as they were fifty years ago, and its description of conditions in Central Queensland at that early stage in the life of the youngest Australian Colony, is of considerable historical interest, but does not

[1] *A Ramble Round: including Six Months in Central Queensland.*

throw much light on its author's mental development. The climate (throughout life he rarely found any place too warm for him) and the opportunities for "roughing it" given by travel in the bush, were much to his taste; and he was alive to the great possibilities of the country's future. But Australia as it then was, in its newness and crudeness, and with its merely rudimentary beginnings of theatrical and literary activity, offered little mental nourishment to one whose spiritual home was in an ancient historic city, and whose chief interest was at that time rather in the essence of human nature as distilled in literature than in its raw material.

Only two things roused the traveller to enthusiasm: the Melbourne Public Library and Sydney Harbour. The Library he celebrates both in prose and in verse;[1] and we have a fine description, too long for quotation, of the Harbour as seen by moonlight, and, on another occasion, at sunrise.

Apart from these two memorable experiences, his first months in Australia are sufficiently summarized in the letter to H. W. G. Mackenzie already referred to:

GRACEMERE,
ROCKHAMPTON, QUEENSLAND,
October 10*th*, 1876

MY DEAR MACKENZIE,

You see I have got to the end of my wanderings at last, and have settled down here for an indefinite (but short) time. . . . This is to certify . . . that in spite of all my toils and perils I am in tolerably good preservation. . . . Melbourne is rather a beastly hole, but I had a very good lark there. Who do you think I saw at the theatres?—Mrs. Scott Siddons at one! J. K. Emmett at the other, in the

[1] See verses: *On Yarra's Banks.*

most degraded piece[1] I ever saw on the stage, "Mesmerism or Quits" not excepted. At the Royal, though, they played "Much Ado" as well as I ever saw a play of Shakespere done out of London. The "Dogberry" was the best Shakesperian clown I have ever seen,[2] Compton always excepted.

This place is about seven miles from Rockhampton, a town of 7,000 inhabitants. It is on the banks of a large lagoon from which it takes its name—that is to say my mother's name is Grace, and mere = lagoon—and to whose margin our garden slopes down, full of all sorts of tropical growths—bananas, pine-apples, oranges, cocoa-nut and date palms, tamarinds, vines, etc. We are great aristocrats here, being the very earliest settlers—in fact my uncles discovered the whole country twenty years ago, and named the spot on which Rockhampton now stands. . . .

I have not yet broken my neck in pursuit of equestrian proficiency, but have skinned my elbow consumedly. However I have got a very nice quiet horse rejoicing in the name of Switcher, with whom I get along first-rate. I have only had one cropper as yet, and that was not off Switcher, but off a horse of notoriously bad principles named Mirza. You should see me in a huge Chinese pith helmet, a blue shirt, a pair of moleskin trousers, leggings and spurs, which is the full dress of these climes—I bet you wouldn't recognize me. . . . I want you to do me a favour—would you mind finding out for me, if you in any way can, the regulations for going to the bar in London—the amount of study and time that is *absolutely necessary* merely to pass or "to be called" or whatever they may call it—also the expense (in

[1] *Jan, the New German.*
[2] The actor so highly praised was Mr. J. R. Greville.

fees etc.) if you can. I hope this will not trouble you much, and I am particularly anxious to know before I make up my mind when to return. . . .

Since coming out I have written a four act drama (some people would say "melo"-drama, but I repudiate the debaging insinivation) founded on a story by Hoffman. I have finished the drama but not fixed upon a title as yet—I think of "The Jeweller's Daughter or the Assassins of Paris" only it reminds one of the Judgment of Paris. "In this work of genius the entranced spectator is introduced to the brilliant court of Louis le Grand at the epoch when the Ancien Régime was at the acme of splendour. We find Racine, Molière and Mademoiselle de Scudéri grouped round the throne of the *Grand Monarque* or bowing at the footstool of Madame de Maintenon. At the same time we are presented with a thrilling picture of the dark mysteries of Parisian life. . . ." The above is an extract from a dramatic criticism in the *Daily Telegraph* sometime in 1878 or 1879. . . . Write me at once on receipt of this, unless you wish me solemnly to devote you to the company of the departed Rockhamptonites. . . .

The inquiries about admission to the English Bar were evidently the outcome of discussions between the young man and his father and mother as to the line he was to take in life. In his own mind there had never been any doubt in the matter—literature and the theatre drew him irresistibly. But it was natural that his parents should at first look with misgivings on his choice of such a precarious calling, and should be anxious for their son to adopt some steadier and more regular profession as his chief stand-by. Even if a man did not practise, it used to be thought in those days, the fact that he could write himself down barrister-at-law gave him a certain standing as a regularly enrolled member of society, denied to those who were mere free-lances of the Press. The upshot of the discussion was a compromise. The parents agreed to their son following his own bent, on condition that at the same time he complied with their wishes by going to the Bar; while the son was prepared to satisfy his parents by eating dinners and passing examinations, provided that his doing so did not seriously interfere with the work on which his heart was set, or commit him to giving it up when "called". It is clear that from beginning to end he never expected to derive any practical advantage from his law course, nor, as it turned out, did he do so—apart from the knowledge gained in reading for the examinations. But his parents no doubt regarded the money and trouble expended in obtaining his admission to the Bar as a sort of insurance against the contingency of his ardour for literature proving, as it has proved in so many cases, a mere fire of straw.

Two long bush journeys made during the later part of his stay in Queensland enriched him with experiences, both of the comforts and amenities of the squatters' hospitable abodes, and of the pleasures and pains of camping in the bush. On the first, travelling alone through trackless bush, he loses himself, and has a charming adventure, reminiscent of Grimm's Fairy Tales, which probably suggested to him a scene in his play, *The Joy Ride*, written fifty years later. On the second, being in command of the party, with a lieutenant who, besides being an accomplished bushman, is also an anointed scoundrel, he learns various useful lessons in bushcraft and human nature, at the trifling cost of £3, stolen by his second in command from his saddle-bags.

The end of February 1877 saw him back at Gracemere, and planning his return to Scotland. Determined, as he says, "not to encounter again the unspeakable monotony of the long sea voyage round either the Cape of Good Hope or Cape Horn", and possessed by "an overpowering desire to see the wonders of American nature and civilization", he decided to take the direct route by San Francisco and New York. His funds were insufficient for a first-class ticket, and he found, on inquiry, that there was no second class on the Pacific Mail boats. But his heart was set on seeing America, and after some deliberation he decided to brave the (in those days very real) discomforts of the steerage passage.

Accordingly, early in April he set sail from Sydney in the R.M.S. *Zealandia*. The description of his preparations is too characteristic to be omitted:

"The steerage quarters I found to be a narrow but tolerably well-lighted cabin, with a plain deal table running down the centre. Four or five sleeping-rooms opened off it, each containing from twelve to twenty bunks, and each bunk containing a straw mattress—the whole sleeping accommodation provided by the Company. One of the rooms was of course devoted to women, and it contained a washing-stand with a couple of basins—the men being supposed to wash on deck. I chose a top bunk in the furthest forward of the men's cabins—a bunk which had a small box at the head of it. . . . 'Acting on information received' from the steward, I purchased four tins of jam, a tumbler, some towels and a piece of soap, with which stores I intended to face the month's voyage. Some luxurious mortals provided themselves with a blanket and a pillow, but such sybaritism was not for me. I made my knapsack my pillow and a couple of large greatcoats my blankets, and in this unsophisticated couch I slept many a night as comfortably as I ever did on spring mattresses or feather beds. My heavy luggage I had sent to London direct by a sailing ship; so that I had all my necessaries in a portmanteau and a japanned tin box, so small that I could easily keep them by me in the sleeping room. As reading is my only occupation, besides eating and sleeping, at sea, I had provided myself with Morley's excellent reprint of *The Spectator*, Mill's *Political Economy*, *Gil Blas*, a cheap German edition of the whole of Schiller, and several of the Waverley Novels. The Spectator especially I found an inestimable and never-failing treasure, but by the time we reached San Francisco I had exhausted almost all my store except some parts of Schiller."

We must pass lightly over the descriptions of the life and the fare on board—the morning struggle on deck for the single tin basin provided for washing purposes, and, when it was captured, for access to the pump where water was served out, besieged as it was by Chinese bedroom stewards, and yielding water only when the ship gave a favourable roll; the rocky meat served on tin plates black with grease; the worse than doubtful butter and the undrinkable coffee. As far as Auckland the amateur steerage passenger subsisted on "a particularly watery kind of vegetable soup served round in the tin mugs in which we got our morning coffee and our afternoon tea," with bread, potatoes, and "unlimited pepper and salt to add a flavour". At Auckland he purchased an enamelled iron plate ("and was so enabled for the rest of the voyage to indulge in the more solid viands without at the same time devouring the oleaginous remains of former generations of steerage passengers"), and laid in a small store of delicacies. "Here it was that I found the advantage of my little box at the head of my bunk. In it I could keep not only my books and my toilet requisites, but my jam-pots and bananas; while my neighbours had to stow their bonne-bouches of all descriptions *under their mattresses*. One who has survived a month's steerage living cannot be accused of squeamishness, but I must confess I would as soon have joined the Cooktown blacks in their banquet of Chinaman, as have shared the red herrings which two of my cabin-mates used to extract every morning from the mysterious recesses of their sleeping-places."

Having touched at Auckland, at Kandavu in Fiji and at Honolulu, the *Zealandia* reached her destination at the beginning of May. Her landfall, as often happens on that coast, was obscured by fog. "About twenty-four hours before we reached San Francisco we became enveloped in a Scotch mist so dense that it was impossible to see the ship's length ahead. For a whole night our speed was slackened so that we had barely steerage way on the vessel. In the morning the Farraleone Islands were looming through the fog, and about ten o'clock a light wind swept the mist away and showed us the Golden Gate standing boldly forth in the cold, clear sunshine."

Twenty-eight years earlier William Archer's father had passed inward through those Gates to seek for gold. Now the son was come, in his turn, on a like quest—not unsuccessful, though, on this first visit, the treasures he sought and found were of the imponderable kind.

The United States offered the traveller all the attractions in which he had found the Australia of that day lacking: a fascinating and romantic history; a literature rich in accomplishment and still richer in promise; a multitude of cities, old and new, in which material civilization could almost be caught in the act of growth; a theatrical life widespread and vigorous, though as yet poor in quality. And in this country of immense possibilities he felt himself from the first, if at all a foreigner, then, as Stevenson expressed it, a foreigner at home. "There was a time", he wrote[1] forty years later, "when I had no friends in America, yet found all America my friend. When I first landed on your shores, a boy of twenty, I knew literally not a soul in the whole continent. I crossed in leisurely fashion from San Francisco to the East, and everywhere I found myself at home. In Europe I am apt to be shy, reserved, somewhat of a victim to the *morgue britannique*. In your country a good deal, at any rate, of that foible seemed to drop off me, and I felt myself, though friendless, in an atmosphere of good nature and good will. This is not the experience of everybody, but it assuredly was mine. Partly, perhaps, because America was already to me a land of romance and of spiritual friendships —the land of Fenimore Cooper and of Bret Harte, of Poe and Hawthorne, of Holmes and Lowell and Emerson. I felt it an enormous privilege, an extension, almost a reduplication, of personality, to find myself in a country which was nominally, and in many ways actually, foreign—which had all the glamour of the unfamiliar—yet in which I could not really feel myself a foreigner. This sensation has never left me. It is as clear to me today as it was forty years ago that America offers to the Englishman, and England to the American, an enlargement of personality—or shall we say a duality of spiritual citizenship?—beyond the reach of any other people in the world. That privilege I have valued the more

[1] Epistle Dedicatory to Brander Matthews (unpublished), intended as preface to an American edition of a collection of War tracts.

as the years have passed, and as mature reason has re-inforced the sentiment, the instinct, of youth."

The traveller found San Francisco Bay disappointing, but the city struck him with admiration and surprise. He found it, he declares, to surpass London and Paris in civilization, magnificence and luxury. As an account of first impressions, this passage is of great interest, but, in view of some of the sights and observations later recorded, it would seem that the word "civilization", if it did not slip in unawares, must have been used in a very restricted sense.

For, though the sense of kinship no doubt predisposed the young critic to favourable judgments, it by no means blinded him to the defects of the Great Republic's qualities; and his remarks on certain American institutions—in particular the Stage and the Press—are inspired by a true kinsmanlike candour. With both of these institutions he immediately came in touch. His first American playbill (*Frou-Frou* at the California Theatre) bears the date May 5th—probably the day after the ship's arrival; while the issues of the *San Francisco Chronicle* for the 8th, 10th, and 12th May contain articles by him, thus referred to thirty-five years later:[1] "California was, to an ardent admirer of Bret Harte, a realm of romance. I so longed to remain in San Francisco that I tried to eke out my slender resources by journalism; and Charles de Young, then Editor of 'The San Francisco Chronicle', did in fact print a couple of articles of mine. . . . In the reporters' room of the 'Chronicle', I remember, a skull was nailed against one of the doors, with a pigtail wound round it, and under it the following legend:

[1] "San Francisco Thirty Years After," *Daily News and Leader*, May 11, 1912.

This is Wong Lee, who did not like an item about himself and was rash enough to say so."

Even though he took this novel form of "Scare-head" for what it no doubt was, a piece of grim humour, it would probably have suggested to the traveller, had he not been under the glamour of Bret Harte, that there were some points in which the civilization of San Francisco fell below even the very moderate level attained by London and Paris. And a commentary yet grimmer than the jest itself is furnished by the sentence omitted from the quotation made above: "Many years afterwards Mr. de Young was shot dead at his desk by a gentleman who differed from him in politics."

His funds thus replenished,[1] the traveller was enabled to give five days to San Francisco—five busy days, in the course of which he saw a play at each of the four English-speaking theatres, and devoted one evening to obtaining his first view of the Chinese drama, a memorable experience.[2] On May 9th he set out across the continent, in what seemed, after the steerage of the *Zealandia*, the luxury[3] of American second-class railway travel.

At Salt Lake City, where he pauses for a day, he is unfortunate enough to miss seeing a service in the great Tabernacle and to find the theatre closed; but going, in default of anything more tempting, to a "Grand Concert", given by the female pupils of the Seventeenth Ward Sabbath School, is richly rewarded by the humours of the entertainment. After

[1] By the large sum of $12. See p. 73.

[2] Described in the London *Figaro* of August 20, 1881.

[3] Comparative only, for most of the journey was made on bare benches, and the traveller took "an immense amount of grub" with him and fed on board the train.

a "Juvenile Oratorio" entitled *Joseph*, two "tolerably broad English farces", *Twice Killed* and *Only Somebody*, were given by the young actresses with great zest, and in some cases with no little humour and effect. Miss Louisa Ellerbeck, a young lady of twelve, in particular, "had a thorough appreciation of her parts, and gave all her points like a practised 'singing-chambermaid' "; and she and Miss Maggie Dwyer, "a snub-nosed, merry-faced little girl", particularly delighted the audience and the critic as "Sarabella" and her devoted admirer Bloggins (pronounced Blodgins) in the second piece. "At one part Sarabella doubts the constancy of her 'Blodgins'. He, again, assures her of his unswerving fidelity, upon which Sarabella says solemnly: 'Swear, Blodgins', and 'Blodgins' with equal solemnity holds up his hand to the heavens and says 'Damn me!' This point afforded especial delight to the audience and was almost encored. Indeed, all through, the performers swore with the utmost freedom and vivacity, very much to the gratification of the audience. I thought it the most edifying 'Sabbath School Concert' I had ever assisted at, and thanked the fates that the theatre was closed. The greatest comedian that ever trod the boards could not have made me laugh more than 'Sarabella' and 'Blodgins'."

The traveller's impressions of New York read strangely at this day, and show how great was to be the transformation wrought by the next few decades. He is "both pleased and disappointed" with the city—disappointed to find it not so handsome as he had expected; pleased with a certain "homely" quality in it (the adjective evidently used in the English sense) which he feels without being able to explain exactly wherein it consists, and with the picturesqueness of the street life. Boston and

Cambridge, where he spends some three days, charm him with their beauty, and are reverend to him from their historical and literary associations. Here the plays he sees are of small account; but he has a glimpse of The Autocrat of the Breakfast Table at a *soirée*, and contributes to the *Weekly Transcript* a sonnet in memory of John Lothrop Motley. And at Boston he indulges in some reflections on the English language which foreshadow much of his later writing on the subject. Considering, at some length, the question whether the English of England and the English of America will ever separate and become distinct languages, he concludes that the probabilities are against wide divergence.

"It is said by foreigners", he goes on, "that Englishmen are immoderately proud of their own nation, and it may be true that pugnacious patriotism is sometimes carried to an obtrusive length. Other nations have had their Blenheims and Waterloos, their Trafalgars and Balaclavas. It is in his language that the Englishman's true point of vantage lies. Who but an Englishman can travel round the world as I did, over two continents—for Australia is nothing less than a continent—through half a score of great cities, and yet be everywhere among people who speak his own language, who read his own literature? Among the things that struck me most in my whole journey were the performances of Shakespeare, mediocre as they were, which I saw in Melbourne and New York. Each time, as I looked round the crowded theatres entranced with the words of the poor player of Blackfriars, I thought what a poor substitute the glory of France or the power of Germany must be for my great birthright of the English language. It is a common reproach that 'an Englishman takes England with him wherever he goes'—in a higher sense, in which there is no reproach, he certainly does so."

Philadelphia seems to the traveller more "foreign" than either New York or Boston; but the quaintness of the streets, with their red-brick houses with white marble basements and doorsteps, appeals to his eye. Here he goes twice, afternoon and evening, to the Walnut Street Theatre—little dreaming how large a part that theatre, in its enlarged and rejuvenated form, was to play in his life forty-three years later—seeing, at the evening performance,

"Offenbach's Latest and Greatest Success in
Three Acts,
L'ARCHIDUC!
Elegant, Chaste and Complete."

Here, too, he attends a spiritualistic séance, and comes away convinced that the whole affair is "a piece of unmitigated and rather clumsy humbug"—though, as he explains, he went to the sitting in no prejudiced frame of mind, since he believes that, in the mass of spiritualistic manifestations, "there are some genuine phenomena, which cannot be accounted for under the hitherto ascertained laws of science, and which are worthy of serious examination, though at the same time I see no reason whatever for supposing that the phenomena are produced by spirits."

An amusing description of a visit to the Tabernacle, New York, to hear a sermon by Mr. Talmage, "the Spurgeon of America" and author of an anti-theatrical book entitled *Sports that Kill*, which had greatly taken the young critic's fancy, leads, by a natural transition, to a summary of theatrical conditions[1] in the America of 1877. He admires the size and handsomeness of the American playhouses, and finds the mounting of the plays almost invariably good. But: "Dramatic art is low enough in England, but I should say that in America it is seventy-five per cent lower. There is much good acting to be seen in the States, but it is even more irretrievably thrown away than in England. The best serious acting I saw in America was English—Miss Neilson's fine Juliet and tolerable Viola at Daly's Fifth Avenue Theatre, and Mr. Rignold's good though melodramatic Amos Clarke at Booth's. For the rest, the serious acting I saw was all more or less weak and loud. . . . In comedy, matters are slightly better. I saw some excellent comedians, notable among them being Mr. Raymond, whose Colonel Sellers, in Mark Twain's execrably bad drama of *The Gilded Age*, was an uncommonly clever character-study. Incomparably the finest comedy acting I saw in America, however, was that of a French opera-bouffe troupe under the direction of Mdlle Aimée, which was playing at Haverley's Theatre, Chicago. One or two of the comedians of this company, and Mr. Raymond in Colonel Sellers, were almost the only noteworthy actors I saw in America. The audiences, too, are inexpressibly bad, and possess the most delicate and unerring taste for applauding in the wrong places. They have, too, a habit of applauding when an English audience would laugh, which is often ruinous to the stage-illusion."

Returning from Philadelphia to New York, he sees "the justly celebrated Evangeline Combination", as the playbill has it, at Daly's Theatre, and *The*

[1] In his five weeks in America he was at the theatre twenty-five times. San Francisco yielded four playbills, Salt Lake City one, Chicago five, New York nine, Boston three, Philadelphia three.

Gilded Age at the Grand Opera House, and, towards the middle of June, sails for Scotland, second class, by the steamship *State of Georgia*, reaching Glasgow a year all but twelve days after his departure from Plymouth on his ramble round the world. Twenty-two years were to pass before he saw the hospitable American shores again.

IIIA

ON YARRA'S BANKS

ON Yarra's banks no storied fanes,
  Impregnate of the past, arise;
No immemorial temple strains
  Its fretted towers to cleave the skies;
No Duomo tells of ages gone,
  No Lateran, no Parthenon.
But lo! a nobler temple rears
  Its modest front on Yarra's leas,
Counting its little life in years
  As others count in centuries;
Yet telling more of ages gone
  Than Lateran or Parthenon.

A fane where every sect and creed
  May worship, all their feuds forgot;
Where Bigotry its doom may read,
  And Superstition lingers not;
Where centres all the glory gone
  From Lateran and Parthenon.

Here History embalms the past,
  And Poetry makes day of night:
Thought toils through problems vext and vast,
  And Science sheds its searching light
O'er cycles ere the sun first shone
  On Lateran and Parthenon.

The history of gloom gone by
  Old Europe's fanes alone can tell;
But this new shrine can prophesy
  Of future history as well;
Of glory such as never shone
  Round Lateran or Parthenon. . . .

IV

1877–1878

EDINBURGH ONCE MORE—*THE FASHIONABLE TRAGEDIAN*

THE influence of the *Wanderjahr*, 1876–77, on William Archer's development was strong and lasting. It would be too much to say that it was his travels alone that set his feet in the paths of Liberalism—the inevitable tendency of all his thought would have guided him in any case into those paths. But this year's experiences helped greatly to open his eyes to the road he must follow. The first-hand knowledge gained of the growth of the great new English communities beyond the seas inspired in him a vivid sense of the brotherhood of the English-speaking peoples, which was a first step, and a long one, towards a realization of the brotherhood of mankind.

In an address on "World Citizenship", delivered in 1905 before the Edinburgh Philomathic Society, he drew an unflattering picture of his attitude to the great questions of politics in the undergraduate days when he was a member of the Society:

"The Philomathic, at the time I speak of, was divided into two parties. One was known as the Evangelical Centre, the other as the Corner. The Evangelical Centre consisted of earnest youths, youths with convictions, both theological and political. Several of them have since taken high positions in the intellectual world; one of them,[1] I believe, is pretty certain to fill a great place in the next Liberal Ministry. The Corner consisted for the most part of

[1] Lord Haldane (?).

flippant, irresponsible young gentlemen, who prided themselves, in some cases with no very apparent reason, on being wits and men of the world. Some of them affected a sort of cynical, disillusioned Conservatism; others were, like Mr. Charles James Yellowplush, 'pokerkranties on plitticle subjix'. Gentlemen, I belonged to the Corner. If not one of its noisier spirits, I at any rate contributed to the debates very little of that high seriousness which now, I doubt not, is the prevailing note of your deliberations. On politics, in particular, I thought, and probably spoke, with amazing ineptitude. In the course of my school life, I had had no sort of guidance or encouragement in political thinking. No one had breathed a word to me of the duties and responsibilities of citizenship which I must one day assume. No one had suggested to me a political ideal of any sort. The miserable smattering of history which I had acquired had come to me tinged with a sort of childish patriotism, which was absolutely devoid of ethical or political inspiration. I saw that there was a great deal of unthinking prejudice and fanaticism in the ordinary party strife of the day, and I fell into a habit of idle scepticism as to the possibility of forming a competent political judgment. At any rate, I felt it was none of my business. Let the earnest youths of the Evangelical Centre excite themselves about the trumpery questions of the day—my mind expatiated in an ampler ether, a diviner air. In a word, I was what the Americans call a mugwump—an impenitent and contemptuous mugwump."

This indifferentism, we may suspect, can never have been much more than skin-deep; and in reading such utterances as the verses on the Melbourne Library and the remarks on the English and American language quoted above, we see him sloughing it off, like a weed outworn. He was never to become—could, indeed, never have become—an active party politician; for that rôle he had neither talent nor inclination. But from this year of his majority onwards a strong Liberalism informs all his thought and all his writing, whether the immediate subject be the drama, or literature in general, or public affairs.

He was himself, perhaps, hardly conscious at the time of the change in his outlook. At least he seems to ignore it in an account, written in 1923, of his second year on the *Edinburgh Evening News*. "Returning in 1877", he says, "I fell into my old place again for another year. . . . What the politics of the paper were in those days I do not remember, and doubt if I ever knew. My impression is that we were Liberal on Mondays, Wednesdays and Fridays, and Tory on Tuesdays, Thursdays and Saturdays." Whatever may have been the general line of the paper, the last sentence certainly gives an erroneous impression of the tendency of his own political leaders of 1877–78. They are consistent in their strong, though independent, Liberalism; anti-clerical, anti-Disraelian, above all anti-Jingo; while friendly to the cause of the Opposition, though critical of some of its spokesmen. From this period, too, we have a confession of faith, in a copy of verses[1] contributed to the *Daily Review*, when war with Russia seemed imminent, which comes strangely from the mouth of one so lately a professed Laodicean. Commonplace enough in form, the lines are remarkable, not to say prophetic, in tenor, with their anticipation of the watchwords of forty years later. "War is but the infant's rattle", one verse begins; and the piece ends:

[1] "England's War Song", February 12, 1878.

Nay, we have enough of glory—
  Glory such as carnage yields—
See, the nation's hands are gory
  From a thousand well-fought fields.
Now, a fame of truer splendour
  Waits us in the coming years,
If our hearts can but surrender
  Childish envyings, childish fears.

Still, with truth and hope to guide us,
  Let us march towards peace and law,
With our sword, yet keen, beside us,
  Lest we should be forced to draw,
Not in vain or wordy quarrel,
  But to war that wars may cease,
Not to snatch a blood-stained laurel,
  But to fight for very peace!

For many years to come, however, he was to remain "adscript" to the theatre and to literature, and his views on life and the world's affairs were to be, as it were, only the undertone in his work. His immediate business was to "make good" in the line which he had chosen contrary to the advice of his elders—to show that he could make of it a worthy and a bread-winning career. Such work as he already had on the *Evening News* and could easily obtain elsewhere in Edinburgh was useful as a stopgap; but for real success it was necessary to gain a footing on the larger stage of London, and on this his mind was already set. The winter of 1877 witnessed a first incursion into the national theatrical arena, which, though undertaken in something of a frolic spirit, was to help him materially on his way.

Looking for a place of abode on his arrival in Edinburgh, he had found a small but snug two-roomed lodging under the slates in a house at the corner of Hanover and George Streets, and here he lived for the next year, under the charge of a lady as diminutive as her rooms. The little woman made an excellent landlady, and her only complaint of her lodger was that when, as frequently happened, his friends gathered in his eyrie of an evening, the party would occasionally (even sometimes on the Sabbath day) fall to playing "at the cartes", the host having brought back with him from Australia a partiality for the game of euchre. (That the games were for love was no sufficient excuse for the practice in her eyes.) Dibdin had left Edinburgh for Liverpool; but Lowe and Halkett were constant attendants at these cold-water symposia, and a new friend, John Mackinnon Robertson, who was to play a large part in the coming years, was furnished by the Insurance Office so fertile in talent. Now and then Lowe would "oblige" with his celebrated impersonation of Irving as Hamlet or Richard III—sprawling across the floor, perhaps, each leg alternately dragged after him, while he mouthed out:

> Juckey of Nurfulk—be nut tuu bawld—
> For Dickon thei master—is bot and sawld!
> A thing deveised by the anamy!—

and it was doubtless on one of these occasions that the two hardened theatre-goers were inspired with the idea that what they had learned in suffering while sitting through many evenings at the feet of the eminent actor, they might teach, if not in song, at least in pointed prose; and persuaded Halkett to lend them the aid of his pencil to barb their shafts. "Lowe, Halkett and I", we read in a letter to Dibdin of October 1877, "have perpetrated an atrocity called 'The Fashionable Tragedian: a Criticism', which you may some day behold, though it is questionable. Lowe did the ideas[1] (figure that!), I the writing, Halkett the illustrations." His correspondent did behold the atrocity in due course. Before the month was out it made its appearance as a buff-covered sixpenny pamphlet, and sold so readily that by November 13th a new edition was in contemplation.

The Fashionable Tragedian was by no means the first severe criticism of Irving's marked and growing mannerisms, nor the first voice raised in opposition to the current laudation of his powers. He had already been treated with some severity by a minority of papers (notably by the *London Figaro*) in most of his Shakespearean characters, and by nearly all the papers in at least one part—Othello. What the pamphlet did was to concentrate and focus all this dissatisfaction, expressing it in pungent, and no doubt youthfully over-emphatic, terms; to draw the uncompromising conclusion that a tragedian with the faults described could not, whatever his gifts, be a great or even a tolerable actor;[2] and to urge the moral always at the tip of the writer's pen—that the deplorable waste of talent in this case proved the necessity for a National Theatre and a School of Acting.

Coming like a bolt from a clear sky, the pamphlet took the theatrical public and the Press much by surprise. The notices, especially those in the Scotch papers, were better than might have been expected; some being positively favourable, while in others

[1] This probably means that the substance of the pamphlet was largely drawn from Lowe's recent experiences of Irving's acting, during his collaborator's absence at the Antipodes.

[2] W. A.'s more mature thoughts on this point may be found on pp. 39 seq. of *Henry Irving: Actor and Manager*, 1883.

the almost obligatory tone of grave reprehension hardly veiled a sly enjoyment of the vigorous invective and the unkind but irresistibly ludicrous illustrations.

The "Second Edition, with Postscript", appeared before the end of the year, in a fresh (blue-green) cover; the postscript dealing with a defence entitled "A Letter Concerning Mr. Henry Irving", which had been issued by an Irvingite partisan, and ending with a measured retractation of some of the remarks on the actor's Richard III, due to second thoughts on Lowe's part. It had not the good fortune of its predecessor. The Irvingite forces had had time to close up their ranks and prepare for its reception; the Press was silent or unfavourable; even the *Figaro*, which had chuckled gleefully over the first edition, was now on the other side. Worst of all, there were rumours of legal action, and one of the collaborators, who was about to marry and settle, feeling, very reasonably, that a libel suit, even if successfully defended, would be ruinous, begged his two friends to consent to the withdrawal of the copies that had been sent out to "the trade". There was, of course, no resisting such an appeal. The sacrifice was made, and the second edition consequently still exists in numerous "remainders", while the first is something of a rarity.

The pamphlet, however, had done its work, and its work was good. By saying with sincerity, wit, and vigour, though with something of youthful cruelty, things that much needed to be said, but which the established criticism of the time was too pliant or too prudent to state in such downright terms, it gave earnest of a new force in theatrical criticism; while it assuredly did no harm to the actor criticized, but on the contrary rendered him a service, by showing him the necessity of curbing and correcting his most flagrant mannerisms.

Though one of the members of the "E. V. Ward"[1] partnership had withdrawn to Liverpool, the operations of that firm were by no means at a standstill. The correspondence of the partners throughout this winter and the years next following teems with references to a swarm of joint and several undertakings, literary, musical, and musico - literary. Numerous poems, originating now in Edinburgh, now in Liverpool, pass to and fro, and are criticized with the utmost candour; and we hear of some of these finding their way into short-lived periodicals, such as H. J. Byron's *Mirth* and Robert Buchanan's *Light.* A characteristic passage in this correspondence shows that Archer was at no time misled by his facility in turning a verse into crediting himself with poetic faculty. His correspondent having complained that his verses are lacking in feeling, he replies: "Your criticism flatters me highly, except in so far that you seem to imagine I want to be a poet, whereas I can imagine no more degrading ambition. My ambition is to write verses for which deluded magazine-editors will give me two guineas a page. As for *feeling,* the lack of that is easily explained by the fact that when by any chance I do happen to 'feel' anything, I am careful not to write verses about it."

In the beginning of 1878, *Our Special Correspondent,* a one-act farce by the partnership, was rejected by the Committee of the Watt Institution Literary Association, by reason of its low view of human nature. "It was not the least objectionable

[1] A *nom de guerre* combining the initials E. R. V. D(ibdin) and W. A. Various brochures by the partnership had appeared in the undergraduate days.

feature about the performance", wrote the Secretary sadly, "that you contrived to make villainy so very amusing." But on February 4th Archer writes: "The upshot of the Watt business is that they play a two-act (!) comedy (!) of mine called *Rosalind*. . . . What say you to that? They wouldn't look at *Our Special*, and quite right too, though they would have played it much better than this, which, though I say it that shouldn't, is a better piece, and is beyond their reach—which, however, isn't saying much for it." *Rosalind* was duly performed on March 1st, Lowe reaping laurels in the part of "Mr. Moncrieff (Manager of the Theatre Royal, Mud-borough)".

The autumn of 1877 had been signalized by the appearance of *The Pillars of Society*, the play in which Henrik Ibsen reopened the vein of modern social drama in which he had made a first essay eight years earlier with *The League of Youth*. The play was received throughout the Scandinavian countries and in Germany with applause almost as loud and unanimous as the abuse which greeted many of the later and greater dramas. It came to Archer "hot from the press", and he received it with enthusiasm, recognizing it for what it was, an epoch-making work, and, like others, over-estimating its absolute value. It seemed to him, too, a play through the medium of which it should be possible to make Ibsen known in England. He at once set to work to this end, making "a hurried translation" which enabled him to inoculate his friends with some of his enthusiasm, but which "no publisher would look at"; and contributing to the *Mirror of Literature* (March 2, 1878) a long and detailed analysis, with copious extracts. There, for the time, he was obliged to let the matter rest.

"THE FASHIONABLE TRAGEDIAN"

(Three of G. R. H.'s illustrations)

MELODRAMA.

(*"The Lyons Mail"*)

A RECOGNITION OF GENIUS.

(*"Statesmen tap him on the shoulder while walking down Bond Street"*)

DIGNITY.

(*Charles I*)

He soon had an opportunity of enlarging his first-hand experience of French dramatic art. On April 21st he writes to Liverpool:

". . . I have just come in to find waiting for me a letter from Ch. de Young of the *San Francisco Chronicle,* accepting an offer I made him about four months ago for correspondence at the Paris Exhibition—10 letters of a column and a half at $10 a letter. . . . I have been busy doctoring Ibsen's play, and have been coming out in a new line of life as contributor to the *Globe Encyclopædia,* in the office of which I last week began three hours' work a day. My work is principally little geographical articles telling how many pigs are annually barrelled in some small town in America, and how many churches and newspapers it possesses. I'm afraid this Paris business may cut short my career of usefulness as an Encyclopædist. My friend Mr. de Young (out of whom I swindled $12 when I was in Frisco) requests a preliminary letter describing the customs and life in Paris, and then remarks: 'Divide your succeeding letters into series so as to take up Arts, Sciences, Manufactures, Machinery, etc. Hunt up and describe fully everything noteworthy in inventions, arts, machinery, and other productions of the Pacific Coast.' Fancy me coming out great upon Sciences, Manufactures and Machinery!!! . . . However, I will get an Encyclopædia and hunt up 'Pacific Coast' under P., and Science etc. under S. and M., and amalgamate them, as the youth in Pickwick did with Chinese Metaphysics. . . .

Yours San Francisco Chronically,

W. ARCHER."

The labours for the *San Francisco Chronicle,* with Paris correspondence for the *Evening News,* and also, no doubt, work for the *Globe Encyclopædia*, must have occupied his time in Paris pretty fully, for from this visit of some five or six weeks we have only thirteen playbills. These include, however, at the Français: *Phèdre* and *Hernani*, with Mounet-Sully and Sarah Bernhardt; *Les Fourchambault*, with Got, Coquelin, Reichenberg, and Croizette; and *Le Marquis de Villemer*, with Delaunay and Madeleine Brohan; and at the Odéon, *Andromaque*—a harvest rich in quality.

Back in Edinburgh, he writes on July 3rd, with reference to a vacancy on the staff of the *Evening News*: "Yes, the E.E.N. rot-riter-ship is no longer open; but another will be this autumn when I secede." And, after his return from a summer visit to Norway, the secession duly took effect. In the middle of August we find him actively engaged in arranging for a like-minded successor to take his place. His intimacy with John M. Robertson had been ripening during the past year, and, in the course of evening talks in the Hanover Street eyrie and long country walks, he had been greatly struck with this new friend's power of mind. Here, clearly, was the man the *Evening News* required. "I introduced him to 'Mr. John'", he writes, "and matters were arranged without the least difficulty; so that I certainly did the paper yeoman's service—in leaving it." September 1878 saw him settled in London, and in November he entered as a student at the Middle Temple.

V

1878–1881

FIRST YEARS IN LONDON

THE state of the English stage in the late seventies is set forth fully in Archer's *English Dramatists of Today*,[1] and we need not attempt to retell the story here at length. So far as the contemporary drama was concerned, the condition of things seemed hopeless enough. Since 1866, when Henry Morley published his *Journal of a London Playgoer*, there had been a great expansion in volume of theatrical enterprise, and considerable improvement in technical means and methods. But of a recovery of native English drama from the state of inanity described by the *Playgoer* there was small sign. The Robertsonian comedy, which had been hailed by some as giving promise of an awakening, had proved to be a false dawn, and ever-during dark seemed to have closed down upon the scene.

Yet there was a new element in the situation which held a germ of promise. Attention had been excited and interest awakened. The Press could no longer afford to ignore the Stage. The troublesome institution was no longer so negligible that editors felt obliged to reassure their readers by disclaiming all intention of wasting space upon so paltry a matter,[2] or to admonish their theatrical critics that, "Whether a play is good or bad, whether a man acts well or ill, is of very little consequence to the great body of our readers."[3] On the contrary, theatrical criticism

[1] See in particular the Introduction and *Playwrights of Yesterday*.

[2] As did the editor of the *World* (of all papers) in his first number, July 8, 1874.

[3] As Delane told John Oxenford.

had become a prominent feature of the daily and weekly Press, so that William Archer could assert in 1882 that "in no country in the world is the drama so much criticized as in England". Moreover, there was a healthy spirit of dissatisfaction abroad, and the question: "Why have we no contemporary native drama worthy of the name?" was constantly being raised and keenly debated. A discussion of the kind, which broke out in January 1879, was the occasion of one of Archer's first contributions to the *London Figaro*.[1]

These stirrings of discontent, however, though in themselves a healthy sign, only served in the meantime to draw attention to the miserable state of things dramatic—to the facts that the only really successful contemporary pieces were either adaptations from the French, or pun-larded farces and burlesques, at best ephemeral, and at worst of a rare puerility and vulgarity, and that the few attempts at "literary drama" which reached the stage were hopelessly anæmic. It is not strange that Archer's determination to devote himself to the culture of this ungrateful plot, where nothing but weeds grew freely, seemed to some of his friends to involve a deplorable waste of power.

No doubt the very fact that the drama of his country had so fallen from its high estate was an attraction to him, as offering full scope to his passion for setting wrong things right. At all events, he went his own way, as was his wont, without paying too much heed to the voices round him; and, being now come to the centre of English theatrical life, set himself to the not altogether easy task of obtaining admission to his chosen field. He had not yet given up entirely the idea of original production, though

[1] See verses, *Competent Dramatists*, p. 89.

none of his attempts in that direction had, in his own eyes, come within measurable distance of success. But the most promising line of approach, and the one most clearly marked out for him by his innate bent, was that of dramatic criticism; and, while entering, with no great ardour, on his studies in the law, working at the British Museum Library for the *Globe Encyclopædia* on the important subjects[1] which were now being assigned to him, and pursuing various dramatic projects, he kept a keen look out for an opening in the critical ranks. The opportunity was not long in coming. A production of *Othello* at Drury Lane, with Charles Dillon as the Moor and Miss Wallis as Desdemona, passed almost unnoticed by the Press; and Archer wrote to Mr. James Mortimer, the editor of the *London Figaro*, calling attention to the fact, and pointing out how unsatisfactory it was that a Shakespearean production of some importance should be ignored, while columns were devoted to ephemeral burlesque and opera-bouffe. In reply the editor, who was in want of a critic, and probably was in the open secret of the authorship of *The Fashionable Tragedian*, sent two stalls for the next production at Drury Lane (*Hamlet*, with Bandmann and Miss Wallis), telling his correspondent to let him have "a practical demonstration of his critical capabilities". In the "practical demonstration", which was published in the *Figaro* of December 14, 1878, Archer made his first appearance in the London Press as a theatrical critic.

The gate thus set ajar, he was not long in effecting an entrance into the charmed circle. The great asset of the *Figaro*, as a theatrical paper, was its editor's unrivalled knowledge of the modern French theatre. Having lived much in Paris (he had been at one

[1] Among others "Shakespeare" and "Spiritualism".

time employed in Napoleon III's entourage), he was a walking cyclopædia of the drama of the Second Empire. It was round him that the critics clustered at London first nights, to learn from what French playwright, famous or obscure, the "new and original" English play they were met to see and criticize had been "conveyed". What the *Figaro* did not know about French plays was not knowledge. Now the visit of the Comédie Française to London, memorable in theatrical annals, was fixed for May 1879, and it was clearly desirable that the paper should make a special feature of it. Possibly of his own motion, possibly on Archer's suggestion, Mortimer decided to publish a series of summaries of the plays announced for production during the visit, which should assist London playgoers to follow the proceedings on the stage. And who so fit to do the work as an aspiring critic, with a competent knowledge of French and of the stage, and ready to go anywhere and do anything that would bring him in touch with the theatre? The commission was given, and Archer left for Paris on February 15th.

In those days there stood, in the Rue St. Hyacinthe St. Honoré, a little, dingy hostelry, the Hôtel Gibraltar, managed by a hostess half or wholly Spanish, whose speech was a strange conglomerate of French, Spanish, and one or two other tongues. Hardly more than a *hôtel garni*, it was cheap, central, and reasonably clean, and Archer had found it answer his purposes well in 1878. Here he settled down to live laborious days and nights, working on the *Figaro* summaries of plays and on his stint of articles for the *Encyclopædia*. A good deal of the work was done in the Bibliothèque Nationale; but much time was of course devoted to seeing the plays he had to summarize—and others. His "bag" of playbills from this visit runs to thirty-five, representing in all seventy-four plays seen, and covering a wide range of French drama, from Racine and Molière to Labiche and Meilhac and Halévy. During the Easter vacation he was joined by his brother (now reading in London for the Indian Service) for a ten days' holiday of the strenuous kind that only youth and enthusiasm could survive. The day would begin with a bowl of chocolate and a roll at a *crêmerie;* the forenoon be spent on some orthodox piece of sightseeing—the Louvre, the Luxembourg, or Notre Dame and the river; in the afternoon the elder brother would be plunged in his work, and the younger in the study of the play for the evening. Then dinner at a restaurant in the Quartier Latin, where one fared sumptuously at Fr. 1.50 a head, *vin compris;* and then—crown and complement of the day—the theatre, which three times out of four meant the Français. At that time the Comédie Française stood at a level of excellence seldom surpassed in the course of its long history. Got, Coquelin, Mounet-Sully, the incomparable Delaunay, Mme Favart, Sarah Bernhardt, Croizette, were but bright particular stars shining in a firmament of minor but yet brilliant luminaries. Some of the productions seemed to come as near perfection as human stage-craft could attain; the acting in the smallest characters was often as masterly as that of the protagonists. For the expert and the tiro alike the fascination of the evenings spent in the sober old playhouse was inexhaustible.

The summaries—twenty articles, dealing with forty-one plays—appeared in the *Figaro* from March 22nd to May 28th, and were republished in book form in time for the opening of the visitors' London season (May 31st). Meanwhile their author had returned to London in the beginning of April, and taken his place as a permanent member of the *Figaro* staff. On May 28th appears the first of a series of sixteen articles on the Comédie Française, which is continued till July 19th;[1] and from this time onwards the new contributor carries on, almost single-handed, the work of dramatic critic and theatrical news editor, while his hand is frequently distinguishable in the book reviews and literary notes.

Meanwhile the editor of the paper had fallen on evil days, through his rashness in admitting to his columns a series of violent articles by Mrs. Georgina Welldon, in which the lady told the story of her incarceration in a lunatic asylum and of her experiences therein. A prosecution for criminal libel was launched against Mr. Mortimer by some of the persons denounced in the articles, and early in July he was convicted on that charge. Strangely enough, his case did not "come up for judgment" till November, when he was sentenced to three months' imprisonment. His preoccupation with the case, and his eventual temporary seclusion from the world, threw much additional labour on the new dramatic critic.

Throughout 1880 and great part of 1881 he remained chained to his *Figaro* desk, escaping only for short runs to Paris at Easter each year, and a somewhat longer holiday in Norway in the summer

[1] In the back row of the Gaiety stalls, which was assigned to the critics for the Comédie Française season, Archer frequently sat next to a large-boned, burly man with a crutch, quite unknown to him, whose remarkable appearance excited his keenest curiosity. "Everything about him was on a large scale, as of a torso rough-hewn by Michael Angelo. . . . I thought of him as a sort of maimed Berserker, dropped by some anachronistic freak of destiny into the Gaiety stalls." Several years later, calling at the office of the *Magazine of Art,* he found his maimed Berserker again, in the person of the editor, William Ernest Henley.

of 1880. But his way of life was greatly changed by the return of his family in 1880 to settle in the neighbourhood of London. This flitting was not accomplished without a misadventure which very nearly ended in tragedy. The 800-ton barque *Scottish Knight*, in which they had left Keppel Bay, touched a coral reef off the east coast of Queensland, and, though the vessel was eventually saved by beaching, she had to be abandoned in open sea by her passengers, who regained their port of embarkation after a trying experience, including a perilous voyage in an open boat and a short sojourn on a desert island.

The family, at length safely arrived, took up their abode at Dulwich, where they remained for a number of years, Thomas Archer having found employment as Agent-General for Queensland; and this became William Archer's headquarters, though he retained a room in London for late theatre nights.

The next year proved a strenuous one. The *Figaro* appearing only twice a week, its critic was not forced to work at quite such high pressure as if the paper had been a daily. But it chanced that the special calls on the London critics, apart from the current productions, were that year unusually numerous. A starring visit from Sarah Bernhardt; a season of Dutch plays; Edwin Booth's visit, culminating in the Irving-Booth performances of *Othello*; the memorable two months "Gastspiel" of the Meiningen Company; another season of French plays—all of these added to the burdens as well as to the interest of the critic's task. All this time the normal productions of the theatrical season had to be dealt with, the column of theatrical news and notes purveyed, and a considerable amount of book-reviewing done; while, from the autumn of 1880 onwards, the work of recasting and amplifying his *Figaro* criticisms of current productions into the comprehensive review of the native drama eventually published as *English Dramatists of To-day*, must have made great inroads on his time. A number of magazine articles, too, were written at this time, and some found their way into print; notably a study of Ibsen, which appeared in the *St. James's Magazine* of January and February 1881.

But critical work formed only a part of the activities of these years. Having failed to find a publisher for his translation of *The Pillars of Society*, Archer had set himself, as the only way of bringing Ibsen to the front, to adapt the play for the English stage; for in those days it was unthinkable that a faithful translation, even of a French piece, much more of a play by an unknown Hyperborean dramatist, should ever make its way on to the London boards. By the end of 1878, an "adaptation", which might have been better described as an abridgement, had been accepted by Mr. W. H. Vernon, who was much struck by the part of Consul Bernick. But Mr. Vernon had no theatre at his disposal, and negotiations for a London production dragged on for nearly two years. At last, since no better might be, the piece was produced experimentally at a Gaiety matinée on December 15, 1880—and fell perfectly flat. The production, as a whole, was inevitably scrambling and ineffective. But the best setting and acting could not have made the play a success with the English critics and audiences of that day. Ibsen's time was not yet come.

The other dramatic attempts of this time need not long detain us. An original one-act drama, entitled *Auto-da-fé*, was praised by the two or three actors and managers to whom it was submitted, but rejected on the ground that there was no market for serious one-act pieces. It would have saved Archer occasional annoyance in after years if the same fate had befallen *Australia ; or the Bushrangers*, a melodrama conceived in something of the same frolic spirit that had inspired his boyish tale, *The Doom of the Destroyed* (with episodes suggested by the exploits of the Kelly gang of bushrangers, and local colour derived from his own recollections of the Bush), which he, and a friend writing under the *nom de guerre* of A. C. Stanley, compounded in dreadful secrecy. This hair-raising piece was produced at the Grecian Theatre on April 16, 1881, and seems actually to have run for three weeks. Before the production, however, remorse had already overtaken him ("I saw two acts of it rehearsed", he wrote, "and that was quite enough for me"), and he had disposed of his share in the venture to his collaborator. But he was not to escape so easily. At odd moments during the next forty years and more, *Australia; or the Bushrangers*, would rise up at the critical banquet and shake its gory locks at him. That a critic who in his youth had shared in the concoction of a Grecian melodrama should venture in after years to speak his mind about other men's melodramas, seemed to some, and particularly to the melodramatists concerned, an outrageous thing. And even in quite recent years the spectre of *Australia*, accompanied by the ghosts of other melodramas which never existed at all, has been known to stalk through newspaper articles and paragraphs.[1]

A pleasant and useful by-product of his relations with W. H. Vernon, which were most cordial throughout, was the formation of an intimacy with Sydney

[1] The curious in such matters may find the tale of Archer's essays in drama after his coming to London summed up in his letter printed in the *Era* of July 19, 1886.

Grundy, the first of many friendships with dramatists. Grundy's robust talent and downright character and utterance were much to Archer's taste; while the dramatist, on his side, though by temperament irascible enough, was a man strong enough to accept and be grateful for blame as well as praise from a critic who took the trouble to understand him.

A large part of the fruits of Archer's two and a half years' labours on the *Figaro* are garnered in *English Dramatists of To-day*, whose pages include the substance of such of his criticisms of contemporary English drama as he considered worth preserving. But much interesting matter—such as his studies of Irving, Booth, and others in Shakespearean parts; of Modjeska's productions; of the Meiningen Company's performances; and of the various French seasons—lies buried in the dusty volumes of the defunct paper. A study of these criticisms would considerably modify the tradition (fostered, it is true, to some extent by himself) of his comparative indifference and insensitiveness to the niceties of acting.

During the latter part of these first years in London Archer's health had begun to cause some anxiety to himself and those about him. Though both physically and constitutionally strong, he was of a highly nervous temperament, and had always been liable to occasional violent attacks of headache, short, but utterly prostrating while they lasted. But there seemed now to be signs of more serious trouble, and his spirits as well as his bodily health were affected. Various causes contributed to this loss of tone. Two years and a half of overwork, and of constant late nights in the unwholesome air of the theatre, might by themselves have sufficed to account for the "liver dyspepsia" which the doctors diagnosed.

But there were other, less obvious, factors in the case. The "coiled perplexities of youth" had him in their grip.

"Both my parents", he says,[1] "belonged to families of a deeply religious cast of mind, ultra-orthodox in dogma, heterodox, and even vehemently dissenting, on questions of church government." The deeply religious cast of mind he had inherited, and the dislike of priestcraft, but not the orthodoxy. The dogmas of Christianity came before him in his boyhood in their most inflexible, least accommodating forms; but, in whatever guise they had been presented to his mind, it is probable that he would have been unable to accept them. His logical sense was too intransigent to be satisfied with any of the current solutions of the, to his mind, insoluble dilemmas which they presented. And one of the chief of them was diametrically opposed to the central article of his creed—the Ascent of Man. With him, as he said long after, "the awakening of thought was the awakening of disbelief. It cost me no struggle, no regret. The only emotion I can recall was the pleasant sense of reassurance with which I discovered that many of the wise and great were no more Christians than I was."[2]

But

> Die Thränen und die Seufzer
> Die kamen hintennach.

As he grew to manhood he found the convictions on things divine on which all his thinking turned more and more at odds with his most intimate affections;

[1] Introduction to *Poets of the Younger Generation*. His mother, though not a professing member of the Glasite Church, held the Glasites' views and conformed to their observances; while Thomas Archer was in general sympathy with the very similar views of the Walkerite or Separatist Church, to which most of his brothers and sisters belonged.

[2] *William Archer as Rationalist*, p. 155.

and the conflict caused him some unhappiness. This it was, quite as much as physical ill-health, that was at the root of the fits of depression to which he was subject during these years. The case was not likely to be mended by the impending return of his family from Australia, the news of which, when it reached him, he received with very mixed feelings. He foresaw that in the constant intercourse of daily life the opposition in religious belief, which carried with it a divergence in social and political views, could not fail to obtrude itself. His forebodings were justified: he and his had to pass through the same ordeal that Robert Louis Stevenson, the "dear and illustrious fellow-townsman" whom as yet he knew not, had undergone some seven years before.[1] The trouble wore itself out in time, as happily is—and was, even in those more rigid days—the way of such troubles, when affection and mutual forbearance are there to help. The young man was able, for the most part, to keep from his parents' knowledge such of his utterances as were likely to cause them serious grief; while they, on their side, viewing the general tenor of his life and work, soon began to take comfort in the reflection, natural to humanity, however repugnant to some schemes of theology, that a tree must be judged by its fruit. In the meantime, however, both parties suffered, and the pain which he was compelled to bring down upon those nearest and dearest to him, and through them upon himself, left lasting marks upon Archer's mind. We have an echo from these days in a twelve-line epigram, written long after:

[1] "If all that I hold true and most desire to spread is to be such death, and worse than death, in the eyes of my father and mother, what the *devil* am I to do?" R. L. S. to Charles Baxter, February 2, 1873. See also his impressive parable, *The House of Eld*.

Above the gates of Hell (so Dante sings)
The institution's origin is dated:
"Before me, saving the eternal things,
Was nought created."

'Tis true; for in the primal nebulæ,
Before they took to clustering round a centre,
There lurked in germ the mind of man—and he
Was Hell's inventor.

Making a fire-drill of his demon-dread
Abject, and vengeance-hunger unforgiving,
He lit the flames that sear, not bad men dead,
But good men living.

It must not be supposed, however, that these years had been on the whole a time of gloom. As with Johnson's old friend, "cheerfulness was always breaking in". The young man's powers of enjoyment were unblunted. He had taken the keenest pleasure in much of his work, and had enjoyed no less the off-days at his uncle's hospitable house at Croydon, the occasional tramps in the north with Edinburgh friends, and the longer holidays, brilliant with sun and summer, in Norway.

Yet by the autumn of 1881 it had become evident to those about him that there was something seriously amiss, and his parents proposed that he should try what a complete change would do for him, suggesting a stay in Germany. He caught at the suggestion, but with an amendment as to place. Italy drew him with many cords: the glamour of the name, his love of warmth, and the knowledge that in Rome he might see in the flesh the poet whom, since the appearance of *A Doll's House* in the end of 1879, he believed more firmly than ever to be the master-dramatist of the time. "Don't talk to me of your health", wrote Sydney Grundy to him in the following December. "You went to Italy simply and solely to talk to Ibsen." Early in November he left England, and, after a short stay in Provence, sent off his luggage by rail to Leghorn, and marched into the enchanted land on foot, knapsack on back.

VA

LETTERS, ETC., OF 1879–1881

COMPETENT DRAMATISTS

(*London Figaro*, February 5, 1879)

"WHERE are our dramatists?" the critics cry.
"Our English dramatists—we cannot find 'em."
"I", says Burnand, and Byron echoes "I",
And Gilbert vows he's not a whit behind 'em.
"We all can write good dramas when we try;
If people say we can't—why, never mind 'em.
We not original! Good critics, hold!
Think of *The Ne'er-do-well* and *Guinea Gold*.

"Feuillet is well enough, and so's Sardou,
Dumas and Augier are clever fellows,
But *we* could teach them all a trick or two—
Look at our *Vagabonds* and *Elfinellas*.
We sometimes take a play from them, 'tis true,
Merely to show we're friendly and not jealous;
So what of that? Our paying plays we bone,
But all our glorious failures are our own."

Truly we do not lack originality:
In *No. 20* there was quite enough;
And as for genius, vigour and vitality,
See Mr. Reade's ingenuous little puff[1]
Of *Ne'er Too Late*: and it, in sad reality,
Might well outlive all France—'tis long and tough;
Well on to midnight it had outlived me,
I left them struggling bravely with Act III.

[1] "*It's Never Too Late to Mend* has outlived a hundred French plays and will outlive a hundred more."

Come, Messieurs the Originals, be plain;
Don't talk of what you might, could, would, or
should do!
What *have* you done? What will you do again?
If you can show one play that's all-round good, do!
Plot new and strong, a deftly ravelled skein,
Whose actors talk as human beings would do—
Produce this one, by whomsoever be it,
And I'll—why, hang it all, I'll go and see it!

Our Boys? A clever farce of strained conceit.
Diplomacy? A glorious—adaptation.
Our Club? A trifle, dull, but short and sweet.
Pink Dominoes? A Boucicaultization.
D. Druce? George Eliot watered—but yet *neat*.
Proof? Celebrated case—of annexation.
Engaged? Original? Who knows? Perchance.
At least we're sure 'twas not annexed from France.

Tom Taylor now's a solid, skilful man,
Though he, we know, *reprend son bien partout*;
That cynic Gilbert's got a simple plan
For humour—just to turn the world askew;
James Albery? Not one since Sheridan
Has done such dialogue as he can do;
But as for plot, such detail he despises,
And lets it worry through as heaven devises.

There's Wills can "bombast out" a fine blank verse
And make dull dramas of distorted history;
Byron will ne'er have empty pit or purse
So long as words remain for him to twist awry;
Simpson's unequal—Merivale is worse,
So strong at times, their weakness is a mystery;
Farnie and Reece excel in—*Stars and Garters*;
Grundy and Matthison are tongue-tied martyrs.[1]

[1] This verse much "edited" for prudential reasons.

What wonder that good *pâtés* fresh from Paris
Our love for home-made pies should somewhat damp?
The English dramatist's a Mrs. Harris,
The English critic oft a Mrs. Gamp.
The playwright *may* come—but as yet he tarries;
Meanwhile French oil sustains our flickering lamp—
And therefore, hail Dumas, delightful *vaurien!*
Three cheers for Augier, and *vive* Victorien!

To George R. Halkett

August 20th, 1880

My dear George,

I returned from Norway on Monday and received your note on Tuesday morning. Many thanks for keeping yours truly in mind in your converse with the literary bigwigs who seem to rain around you wherever you go. I enclose herewith a wise, witty, learned, profound, moral, religious, philosophical and generally invaluable article which you will greatly oblige me by forwarding to Principal Tulloch.[1] You might look it through yourself first, correct the grammar and spelling and dot the i's and stroke the t's. The title, you may mention, is only provisional. Also you may state that if this will not do—or "fither or no" in fact—the same sublime genius has unlimited stores in hand and would be only too glad to supply articles on any possible subject in the English, French or Scandinavian drama, or any other subject whatsoever down to Chinese metaphysics. Just as a first instalment I could let him have three papers on Augier, Sardou and Dumas, and some half a dozen or so articles on Ibsen and Björnson, with a series of eight or ten papers on a national theatre. In short you may tell him to keep

[1] Editor of *Fraser's Magazine*, published by Longmans.

up his spirits—I won't desert him while the Longmans have a guinea in their coffers.

What about our *magnum opus*? Shall I set to work?

With kind remembrances,

Yours,

W. A.

To J. M. Robertson

October 21st, 1881

You ask me why, though ill at ease,
Within these regions I subsist
Whose spirits falter in the mist
And languish for the purple seas:

To which I reply that

I will see before I die
The palms and temples of the south—

if I don't die first that is to say. All this poetic and figurative language is intended gently to break to you the fact that I am going to cut my ungrateful country for the winter, and wander southwards. I haven't quite decided where, but as every road leads to Rome, I shouldn't wonder if you were one day to hear from me in the Eternal City. My health is the immediate cause of this move. I have been in a sort of broken down condition for ever so long. The doctor calls it "liver dyspepsia"—I was afraid of my heart, the action of which was anything but pleasant and satisfactory. In any case I was far from well, and my people were very anxious for me to go abroad for a time. They suggested Germany, but *pas si bête*, say I—if I'm to be frozen anywhere it may as well be in London. My determination to go has been clinched by the discovery that the *Figaro* is in anything but a flourishing condition, so that I don't think I am losing much in giving it up. *Enfin*, I'm off. . . . You may announce to the faithful in Edinburgh my approaching departure, so that they may have lots of time to subscribe for the gold watch or silver-mounted dressing-case which they will no doubt feel impelled to present me with. . . .

From J. M. ROBERTSON

23rd Oct., 1881

MY DEAR ARCHER,

You have given me a distressing surprise. I have told you the last two times you have been down that you weren't looking quite satisfactory, though I thought you better lately; but I didn't think you would need to change your climate to come round. I will, however, give myself the satisfaction of thinking that you will not only get set up abroad but enjoy the process in more ways than one. . . . Really, you are rather to be envied than otherwise. "Liver dyspepsia", I trust, doesn't take long to cure (by the way, wouldn't it be wise to see one of the best Paris doctors?—"liver dyspepsia" sounds slightly puzzle-headed); and who wouldn't get well in Italy! My best wishes go with you, my dear fellow. I shall often think of you, going about in Genoa and Venice —of course you'll see Venice—and Florence and Naples and Rome! living in the past without any liver complaint, and in the present, by consequence, in a state of progressive convalescence. . . .

Many, many thanks for all the trouble you have taken about my paper. Martin told me of your split with the *St. James's* man. When he returns my MS. I *may* possibly send it to the *Magazine of Art*. I met, the other evening, the man who has just been made editor—Henley, a pleasant, brilliant fellow, who goes with a crutch. He says he's going to introduce a new régime. But I have a notion he'll ruin the Magazine in six months, if he doesn't get sacked in three. He is considerably too good for the place, I should say. . . .

The E.N. staff express sincere concern about your health—everybody is too dejected to think about presentation watches. . . .

Poor old *Fig*! I must treasure the numbers till you go.

Your friend,

J. R.

Let me reiterate my suggestion about consulting a Paris doctor.

To J. M. Robertson

October 26th, 1881

Thanks for your letter and for the cuttings, which interested me much. I shall have an extensive correspondence to keep up in Italy, but if my correspondents of this side do their duty, I don't think they will find me remiss. You don't know how a letter from home cheers the wanderer in foreign parts—I do.

I am sorry the phrase "liver dyspepsia" does not commend itself to you. I am highly pleased with it myself, and think it most satisfactory. If I went to a Parisian doctor he would no doubt find out something more imposing for my complaint, but I am modest in my aspirations, and liver dyspepsia quite suits me. There is an aesthetic lowness of tone about it which seems to me eminently pleasing. Moreover, I do not see why a man who lives in London should go to a Parisian doctor, unless indeed the latter can minister to a mind diseased and pluck from the memory a rooted sorrow, which I am not aware to be a branch of French medical science any more than of English. Don't suppose I have been ordered to Italy by the doctor—I have been ordered by my father and mother, who don't know that I have consulted a doctor at all. The doctor prescribes strong ammonia and various other horrors—they prescribe a thorough change, and I think they're right.

I shall bully the *St. James's* man either to print your article or to return it to me at once.

I heard Foote lecture for the first time last Sunday night: what a first-rate speaker he is!

They say Italy brings spiritual regeneration to some people. When you next hear from me I hope I may be regenerate, but I don't much believe in new births until we've quite got over the effects of the old one, which I haven't as yet.

Yours ever,

W. A.

From HEINE

DAS GLÜCK IST EINE LEICHTE DIRNE

O Joy is but a lichtsome hizzy,
She winna bide wi' ye ava;
She stroks yer broo an' maks ye dizzy,
Then kisses ye, an' flees awa.

Dame Sorrow is a canty kimmer,
A warm embrace ye's hae frae her;
She vows she isna thrang—the limmer!
Knits by your bed an' winna stir.

VI

1881–1882

LETTERS FROM ITALY

A CENTURY of praises of Italy might easily be compiled from William Archer's writings. He admired many foreign countries and was grateful for their gifts—with two of them, Norway and America, his ties were so close that he hardly thought of them as foreign—but his feeling for this country was a thing apart and beyond compare. For Italy and what he found in it worked in him something like the miracle of regeneration of which he had felt so incredulous. Before he had been long in the country he was writing to his mother: "Italy has made a new man of me, in body and mind."

His first letter from Italian soil shows that the process had set in even before he crossed the frontier. Writing to Robertson from Ospedaletti, after an enthusiastic account of his walk along the Riviera from Cannes, he winds up:

"... I must apologize for all this gush, but if you had had such a week of sunshine you would gush too. My internal mechanism is not what it should be yet, but in spite of the depressing effects of utter solitude, I have actually been enjoying life, which is a sensation I had almost forgotten. There have actually been several moments of every day when I should have liked to possess Joshua's power of bidding the sun to stand still. But, short of standing still when I wanted him to, the sun has been all that mortal man could desire. I don't know why any one lives anywhere else but on the Riviera. ..."

Marching along the Italian Riviera, with a short halt at Genoa, he reaches Leghorn in about a week, and thence takes train to Florence.

To CHARLES ARCHER

HOTEL PORTA ROSSA,
FLORENCE,
November 25th (1881)

MY DEAR C.,

Although you don't deserve it after your shameful conduct, I can't leave Florence without sending you a hilsen [greeting] from the home of Romola. I came across from Leghorn yesterday *d'une humeur massacrante,* partly owing to the non-appearance of my traps at that beastly hole, and consequent anxiety about them, partly arising from the feeling of sheer loneliness which is the most persistent form taken by *atra cura, post equitem* who rides alone. The day was dull, and as the wretched "treno omnibus" dragged on, I could hardly keep my spirits half a degree above zero by the sad mechanic exercise of looking up every second word of *I Promessi Sposi* in a pocket dictionary. At last we got into Florence, a little after two, and the moment I walked down the Via dei Tornabuoni en route for this hotel, I began to feel at home, for the very name had a familiar ring about it. Who Lorenzo Tornabuoni was precisely I forget, but I know the name figures in *Romola* pretty largely. And indeed the feeling of having been long familiar with the whole affair has been growing upon me in the thirty-six hours I have been here, though of course everything is quite different from what I imagined it. . . .

If it weren't for the cold I would fix here instead

of Rome, but this morning was a warning, and I wasn't sorry to get the intimation from the railway people that my luggage was at Leghorn, though I am rather alarmed to see that it has arrived in five packages, whereas it left Marseilles in four. I hope this increase has not been effected by the division of my book-box into its component parts, viz. box and lid, and the elimination of the books in the process.

. . . At Genoa I went to the Norwegian Consulate, and asked the Consul if he knew anything of the whereabouts of Henrik Ibsen. He said that about two months ago he heard he was in Rome, and believed that was his headquarters if not his regular home. If so, I must certainly beard the lion in his den, even if I get kicked downstairs for my pains. I expect when he hears my name he will recommend me to

> Gaa glemselsgang fra havn til havn
> Og list mig til et fremmed navn
> Og gjem mig for mig selv.[1]

My address until further orders is:

"Ferma in Posta, ROMA." *Verb sap.*

Your affecte. brother,
W. A.

I have forgotten to mention the house with the inscription: "In questa casa degli Alighieri nacque il Divino Poeta."

[1] Freely translatable: "'Neath changing skies forget thy shame, And steal thyself some stranger's name, And from thy conscience hide." Ibsen, *A Brother in Need*. The allusion, of course, is to W. A.'s "adaptation" of *Pillars of Society*.

HOTEL LAURATI,
ROME,
November 30th/81

MY DEAR C.,

Though I am now beginning to know Rome—at least a certain part of it—like a book, I find it difficult to realize that it *is* Rome. Somehow you don't think of Rome as a city of dwelling-houses, but as a city of temples and fora and baths and theatres and amphitheatres. But there is no doubt of its being Rome. This hotel is on the Quirinal Hill. I look out of my bedroom every morning at a fragment of the wall of Servius Tullius, or whoever Niebuhr and Mommsen have substituted for him—you may take your choice as to the man, but there is no doubt as to the wall. From the hotel you look down upon the forum of Trajan and his column. I got my watch mended today at the foot of the Capitol, within a pace or two of the steps where Rienzi was murdered, and at the foot of the stairs of the Ara Coeli, which occupy the place of the stairs which Julius Cæsar ascended on his knees during one of his triumphs. At the top of the stairs is the place where Brutus harangued the mob—do you remember: "Und ist gewiss ein ehren*werther* Mann"[1]—and I'm quite sure his speech wasn't nearly as good as Shakespeare's. You see I've mixed up Brutus and Mark Antony, but it's very characteristic, for everything gets mixed up here—it's like a willow-pattern plate—history without the least perspective, or rather frightfully foreshortened. As someone or other says, Time has crossed and recrossed his records here until they have become absolutely illegible. In other towns a few occasional odds and ends of history crop up,

[1] The reference is to Barnay's masterly delivery of Antony's oration in the Meiningen Company's production of *Julius Cæsar*.

but here every stone in the streets reminds you—or would remind you if you could remember—of someone or something, from Romulus to Goethe, or rather from Janus to Daisy Miller.

. . . . .

It is perfectly overwhelming—it is like looking straight into the eyes of "the stony face of Time"—I feel a good deal like Peer Gynt with den store Böjgen—I say: "Ak, Böjg, hvem er du?"[1] and invariably I get the Ekko paa Tydsk, dialekt fra Berlin,[2] "Ach, Sphinx, wer bist du?" I am even haunted with voices singing "Vi ere tanker, du skulde taenkt os",[3] or more often "Vi ere fakta, du skulde vidst os".[4] And the worst of it is that it is impossible to "staenge for arrige nissebuk-tanker"[5] —whether you will or no your imagination and memory are kept constantly on the strain.

Today I have begun to "gaa udenom".[6] A Signor Senesi, to whom Mr. Robert Waterston gave me an introduction, was going on business to Frascati . . . and he asked me to go with him. So we started at 7.30, and I never saw anything more lovely than the morning over the Campagna, with our old friend Soracte, not "nive candida" this time, standing out alone to the northward, and the ruins of the great aqueducts close to us to the south. As you mount the hill from the station to the town of Frascati, you get a magnificent view, and I saw lying away to the right a white village with a church with a dome. I was just on the point of remarking: "All the villages here

[1] Hei, Boyg, who are you?
[2] Echo in German. Dialect Berlin.
[3] We are thoughts; thou shouldst have thought us.
[4] We are facts, thou shouldst have known us.
[5] Shut out cantankerous hobgoblin thoughts.
[6] Go round about.

seem to go in for miniature imitations of St. Peter's", when Senesi pointed to the village and said: "Ecco Roma!"—and I found that the miniature imitation was St. Peter's itself. . . . Then dined off becaccia (woodcock I believe) and some awfully good vin du pays, and returned to Rome about 2 o'clock.

Og dermed basta for today.

VIA DELL' ANIMA, *Sunday*

The great event has come off, satisfactorily, but not in the manner I expected. In the letter in which I shall enclose this I shall explain all about the [Scandinavian Club] at whose swarry I was present last night. Well, I had been about a quarter of an hour there, and was standing close to the door, when it opened and in walked unmistakably the great Henrik. My photograph is very good so far as the face is concerned, but it gives you the idea of broader shoulders and a fuller chest than he really has. He is of middle height, rather under than over—at any rate in talking to him I feel myself noticeably taller. Apparently he is nothing at all of a lion among the sönner af Norge (and döttre too) who patronize the association, who, forresten, are in a minority among the Swedes and Danes. He went about for a while talking to different people, and gave you the impression, which I was prepared for, of extreme quietness. The red ribbon which excited young Björnson's contempt was very prominent in his buttonhole. After a little, I got Professor Ravnkilde [Chairman of the Committee] to introduce me to him. I saw at once that he did not connect my name with *Samfundets Stötter*, so after a little I told him about it. He had heard of the production, but not my name, and took my rather lame excuses for not having got his permission very readily. . . . He invited me to call at his house, which I shall do some day this week; and besides I daresay I shall see him again at the [Club], when I hope to get a little more under the surface, if it is at all possible. One question which you and I have discussed I got a solution of—he does not read any of the French dramatists, and moreover he hardly ever goes to the theatre—and small blame to him in Italy say I, though he says there are some very good Italian actors, besides the famous ones. Altogether the interview was a success. Though I can't say that L's description of him as a spidsborger[1] is quite justified, he certainly is not the man you would imagine to have written Aase's death-scene and the fourth act of *Brand*. Perhaps some day I may say of him: "Hvor han vokste mens han talte",[2] but at first sight there is an absence of anything Titanic about him. It will be all the more interesting to try and get a little into his real character, but I am not sanguine, as I haven't the knack of that sort of thing. However, for the present "the old min's friendly", and that's the main point.

He says *Gjengangere* should be out in Copenhagen by this time.

To J. M. ROBERTSON

55 VIA DELL' ANIMA (3° piano) ROME,
January 8th, 1882

MY DEAR ROBERTSON,

Though I am by this time quite an Ancient Roman, I confess I can't even yet write the above date without a certain sense of strangeness. The

[1] Bourgeois or Philistine.

[2] "How he grew while he was speaking." Agnes's words in *Brand*, Act I.

idea of Rome as a place where Brown, Jones, Robinson and Archer eat, drink, sleep and generally vegetate, just as they might in Portobello or Pentonville, is still a marvel to me. One somehow thinks of Rome as a city of temples and theatres and porticoes and forums—anything but a city of dwelling-houses. As a matter of fact it is the dwelling-place of some 200,000 god-forgotten Italians and some 50,000 god-forgetting foreigners, who go about their daily business and think deuced little of Scipio or Cæsar, or Nero or Marcus Aurelius, or Rienzi, or Tasso or Michael Angelo. I, on the other hand, in spite of the colossal ignorance which one cannot possibly realize until one comes to Rome, am haunted at every turn by the feeling that every stone is speaking to me, or would speak if I only had ears to hear. You feel that the earth is impregnated with the whole history of the world, sacred and profane. George Eliot says the last word on Rome, as she does on many things. She calls it: "Rome, the city of visible history, where the past of a whole hemisphere seems moving in funeral procession, *with strange ancestral images and trophies gathered from afar*." You may think the phrase commonplace, but you do not know its beautiful fitness until you have seen the ancestral images and the trophies gathered from afar. Only she might have said a whole sphere, for America too is represented. I live quite close to "Hilda's Tower" of *Transformation*, and it carries one back in a flash of association to the Puritan Fathers and Plymouth Rock. The roof of Santa Maria Maggiore is gilded with the first gold sent by the Spanish adventurers from Peru. A common walk of mine is past a church from the steps of which Augustine departed to convert Britain, while Gregory the Great solemnly blessed him. The sight of them brings back to you the whole of British history down to the Bradlaugh struggle. Of course there is much that is apocryphal in Rome, even outside the churches, but there is also much that is genuine and undoubted. . . . In short the whole history of the world converges in Rome, and if one weren't well padded in ignorance it would be quite ruinous to the nerves.

. . . Many thanks for the magazine [containing W. A.'s article on Henrik Ibsen], which is at present in the hands of the mighty Ibsen himself. I see that great man almost every day at a café which he and I both frequent for an afternoon glass of vermouth, and I have a yarn with him occasionally. He has just published a play called *Ghosts*, which is playing the devil's delight in the North. [Follows a short account of *Ghosts* and of its repercussions in Scandinavia.] . . .

Having now given you some information about the great dramatist my friend Henrik Ibsen, I want you to give me some information about another great dramatist my friend—Robert Lowe. It is a proud position for me to be as it were a sort of connecting link between these two great ornaments of the art I honor. But how is it that none of you scoundrels have sent me notices of Lowe's pantomime?[1] What is *Ghosts* to *Whittington*? . . . I call it perfidy to let the unhappy exile linger so long without news. . . . Remember me to everyone—Wilson, Martin, and all your godless crew at the *E.N.*

Yours ever,

W. A.

[1] Lowe had written the Christmas pantomime for the Theatre Royal, Edinburgh.

February 12th/82

What a rum old see-saw this world is! There is an original reflection for you, to begin a letter which I warn you will be as egotistical as the correspondence between X. and George Gilfillan used to be. The reflection is engendered by the circumstance that I, even I, find myself sitting down to write a letter, impelled thereto by sheer high spirits, and the necessity of working them off upon someone. You are the victim this evening, because I don't remember having raved much about Italy to you, and all my other friends must by this time be beginning to curse the hour in which Romulus was born and the wolf's pap which gave him suck. There is a certain amount of Mark Tapleyism in my jollity which gives it additional zest. I have got a cold through every fibre of my body, my head is heavy, my erst mellifluous voice is reduced to a rasping whisper; I am sitting with a fez on my head, two great-coats on my body, a railway-rug over my knees, and a bed-quilt between my feet and the brick floor. Yet withal am I passing merry. I have been basking all afternoon in the sunshine of the Borghese Gardens, watching an ant carrying out to the letter Mark Twain's description of the idiotic proceedings which render that over-rated insect a moral fraud. Then I have been having afternoon tea (Russian fashion, with lemon instead of milk) at the house of some friends, and from their windows watching the Romans making idiots of themselves in fancy dresses; for the Carnival has begun. Now I have come home, and this letter is to prevent me going to sleep before it is time to go to the Caffè del Senato and have a glass of "vino caldo" before turning in with a cold compress on my throat.

It was indeed a happy thought which brought me to Italy. You have no conception of the effect this marvellous country and city produce upon the barbarian mind. At present I am reading Hawthorne's *Transformation*, which I had almost forgotten, and find it by far the best book about Rome. . . . It gives you to perfection the *sensation* of Roman life. One speech of Hilda's struck me very much this morning. She says: "I sometimes fancy that Rome—mere Rome—will crowd everything else out of my heart." That is precisely the effect it has upon me. I feel an absolute lack of interest in anything beyond the Sabine Hills to the north and the Alban Hills to the south. (Don't take this admission as an excuse for not writing, for I go to the Post Office every evening and am jolly disappointed when I find nothing for me.) Well-meaning friends send me the dramatic papers now and then—I read them as a duty, but I believe I would hear that Irving had been hissed in Romeo, or that Clement Scott was hanged, without more than the languidest satisfaction. When I read in the *Popolo Romano* the other day that Sir Bradlaugh had again failed to take his seat, I did feel a certain glow of indignation, but it didn't go the length of smashing the crockery or sending an explosive letter to Sir Stafford Northcote. As Benvenuto Cellini says: "I uttered a horrid imprecation", and thought no more about it. There has not been a cloud in the sky for a month past—the stone-pines glow in the sunsets, and the fountains plash lazily among the ilex avenues of the villa gardens—the hills are sometimes blue, sometimes lavender, sometimes purple—the music on the Pincian sounds lovely when you're far enough away from it, and through the fretwork of trees in the Borghese Gardens even St. Peter's looks beautiful—these facts, with many similar ones, are the only things in the world that matter two straws to me. Only two things trouble me—the Carnival is turning *my* Rome topsyturvy, and when the Carnival is over I suppose I shall have to go to Naples. You will probably remark that the man whose one trouble in life is the necessity of going to Sorrento and Castellamare and Capri is in a very bad way—and so I am. I feel some great catastrophe hanging over my head like the sword of Damocles, because I have so much fatalism in me as to believe that no man can be so perfectly jolly as I have been for the past two months without paying dearly for it. If the catastrophe were to take the form of a Roman fever (I insist upon its being Roman) which should lay me in the Protestant graveyard beside the heart of that eminent Protestant, Shelley, I should say "meno male"—one of the few Italian phrases which please my pessimist soul, for I think "less bad" is a much more exact expression than "so much the better" or "tant mieux".

In short, in sending me to Italy, "as luck would have it, Providence was on my side". You know my somewhat snail-like habits in the matter of making, or rather not making, friends—how I draw into my shell on the slightest approach of the Philistine—well, here I have made no less than three friends, one male and two female, with whom I am as intimate as if I had known them all my life. The first, Bond,[1] a Cambridge law tutor, has unfortunately left for England, but for about a month we were inseparable, and I never knew a more thoroughly good fellow in all my life. . . . With him I had high old times indeed, and his ghost is still with me as I take my walks abroad and think of the stories we used to tell each other and the vermouths we used to have at the different cafés. . . .

[1] Now Dr. H. Bond, sometime Master of Trinity Hall.

Now that Bond is gone I have taken to cultivating two girls whom I knew before but rather neglected, and I find them an uncommonly good substitute. . . . They are both well-educated, as girls go, and one of them is unusually clever, with a finely developed sense of humour. . . .

Greet all the brethren. I wish some of you could have a little of the sunshine which as I write is bathing my beautiful prospect of tiled roofs.

Yours ever,

W. A.

Amidst all this sunshine and idyllic felicity, *English Dramatists* had been steadily progressing towards completion. On Bond's lamented departure in the end of January part of the manuscript goes with him, and by the beginning of March the last pages have been finished and dispatched. In the retrospect of the Roman days scribbled in the train on the way to Naples, we have the author's anticipations of the fate of his work.

To CHARLES ARCHER

IN THE TRAIN BETWEEN
ROME AND NAPLES,
March 5th/82

Just to show the forgivingness of my disposition I am going to inflict upon you one of my illegible train letters—the fact being that I am utterly tired of Daudet's *Numa Roumestan* (in Italian), Sawedwadgeorgeearllyttonbullwig's *Rienzi*, and Sandars' *Institutes of Justinian*, these being the varied reading I had provided myself with. . . .

"Eccomi qua", as we say in Italy, among the Apennines, with rain-clouds sweeping round the snow peaks, and strange old towns and castles and monasteries perched in mid air on the most inaccessible rocks discoverable above the vineyards and olive terraces. I had an idea before I came here that Italy was a Gjenganger; but it isn't—it is a solid reality. As I left Rome this morning and watched the dome of St. Peter's gradually receding as we wound round the Campagna to Albano, I felt a sort of *attendrissement* such as I never felt before on leaving any place whatsoever. I could scarcely believe that this was actually Rome, which three months ago was only a name to me, and seems now almost the only reality in the world. For you have no idea how Rome takes hold of you, and makes everything else seem remote, and as it were insignificant. Not that I am altogether sorry to leave it. I suppose the saying "tout lasse, tout casse, tout passe" applies to Rome as to everything else. I can't imagine myself tiring of the gardens and the fountains, and the ilex avenues and cactus hedges, but I suppose I should all the same. As it is, I shall look back to Rome as the most unbrokenly delightful episode in my life. Three months of perfectly undisturbed, quiet, unemotional and consequently even and non-reactionary enjoyment don't fall to the share of everyone at the advanced age of five and twenty. The strongest emotion I had to disturb me was the anxiety to know whether "the old min was friendly"—and even that wasn't of a very absorbing character. Fate seems to have come to the conclusion that it "owed me one", which on general principles it did, and so conspired even with the clerk of the weather to put things straight for me. Everyone says the season has been a very exceptional one, and for me the sunshine was half the battle, as I don't care two straws for the museums and galleries in comparison with the villa gardens and the Campagna and the hills. Then, in the matter of friends my luck has been unparallelled (is that rightly spelt?). I, who have gone round the world without making a single friend, and imagined that I never should pick up more than a passing acquaintance in travelling, have made three friends in Rome, all by the merest chance, than whom I couldn't imagine pleasanter or more congenial companions. I think there must be something in the air of Rome which softens characters as it does forms and colours. In the first place, Bond was one of the best fellows that ever trod shoe-leather, and his enthusiasm for Rome rendered him simply perfect as a companion. "Now this is what I came to Italy for!" was his favorite phrase whenever we got to one or other of our habitual coigns of vantage.—"Blow museums—this is what I came to Italy for!" This saying has become a stock phrase with my other two friends—two girls whom I had known a little before, and cultivated in a small way, but who began to cultivate me from the very day that Bond left, so that in a week they and I were as inseparable as he and I had been. The proverb that "two's company and three's none" is an even smaller half-truth than most other proverbs, for better company than we three couldn't be imagined. Every afternoon with the utmost regularity we went to some villa or other (there are half a dozen near Rome, each more lovely than the other) and sat beside some fountain looking out over the Campagna and yarning or reading or drawing or eating "pasticci" and figs—and always saying: "Now this is what we came to Italy for". . . .

I don't know if you notice an improvement in the handwriting of the last few lines—the fact is we have stopped at Capua, and by the same token we're getting near Naples. I'm afraid Rome itself may prove to have been *my* Capua, for I don't expect it has done much to develop my genius for dramatic criticism, and I have an impression that my Dramatists, whom I polished off last Monday, are a very poor and scrappy production indeed. Braekstad[1] is trying to work them with some publisher, but I don't expect he'll manage it, though he has a great "Kongetanke"[2] with which they are intimately connected (namely the publication of a series of English plays) and no man I know has less of "tvivlens gave".[3] But I have an impression that Ibsenian metaphysics fall through when brought in contact with London publishers. . . .

I have seen a good deal of "the old min" lately. I took an affecting farewell of him yesterday, and he gave me his photograph, with, written on the back: "Til Herr William Archer, venskabeligst og forbindtligst fra Henrik Ibsen." He sent me a pile of criticisms on *Gjengangere*, mostly Swedish, and these, together with a third reading of the play, have confirmed my belief in it as a great achievement, with all its faults. . . .

Have just caught my first glimpse of Vesuvius.

Yours Neapolitanly,

W.

NAPLES, *March* 14*th*/82

. . . This letter was begun in the Villa Nazionale on the Chiaja—the Pincio of Naples—it is useless to try

[1] H. L. Braekstad, a son of Trondhjem settled in London, and a devoted friend to Archer, who, on his part, wrote of him some years later as "that honour to Trondhjem and best fellow among all the sönner af Norge".

[2] Kingly thought: *The Pretenders*, Act IV.

[3] The gift of doubt: *The Pretenders*, Act IV.

to sit indoors on these brilliant days. Your recollections of the Bay of Naples do not deceive you—it is wunderschön; but after all it is not Rome, and I am dépaysé. I tire of the eternal blue sea and the irrepressible Capri, and importunate Posilippo and ubiquitous Vesuvius. It hasn't half the variety and charm of my dear old Campagna, and Soracte, and Tibur, and Praeneste and the Alban Mount. Naples is *oleographic*, in fact, compared to Rome—it is like enamel upon papier-mâché, while Rome is a delicate water-color. Natheless, I am bound to admit that I have seen sights here I shall never forget. . . .

Do you know that I am probably going to Germany for the summer? . . . If Braekstad gets anything done with the Dramatists, I want to await the effect of the *grand coup*—if he doesn't do anything with them *tanto peggio*—I should all the more certainly fall into the old rut. So I shall go to Germany and *read law*. . . .

I should like to have seen Bradlaugh's manifesto, though it is no news to me that he is one of the ablest men going. I have thought so ever since I read his first speech at the bar of the House—I don't believe a more masterly speech was ever spoken at Westminster. It was perfectly monumental English—there wasn't a word thrown away, not a word of false logic, not a word in bad taste. I remember now the *frisson* which it gave me as I read it in the train one morning coming to London Bridge. The last night I was in Rome, I dined with the Tricketts, and old Mr. Trickett announced that he was disgusted to see at the reading-room that Bradlaugh had been re-elected. Like Brer Rabbit, I "lay low and said nuffin' ", but I had a second helping of spaghetti on the head of it. It is really a desperate situation in England when this sort of thing goes on from session to session.

You should hear Ibsen on Bradlaugh—he has the most vivid sympathy for him. . . .

Yours,
W. A.

HOTEL CENTRALE, NAPLES

Would you like to see the latest addition to Italian literature? You must know that one of the tastes Miss Taylor, Miss Trickett and I had in common was an enthusiasm for macaroni. Consequently we agreed that by far the most pathetic ruin in Rome was that of a macaroni-factory which was burned down some time ago, whose gaping windows are to be seen from all quarters, but especially from the Tarpeian Rock. We agreed, too, that it was a shame this should be the only ruin uncelebrated in song, and I undertook to set that right, with the following touching result:

PERCHÈ QUESTE LAGRIME?
(Un Dialogo alla Rupe Tarpeia)

La Signorina Taylor

Sei melanconica
Carina mia—
Perchè hai bandita
Qui l'allegria?
Forse che pensi a
Tant' infelici
Arrovesciati qui
Dai nemici?

La Signorina Trickett

Niente affatto! La
Mia tristezza
E piu profonda, ha
Maggior' grandezza.

Una rovina là
Maestosissima
Mi rende l'anima
Tutta tristissima.
Ecco quel muro, pa-
tetico tanto!
Non posso vederlo
Senza pianto,
Perchè per sempre è
Stata perduta
Tanta dolcissima
Pasta asciutta.
Penso con lagrime
Agli spaghetti,
Ai capellini ed
Ai capelletti,
Ai fitticini si
Grossi e belli—
Piango la sorte del
Buon vermicelli . . .

(La voce viene soffocata nelle lagrime.)

In case your Italian doesn't run to it, I may explain that the mysterious articles mentioned in the last verses (spaghetti, fitticini, etc.) are different sorts of macaroni.

Early in April he is in Florence, and this time, in the balmy spring weather, is able to appreciate the Tuscan city to the full.

FLORENCE, WEDNESDAY.
[*Mid-April*, 1882]

My letter to . . . has spun out to such a length that I have only energy and room in the envelope for half a sheet to you. My *Dramatists*, Braekstad says, have been accepted by Sampson Low & Co. on sharing terms, and, if there is no hitch, which a prolonged silence on his part leads me rather to fear, I want you to read the proofs carefully for me. . . . Now that there is really a chance of the book appearing, I am inclined to think that its probable effect will be to ruin for ever my chance of ever doing anything in dramatic criticism—in which case I shall set up as a courier for the nobility and gentry travelling in Italy, that being the *métier* for which I believe I shall be best fitted.

. . . In my one day in Rome (of which I am writing an account which I shall call "A Sentimental Journey", with motto from Heine something like this: "Ich stehe an des Berges Spitze, Und werde sentimental") I saw Ibsen at the Caffè Nazionale, and the old min was not only friendly but effusive. He says he's at another play already—I hadn't the pluck to ask him what it was about, though I'd give my ears to know what is to succeed *Gjengangere*. . . .

If anything could console me for Rome, Florence would. As I write I can see the white marble of Giotto's tower shining through the darkness opposite my window. Today I have been to Vallombrosa—loveliness itself—tomorrow I am going to get up early and walk to Fiesole before going to the convent of San Marco (Savonarola's convent). . . . We took up *Romola* to San Miniato the other afternoon, and I read the introduction on the spot. . . .

Yours affect.

W. A.

The next letter is dated: "Venice, April 26th (I believe, but we don't count time here; we only know jolly well that it is April and Italy)." But failure to count the steps of Time avails nothing to hold his swift foot back. Ten days of early May, spent at Milan and Varese and on Lake Como, brought the Italian idyll to an end; by mid-May he is at Munich, and in September in England once more, taking up the tasks of the workaday world.

VII

1882–1884

LONDON AGAIN—ENTER G. B. S.—*HENRY IRVING*—THE *WORLD*—THE *PALL MALL GAZETTE*—MARRIAGE

READING the letters from Italy in the light of after events, we may detect in the later ones a tone of elation not to be wholly accounted for even by the magic of Rome and Florence and Venice. It will not have escaped notice that much of the enjoyment of the later days in Rome was intimately connected with the company of "two girls, both well-educated as girls go, and one unusually clever, with a finely developed sense of humour". The latter lady, Miss Frances Elizabeth Trickett, was spending the winter in Rome with her parents; her companion was her close friend, almost her adopted sister, Mdlle Blanche Taylor. Mdlle Taylor returned to her home in Paris in the spring, and, as the hot weather approached, the Trickett family, after a short stay in Naples, wandered northward into Tuscany. Here, by a not quite fortuitous coincidence, the young Scots traveller again struck into their path and made it his, and the idyll begun in Rome *à trois* was continued *à deux* in Florence, in Venice, on Lake Como,[1] and, during the summer, in Switzerland. When William Archer returned to England he was virtually, though not officially, engaged, and he thus brought back with him not only renewed health and vigour, but also a fresh incentive to make good his footing in the world as early as might be.

[1] "You don't know what Italy can be, Sir", he wrote to Bond from Munich, "in the spring, with the vine-leaves just sprouting and the violets giving way to the roses, and a little girl with a Luca-della-Robbia face to say witty and beautiful things about it all."

His first care was to complete his part of the bargain with his parents by passing the Bar examination. On January 3, 1883, he writes in the full conviction that he has failed in "the iniquitous Equity paper", but adds that he has scored off the examiners in Roman Law: "80 or 90 p.c. I should think—in fact I had old Justinian at my fingers' ends." Roman Law must have redeemed Equity, for next week his name duly appeared in the pass lists. "I am glad to get the beastly thing off my mind", he writes, "though I am convinced it has all been a gross waste of emotion." He goes on to say that he is now going to represent to his father that it is hardly worth while to spend the extra £100 required for his "call" to the Bar. Thomas Archer, however, was as capable as his son of sticking to his point, and the "call" (at the Middle Temple) followed in due course in the following November.

English Dramatists had been well received by the Press, but had, to all appearance, produced no great impression in the theatrical world, and there was, for the present, no opening which its author cared to seek for in the critical ranks. During the winter and spring he was hard at work on a *Readable Guide-book* to Florence—an attempt to realize an idea in which he had vainly tried to interest Messrs. Cook three years before—and on an elaborate study of Wagner and his theories. Each of these works involved a large amount of laborious but interesting reading; each was carried to an advanced stage; and each in turn failed to commend itself to the undiscerning British publisher.[1]

[1] That the *Readable Guide-book* idea was in itself a sound one was to be shown in the fullness of time by the success of Mr. E. V. Lucas's delightful "Wanderer" books, which, though they give more attention to art and less to history than Archer had contemplated, are much on the lines of the series he had conceived.

This winter and spring were notable for the acquisition of a new friend, and for the catastrophe which befell an old one. "In the winter of 1881–82",[1] Archer wrote long after, "I used to go almost every day to the British Museum Reading Room in London. I frequently sat next to a man of about my own age (25) who attracted my attention, partly by his peculiar colouring—his pallid skin and bright red hair and beard—partly by the odd combination of authors whom he used to study—for I saw him, day after day, poring over Karl Marx's *Das Kapital* and an orchestral score of Wagner's *Tristan und Isolde*. How we first made acquaintance I have forgotten; but one did not need to meet him twice to be sure that George Bernard Shaw was a personality to be noted and studied. . . . At any rate we became fast friends." This friendship, founded on a common idealism in fundamentals, was to endure for more than forty years, standing the strain of radical difference of temperament and wide divergence of views, and was to be of great moment in Archer's life and of some consequence in literary history.

The misfortune which at this time overtook the Secularist writer and lecturer, G. W. Foote, with whom Archer had associated on terms of some intimacy during his first years in London, and whose breadth of reading and powers of mind he greatly admired, threw upon him a good deal of unpaid work of a kind which only loyalty to a friend and a sense of public duty would have induced him, at this juncture, to undertake. He had willingly agreed to contribute to a monthly magazine, *Progress*, started by Foote; but, before many numbers had appeared, a prosecution for blasphemous libel, founded on a series of illustrated articles in the *Freethinker*, Foote's

[1] This is clearly a slip of the pen. We should read "1882–83" and "(26)".

weekly journal, sent the editor to prison for twelve months. The magazine, a struggling undertaking at best, was threatened with extinction, for the friend in whose hands the editor had left his affairs was (temporarily) driven out of his mind by the shock of the conviction and sentence. Disapproving strongly, from the point of view of taste and policy, of the incriminated matter, Archer disapproved yet more strongly of the use of the criminal law in what seemed to him an attempt to suppress freedom of speech. He threw himself, then, into the effort made by Foote's friends to carry on the magazine, with his name on it, during his seclusion; and to this end not only wrote regularly for it himself, but also exerted himself to induce others to contribute. His work for *Progress* was continued until the editor's release in February 1884, and for some time after.

Two other notable friendships date from about this time. Some contributions sent to the *Magazine of Art* (including a lively parable in verse, "The Marvellous Madonna") led to the acquisition of a new acquaintance holding views as far from Foote's as the east is from the west—the "maimed Berserker" of the Gaiety stalls, W. E. Henley. The end of the first interview between Henley, then editor of the magazine, and his contributor was characteristic of both men. "I had shaken hands with him", says Archer, "and was opening the door to go, when he turned sharp round upon me and said:

"'By the way—one thing more. What are your politics?'

"'Well!' I replied, taken aback . . . 'that is rather a large order.'

"'In one word,' he said, '. . . . are you a Conservative?'

"'In one word,' I replied, '. . . no!'

"'Oh!' was his sole comment; and though the vowel rhymed to the ear, it expressed to the mind a sharp and untunable dissonance."

The dissonance was not confined to politics, for Archer, as he says, "never had any love for the swashbuckling style of journalism". But the rugged force of Henley's character and the gallantry with which he faced his many misfortunes were strongly attractive; and a common affection for Stevenson was soon to draw the two men closer. "When I come across a man", wrote Archer after the older man's death, "who can see and feel, and rejoice and suffer and talk and sing, as Henley did, I am very willing to take him as God made him, and not as I myself might wish to have made him."

As in the case of Bernard Shaw, the British Museum Reading Room was the go-between in the genesis of the other acquaintanceship. A fortunate encounter there led to a cordial and lifelong intimacy with Brander Matthews, then at the beginning of the distinguished career which did so much to foster good literature and good drama in the United States. Community of tastes and congeniality of temperament soon drew the two men close, and it was not long before they looked to each other, and never looked in vain, for help in the frequent conjunctures in which a friend across the seas could be of use. Matthews, in particular, did much to introduce Archer to the American literary public. The connection helped to keep undimmed what Archer himself called his "American patriotism"—his understanding of and sympathy for things American.

None of the varied employments of this year was allowed to stand in the way of diligent theatregoing; and the critical impulse soon reasserted itself.

Early in July he writes: "I am going to have out a little book about Irving in Field and Tuer's Parchment Library, in which 'English as She is Spoke' was published. Someone suggests that the title of my Irving business should be 'English as She Should not be Spoke' (referring not to my style, please note, but to Irving's dialect)." And again, his correspondent having referred to the forthcoming book as "a skit": "N.B. my Irving business is not a 'skit', but perfectly serious and sober criticism. My 'skittish' days are over."

Henry Irving: Actor and Manager, while not without a certain liveliness, proved indeed to be a much more sober and judicial pronouncement than its predecessor of six years before. The invective of *The Fashionable Tragedian* has given place to a measured, respectful, though certainly not over-cordial, estimate of the eminent actor's qualities and defects. The little book may stand as giving, in essentials, Archer's final view[1] of Irving's talent, a view which, though it may err somewhat on the side of severity, will probably be found not very far from the mark, when the actor's career comes to be finally judged.

A holiday in Norway, prolonged, in default of regular work in England, into the late autumn, gave Archer his first opportunity of seeing Ibsen's work brought to the test of stage performance. Braving the autumn storms in the small coasting steamers which were then the regular means of access to Christiania from Larvik, he was able (at the cost of

[1] Though he warmly admired some of Irving's later impersonations, e.g. Wolsey and Becket, and had an unfeigned respect for his personality. "He has long been recognized", he wrote on the occasion of Irving's knighthood, "as a man of such essential and, so to speak, inward dignity, that no outward dignity could possibly misbecome him."

several days' utter prostration from seasickness) to see *Et Dukkehjem* at the Christiania Theatre, and *Gjengangere* played by a visiting Swedish company. His letters give a minutely critical account of these memorable experiences, and a somewhat harrowing one of his coastwise voyages and of his return across the North Sea to England, where he found that the Irving book was having a good reception both from the Press and the public.

But man cannot live, and still less can he assume responsibility for other lives, on critical booklets alone, and it hardly needed the additional incentive supplied at this time by his father's loss of the Agent-Generalship of Queensland (following on a change of Government in the Colony) to spur Archer on in the search for remunerative work. We find him turning his hand to many things: a bi-weekly batch of paragraphs for the *Edinburgh Evening News*; "turnovers" for the *Globe* ("far too good for that pink abortion", he says, "but still wretched enough"); articles, not always accepted, for other "confounded Conservative prints". "Altogether", he writes in February 1884, "things are not as flourishing as they might be, but I daresay they'll improve." The lane was not long in turning. In the next letter, written a fortnight later, we find him with a footing on the *Pall Mall Gazette*, and, "for three months' trial", dramatic critic of the *World*. On the latter office he entered with even more than his usual misgivings. He had no love for the class of journal of which the *World* was the prototype; he had something of a prejudice against the editor, Edmund Yates, founded, characteristically, on the fact that Yates had been the occasion of a quarrel between Dickens and Thackeray; and he knew himself incapable of furnishing the "light, and even perhaps flippant", style of criticism which the editor seemed to desire. "I question whether it will last even the three months", he writes. In the event "it" lasted about twenty-one years, and furnished Archer with a platform which could hardly have been bettered for the setting forth of his views—a firm fulcrum for his lever in his efforts to move the theatrical world. Yates proved to have one of the greatest virtues of an editor—that of giving his contributors, when once they had proved their value, a free hand. The relations between editor and critic were cordial throughout; and when, ten years later, the editor died, Archer, writing of his death with sincere regret, added, in the words of Joe in *Bleak House*: "Well, 'he wos wery good to me, he wos!'"

The *Pall Mall Gazette*, then at the height of its fortunes, might have seemed a more promising organ for a critic of Liberal tendencies. But it followed, at this time, a somewhat haphazard system in theatrical matters, having no regular dramatic critic, but getting notices of plays done by anyone who came handy. Archer, however, became from this time a constant contributor, doing occasional theatrical criticisms and very numerous book reviews. His connection with the paper lasted through the stormy closing years of W. T. Stead's editorship, and the more tranquil reign of E. T. Cook; and when, in 1892, the paper changed owners and politics, he was one of the faithful who passed on to the journal founded to fill the breach, the *Westminster Gazette*. Archer's work on the *P.M.G.* was well paid, and did much to bring him into notice as a literary critic; but it was by no means an unmixed blessing, for much of it had to be done at harmfully high pressure. There lies before me a two-column notice of Browning's *Parleyings with Certain People of Importance in*

Their Day, of date February 1887, with the significant pencil subscription: "W. A., between midnight and 7.45 A.M."; and though this, owing to the exceeding toughness of the subject, was doubtless an extreme case, all-night sittings of the kind must have been far from uncommon.

His doubts of the security of his footing on the *World* did not long endure. Writing on March 20th, he tells of the formal announcement of his engagement to Miss Trickett—in consequence of his "having got a sort of opening at last (for I think my position on the *World* is tolerably secure)". He is still, however, sceptical of the value of his work. "I have not been sending you my *World* articles, because I suppose that blackguard print is the very one you're sure to see in military circles. Besides, to spend 6d. on such little bits of rot isn't good enough. Yates seems pleased with my work, and certainly he has never altered a comma of it, which is so far satisfactory." But on April 18th he is "rather pleased" with his notice of *The Ironmaster*.

All the time that could be spared from work this summer was spent in Derbyshire with the Trickett family, who had returned to England the year before. And, the future now seeming reasonably secure, William Archer and Frances Elizabeth Trickett were married on October 23rd, and established themselves in an old street of Bloomsbury. The marriage was doubtless one of the chief of the strokes of fortune which Archer, in reviewing his life at its end, looked back to with grateful surprise; for, as things then stood in England, it might well, beforehand, have seemed unlikely that he should find a life's companion combining, in such a high degree, character and charm with intellect and a sympathetic understanding of his unfashionable ideals and outlook on life.

VIIa

LETTERS, ETC., OF 1883–1884

To Charles Archer

B.M., *Friday, July 28th* (1883)

. . . . .

I am seriously contemplating a book or series of articles (the latter, if I can possibly get anyone to take them) on Shakespeare and the Stage, or something of that sort. I haven't got the idea quite formulated yet, but I think something of the sort wants to be done—an estimate of Shakespeare's actual value for our stage of today, and a sketch of the position he *should* occupy on a more or less "emancipated" stage. An advisable preliminary to this end will be to read Shakespeare, and that is what I intend to do in Norway—besides some other reading in the shape of Lessing's "Hamburgische Dramaturgie", Freytag's "Technik des Dramas", etc. Meanwhile I have been reading up some of the Elizabethans—all Marlowe, a good deal of Ben Jonson (his "Sejanus" is very fine), Webster's "Vittoria Corombona", Beaumont and Fletcher's "Maid's Tragedy", etc., etc. They were no fools, these fellows. What I should like to do in the first place would be to write a paper on the details of Elizabethan stage representation. I think one can get very little way in fairly appreciating Shakespeare as a playwright, until one knows minutely the conditions under which he worked.

. . . . .

Tolderodden [1883]

. . . . .

Sunday, Oct. 14th. Meeting is just over, and I have been utilizing the enforced hour of idleness to put the finishing touches to a sonnet which has been running in my head during the daily "readings" for a week past. It is the first verse I have written for ages, and is indeed merely a "sad mechanic exercise, like dull narcotics numbing duller" theology. Such as it is, however, I give it unto thee.

On Reading Green's "Short History of the English People."

England! thou paradox of history,
 How shall we read thy hieroglyph aright?
 Imperial in thy paltry soul's despite,
Conquered, yet by thy very chains made free!
Bat-eyed, yet eagle-pinioned, soaringly
 Thou greet'st the day, regretful of the night;
 And rulest, insular-cosmopolite,
Thy all-repelling, all-embracing sea.
Hating ideas, thou hast hurled abroad
 Thought-brands that lap the earth in cleansing fire
  Till thou thyself dost shrink before the flame.
Thou art the nations' mockery and desire;
 And we, thy sons, with passionate pride and shame,
  Despise and reverence our fetish-god.

I think it will do for *Progress*, if that enlightened periodical still exists and has not progressed off the face of the earth.

. . . . .

B(RITISH) M(USEUM), 28 *Feb.* 84

. . . . .

Jones and Herman have done a so-called adaptation of "Et Dukkehjem" to be produced next Monday at Edgar Bruce's theatre under the title of "Breaking a

Butterfly". Seeing this I wrote to Yates, and said that I had sent him some time ago an article called "Henrik Ibsen at Home in the Via Capo le Case" which he had not unnaturally declined; now, however, Ibsen had a certain *actualité*; was it worth while re-writing and submitting it to him? A day or two after he wrote: "My dear Sir, Ibsen won't do, but,—if I am addressing the author of English Dramatists of Today—you will", and made an appointment with me. I went, and found him very pleasant, the result being that I am, for three months' trial, dramatic critic of the *World* at 3 guineas a week. He said Dutton Cook had been with him since the beginning of the *World* (a long tenure of office!) and he thought him the best critic of his kind in London, but not *precisely* what he wanted, his idea being something lighter and even perhaps flippant. I told him plainly that that was not precisely my line of business, but said I would do my best, and there it stands. I question whether it will last even the 3 months, for it is *not* my style. However, speriamo! Meanwhile Morley[1] had arranged for my interview with Salvini, which came off at 10 p.m. the day before yesterday at the office of his manager Chizzola. I was a little nervous about my Italian, for, barring an occasional word to F., no syllable of modern Italian has crossed my lips since our walk over that double-damned[2] Gotthard 18 months ago. F. and I have read through the Inferno this winter, but it would have astonished Salvini considerably if I had addressed him in terza rima. However, I read up a little modern Italian (one or two plays of Cossa, a remarkable play of Paolo Ferrari, etc.) and, gudskelov! found my tongue

[1] Of the *Pall Mall Gazette.*

[2] As the road that led out of Italy, and the scene of a violent attack of toothache.

surprisingly limber, though there was a Dantesque unconventionality about my grammar. Salvini was amiability itself, and as for *his* Italian, era bellissimo, proprio un piacere. . . . I forget whether you have ever seen Salvini—I have seen his Othello twice, and began by detesting it, to end in great enthusiasm for it; but I am very curious as to its effect upon me tonight.

VIII

1884–1889

GOING AHEAD—*ABOUT THE THEATRE*—SHAW AND *WIDOWERS' HOUSES*—*MASKS OR FACES?*—NEW FRIENDSHIPS (STEVENSON, PINERO, WALKLEY)—IBSEN'S FIRST FOOTING

THE years that followed, though laborious, were prosperous and happy. Archer soon found his feet on the *World*, and as time went on signs were not wanting that he was more and more winning the ear of an audience, small in comparison with that commanded by a critic of one of the great dailies, but influential out of proportion to its numbers. And though it was his signed work—his dramatic criticism in the *World*, and in numerous magazine articles[1]—that drew most attention, those behind the scenes were soon able to distinguish his hand in anonymous reviews in the *Pall Mall Gazette* and elsewhere, showing, as Stevenson was to put it, "a sober, agile pen; an enviable touch; the marks of a reader . . . thoughtful, critical and kind; and a greater readiness to describe the author criticized than to display the talents of the censor". It is true that he showed himself capable of dealing more faithfully than kindly with what seemed to him bubble reputations,[2] but this by no means lessened the respect in which his criticism gradually came to be held. His reputation was thus steadily growing, and with it his worldly fortunes improved. For, though his habit of taking on his

[1] There were no less than twenty-nine of these in 1884–88, all but five on theatrical subjects.

[2] In such cases (as in his criticism of Rider Haggard, *Pall Mall Gazette*, October 25, 1888) he was apt, when possible, to discard the veil of anonymity, which he disliked.

shoulders masses of unpaid or greatly underpaid work was never quite in abeyance, the proportion borne by such work to his total output was smaller at this time than it was to become later, after the entry of Ibsen on the English scene. To crown all this, he had the satisfaction of feeling a movement in things theatrical, slight and intermittent, but distinct, in the direction he deemed the right one.

The young couple soon left their first abode, but remained faithful to Bloomsbury, moving first to John Street, Bedford Row (to rooms once tenanted by John Oxenford and, it was rumoured, haunted by his ghost), then to Gordon Square, and finally to Queen Square. At John Street, on August 2, 1885, a son, the only child of the marriage, was born to them. Named by his parents Thomas, and by himself Tomarcher, the boy soon became known to a large circle of friends as one of the quaintest and most brilliantly fanciful of children. The friends who frequented the house included several of Archer's early allies, who by this time had been drawn to London or its neighbourhood. Lowe had settled at Dulwich, handy for mutual help or collaboration in work in which theatrical history was involved; and Mackenzie and Robertson were then, or soon after, established in London. Among the most constant visitors was the new friend, Shaw, who became one of Tomarcher's greatest allies, as ready as the boy's own father to share his adventures in the cloudland of Peona, or listen to the exploits and misdemeanours of his large and unruly family of imaginary brothers and sisters.

The publication in 1886 of *About the Theatre: Essays and Studies,* a selection from his magazine articles, prefaced by a review of the course of the English drama since the appearance of the *Dramatists* in 1882, did much to establish the new critic's position. The prefatory article—"Are We Advancing?"—shows him, as always, mainly occupied with the general movement of things dramatic, and, as always, keenly alive to any hopeful symptoms. On the strength of the work done in the period by Grundy, H. A. Jones, and A. W. Pinero (the last rated as, with the possible exception of W. S. Gilbert, "the most original and remarkable of living English playwrights"), he opines that "on the whole, WE ARE ADVANCING"—a conclusion which must, at the time, have seemed to most observers unduly bold. The second essay—the first shot in a battle that was to rage for many a year to come—was an assault on an institution, the Censorship of the Stage, which he held to be one of the chief obstacles to further progress. But the most important paper, and the one which attracted most notice, favourable and unfavourable, was "The Ethics of Theatrical Criticism", notable as the first formal utterance of Archer's high conception of the importance to the commonweal of dramatic criticism, and as setting the standards up to which, as critic, he aspired to live. Such a passage as that on the influence wielded by the critic of a great daily paper[1] might seem to

[1] "All things considered, it is no exaggeration to say that there are in the literary world few more responsible positions than that of the dramatic critic of an influential daily paper. He has an immense power of dealing out personal pleasure or pain to those whom he criticizes; a few strokes of his pen may involve the gain or loss of hundreds, nay thousands, of pounds; and thousands of people are guided by his judgment in the selection of their theatrical fare. He may guide them nobly or ignobly, to the tables of the gods or to the troughs of the beasts that perish. In the course of time he may even create in the minds of his readers a certain habitual attitude towards the stage, on which the future of the English drama may in no small measure depend."

many to overstate the case, but could not fail to be recognized as striking a new note in English theatrical criticism.

In his next book, *Masks or Faces? A Study in the Psychology of Acting,*[1] he left the beaten ways of criticism for an attractive by-path. The book is an attempt to clear the issues in the perennial dispute started by Diderot's *Paradoxe sur le Comédien* as to the helpfulness or the reverse of "sensibility" in acting, and to contribute to their settlement by an inductive study, based not only on theatrical records, but also on evidence drawn from the experience of as large a number as possible of living artists. His attempt to enlist as helpers the actors and actresses of the day, by obtaining from them answers to a carefully drawn set of "Questions on the Art of Acting", was only partially successful; for a good many of them, failing to understand the drift of some of the questions, were disposed to receive them with ridicule—even, in some cases, with resentment. And as the two leading French critics proved unwilling to assist, the only foreign contributions were from actors to whom Archer had personal access.[2] His letters illustrate amusingly the troubles of a scientific inquirer into questions of histrionics.

"My catechism business", he writes in December 1887, "is causing me a good deal of worry and annoyance, but also giving me some fun. I'm afraid I won't make a very good job of it; and if I don't the enemy will say 'Aha' and the wicked triumph—but it's all in the day's work. I had no notion when I issued them that anyone would be offended by the questions, though I quite expected them to be chaffed. But

[1] 1888. The substance had appeared in three articles, entitled "The Anatomy of Acting", in *Longmans' Magazine* for January, February, and March of that year.

[2] These included, however, the two great Italians—Salvini and Ristori.

I believe lots of people have been quite offended by them. Lady Martin (Miss Faucit) wrote a savage letter to Longmans about them; and though she has since calmed down in a letter to me, she still declines to answer. I have taken revenge by quoting a phrase from her letter with high approval (of course not giving her name). Lady Martin and the Savile Club set I don't care two straws for, but when Sarcey takes something of the same view, I begin to 'hae my doots'. . . . All the swells of the profession here have been amiability itself—the Bancrofts, the Kendals, Clayton, Mary Anderson, etc. You should have seen me perambulating Hampstead Heath with the divine Mary one brilliant day a fortnight ago. It was a memorable sight." To Brander Matthews, whose aid he had enlisted, he writes: "I replied to Sarcey" (who had written: "Je regarde ce procédé, qui est américain, comme fâcheux à la critique et à l'art") "in a letter of such classic French as Renan might have envied, that in my opinion the proceeding could neither help nor hinder criticism, which is concerned simply with the effect an actor produces, not with the internal mechanism he sets in motion. Indeed, its total lack of bearing upon criticism is my own objection to the whole affair. The question is of *no* practical importance. . . . But as it has been, and is constantly being, raised, it seems to me worth thrashing out."

Thrashed out it accordingly was, in spite of all hindrances, with great thoroughness, and the result was a book which, if it did not finally lay the question to rest (as what book could, while paradox retains its fascination?), is at once a storehouse of entertaining anecdote, and of definite value as a study in psychology. In this respect it has not lacked recognition. Quoted with appreciation in William James's standard work, *The Principles of Psychology*,[1] it is still held in esteem by authorities[2] on the subject, who find the general argument entirely in harmony with the trend of modern psychology, and remark in it notable anticipations of recent doctrine—as in the distinction drawn between simple emotions and attitudes of mind, and the stress laid, in the solution of the question, on the multiplicity of consciousness.

Before he had been long on the staff of the *World* Archer had provided himself with a brilliant colleague. Yates, who soon recognized his new recruit's power of turning out acceptable "copy" even on subjects out of his line, furnished the occasion, and Archer was not slow to grasp an opportunity to do a turn at once for himself, for a friend, and for the paper. The story can best be told in his own words. "The post of art-critic of the *World* fell vacant, and Edmund Yates asked me to undertake it. I told him I knew nothing about painting: he said that did not matter. I did the work laboriously and infamously for some weeks, until my conscience could endure it no longer. I then got Shaw to do a specimen article, which I sent to Yates, and thus easily secured him the post. He didn't know much more about painting than I, but he thought he did, and that was the main point. I had, as a matter of fact, already forced upon him a good deal of work as a reviewer of books. Then[3] the post of musical critic fell vacant, and I secured it for Shaw, by the simple process of telling Yates the truth: namely, that he was at once the most competent and the most brilliant writer on music then living in England." Archer has spoken

[1] Vol. ii. p. 464.
[2] It was the subject of a paper read to the British Psychological Society by Dr. William Brown, February 1913.
[3] In 1890—some four years later.

somewhere of the joy a dramatic artist must feel in conceiving such an idea as that of the threatened blindness of Hedvig in *The Wild Duck*—"a trait by which he could serve so many purposes at one time". As something of an artist in life, he must himself have felt a touch of similar joy in this stroke.

The close association of the two men as colleagues and friends led to an attempt at collaboration, of some consequence to the future of the English drama, though in itself abortive. "Of course", writes Archer, "Shaw and I used often to discuss the stage, and the possibility of his writing for it. He told me that he had a great genius for dialogue, but was not very strong in the matter of invention and construction. At that time I rather fancied myself as a constructor of plots, so I offered to provide him with a scenario which he should work up. He agreed to this collaboration, and I cast about for a story. In spite of my self-confidence, I did not invent the germ of the plot: I borrowed it—shall we say?—from an early play of Emile Augier's, entitled *Ceinture Dorée*. I developed it after the style of T. W. Robertson, with a serious and a comic heroine; and I placed the scene of the first act in a hotel garden on the Rhine: the title was to be 'Rhinegold'. Having handed the scenario to Shaw, I heard no more about it for six weeks or two months. I saw him every day at the British Museum, laboriously and very slowly writing shorthand in a reporter's notebook; but I had no idea what he was about." Then one day he is surprised by Shaw producing two acts in which the whole of the plot has been used up, and asking for more. "I told him", Archer says, "that this was quite absurd—that my plot was an organic whole, and that to ask me to add to it was like asking a sculptor to add a few more arms and legs to a statue which was already provided with its full complement. . . . So I had to leave him, as we say in Scotland, to 'make a kirk or a mill of it'; and when at last the manuscript was placed in my hands, behold! my *Rhinegold* had become *Widowers' Houses*, and my sentimental heroine . . . was transmuted into a termagant who boxed the ears of her maid-servant. Still, however, it is possible to discern in the play fragments of my idea, and to trace its relationship to 'Ceinture Dorée'."

New friendships not a few date from these years, three of them too notable to pass by.

The story of how a *Pall Mall Gazette* notice of "A Child's Garden of Verses" brought the reviewer acquainted with Robert Louis Stevenson, and of how the acquaintance was drawn closer by Stevenson's magnanimous reception of the "severe but inspiring analysis"[1] of his work contained in an article contributed to *Time*, has been told elsewhere.[2] The two men were fated to meet face to face but seldom, for Stevenson's ill-health kept him as a rule at a distance from London, and, little more than two years after the first meeting, took him on his last journey to the other side of the world. And their views on life were, at first at least, so divergent, that any sympathetic intimacy between them might have seemed out of the question. "Our relation", Archer wrote[3] to the exile seven years later, "has been from the first—since before we set eyes on each other—one of harmony in discord." But from the time when they first met and talked, face to face, on that visit

[1] Graham Balfour, in *The Life of Robert Louis Stevenson.*

[2] See Stevenson's letters of March 29, October 28 and 30, and November 1, 1885. *The Letters of Robert Louis Stevenson,* vol. i. pp. 358–371 (Colonial Edition); and the *Life of Robert Louis Stevenson,* by Graham Balfour, vol. ii. p. 8.

[3] Notice of *Across the Plains, Pall Mall Gazette,* April 20, 1892.

of the critic to Skerryvore in November 1885 which was Stevenson's revenge for the *Time* criticism, the harmony began to seem to the younger man all the rarer and more precious for the elements of discord resolved in it. Other meetings followed, both in London during Stevenson's rare visits, and at Bournemouth, to confirm the impression—other disputatious *Noctes Skerryvorianae,* when, as Archer wrote: "You would pace the long drawing-room up and down, a cigarette between your fingers and your arm in its (I hope long-disused) sling; I, meanwhile, quiescent in body on the low divan, and revelling in the intellectual gymnastic of coursing, so to speak, your nimbler wit." The appearance of *Underwoods* completed the conquest. The cool, clear-cut grace and noble feeling of the poems filled Archer with delight, and, while in his public utterances he strove with some success to maintain the critical integrity which was in him both first and second nature, in his heart, as his letters show, he was "sealed of the tribe of Louis" from that time forth.

Then came the parting. The story of the last meeting, late of a Saturday night, in a bedroom of that City hotel "called Todgers's for short", is told in the letter here printed, with some details naturally omitted from Archer's published account[1] of it. The next day but one the Stevensons sailed, and henceforth occasional letters had to serve, in place of those eager encounters of wits (somewhat, one fancies, of the Spanish galleon and English man-of-war type) which had illuminated the visits to Skerryvore.

In his paper on "The Ethics of Theatrical Criticism"

[1] In his contribution to *I Remember Robert Louis Stevenson.* It is a curious illustration of the width of Archer's range in literature and friendship that he had come to this affectionate parting with the great Romantic fresh from sitting at the feet of a poet for whom Stevenson and his school had nothing but disesteem—Henrik Ibsen. See letter, p. 152.

Archer has given his reasons for rather shunning than seeking the society of actors, rather seeking than shunning that of dramatists—these being, briefly, that personal acquaintance with actors tended to unsettle his estimate of their acting, while his judgment of plays was so decided as to "formulate and express itself, rightly or wrongly, in spite of all possible friendship or enmity". It is possible that his comparative tardiness in seeking personal acquaintance with the dramatist whose career he was to follow in later years with special interest and admiration was due to this feeling. His cordial intimacy with Henry Arthur Jones, which lasted to the end, undisturbed by their occasional skirmishes, had begun as early as 1884. But in those days Arthur Wing Pinero was still actor as well as dramatist, and it was not till 1887, when Pinero had finally quitted the stage, that Archer sought him out. Then, indeed, he did so mainly in order to obtain the benefit of his experience as an actor, for the purposes of the *Masks or Faces?* inquiry. The friendship that followed, fostered by long country walks and talks in the next few years, was a happy by-product of that troublesome piece of work.

Not the least notable event of the year 1888, from Archer's point of view, was the appearance of a doughty ally, in A. B. Walkley, the dramatic critic of a newly founded evening paper, the *Star*. Walkley has recorded that it was Archer's books (doubtless reinforcing an instinctive love of the drama) which first convinced him that the English theatre was a subject worthy of critical attention, and, when the two men met in 1887, they soon became close friends. But it was Walkley's criticisms in the *Star* (under the *nom de guerre* of "Spectator"), rivalling in penetration and vivacity those of the musical critic, Corno di Bassetto (otherwise G. B. Shaw), and later his articles in the weekly *Speaker*, that revealed him to Archer as a new and important force. The gifts of the new-comer appealed to him all the more because they were widely different from, and in a sense complementary to, his own. There were skirmishes in plenty between them in their long association, for not only their gifts, but also their attitudes to the drama and to life, differed widely. "To me", Archer wrote in after days, "dramatic criticism is a campaign; to Mr. Walkley it is an art—I had almost said a hobby." But he recognized at once the value to his campaign of the wide knowledge, alert perception, gaiety and lightness of touch that this new comrade brought to the practice of his art, and did all he could, in the years to come, to ensure for him as wide an audience as possible.

Before this year of 1888 was out, the first effective step towards the introduction of Ibsen to the English public had been taken. Translations by various hands of one or two of the prose plays had already appeared singly, but these were painfully amateurish and often inaccurate productions, giving no adequate notion of the originals; and they had attracted little attention. Now Ibsen's name had become so far known, largely owing to its frequent recurrence in Archer's criticisms, that a publisher[1] ventured to issue three of the plays (*The Pillars of Society, Ghosts,* and *An Enemy of the People*) in a volume of the Camelot Classics series; Archer's translation of the first play being used, and the second undergoing a very thorough revision at his hands. At last a sample of the goods, the merits of which he had so insistently proclaimed, was before the English public, and that *a* public at least found the sample to its taste the next year was to show.

[1] Walter Scott.

VIIIA

LETTERS, ETC., OF 1885–1888

To CHARLES ARCHER

3rd April, 1885

. . . . .

Two days after the notice of Stevenson's verses appeared in the *P.M.G.*, a letter was forwarded to me from the office addressed "To the writer of the review of Mr. Stevenson's 'Verses for Children', care of Ed. *P.M.G.*, etc."—and inside was the following "cream of the correspondence":

"BOURNEMOUTH, *March 26th*, 1885

Now. *Who* are you?

ROBERT LOUIS STEVENSON."

I replied to this effect: "Dear Mr. Stevenson, If the 'now' in your note implies a suspicion that we have met before in the relation of reviewer and reviewed, you are wrong. So far as I remember, I have printed nothing else about your writings. You have probably heard my name from your friend, my valued acquaintance, W. E. Henley. It is

W. A."

By return of post I received the communication which F. has copied for you, capitals and all. It took me aback almost as much as it gratified me, for it had never occurred to me that the review was anything but a rather second-rate production even for me—I sent it to you merely for the interest of the subject, and especially for the exquisite:

The world is so full of a number of things,
I'm sure we should all be as happy as kings,

which seems to me a joy for ever. But R. L. S. has given me so much pleasure that I am glad to have paid him back a little (I am told he is dying, poor fellow)—and to have him praise one's turn of style is "praise from Sir Hubert Stanley". I'm afraid he wouldn't appreciate so much an elaborate article on his style and thought which I have had knocking about for some time—praising the former, of course, but pitching into him hot and strong as an aggressive optimist, or what an Indian friend of his own (he says) calls a "faddling hedonist".

. . . . . .

[*Enclosure*]

March 29th, 1885

DEAR MR. ARCHER,

Yes, I have heard of you, and read some of your work; but I am bound in particular to thank you for the notice of my verses. "There", I said, throwing it over to the friend who was staying with me, "it's worth writing a book to draw an article like that." My friend (Sidney Colvin) was of the same mind; we debated who should be the author, and thought it must be Symonds in an unusually workmanlike humour: of no one else could we think who had the requisite turn of style and turn of thought. Had you been as hard upon me as you were amiable, I try to tell myself I should have been no blinder to the merits of your notice. For I saw there, to admire and to be very grateful for, a most sober, agile pen: an enviable touch: the marks of a reader such as one imagines for oneself in dreams, thoughtful, critical and kind; and to put the top on this memorial column, a greater readiness to describe the author criticized than to display the talents of his censor. I am a man blasé to injudicious praise (though I hope some of it may be judicious too), but I have to thank you for THE BEST CRITICISM I EVER HAD, and am therefore, dear Mr. Archer, the most grateful critickee extant.

ROBERT LOUIS STEVENSON

To CHARLES ARCHER

12 *Novr.* '85

My *fourth* editor[1] is in prison! I am beginning to think it unwise to mention this fatality, for fear editors decline to have me on their staff, believing me to have the evil eye. The Armstrong case has proved a deplorable business, but it seems to me that Stead's personal character comes out admirably in it, and I am inclined to say with Cato (slightly improved)

> "When vice prevails, and infamous men prevail,
> The post of honour is in Coldbath Prison."

My own present view of the matter is pretty accurately given in two articles in the *Pall Mall Budget* which I post along with this; the one, "After the Verdict", by Stead himself (a really noble utterance, I think, barring the inevitable touch of spread-eagleism), and the other, "After the Sentence", by Cook, the acting editor. There is no possible doubt that the whole prosecution has been simply a dodge on the part of the enemy to discredit the truth of the revelations, and there is as little doubt that the revelations are in substance and fact absolutely true.

[1] The victims were Mortimer, Foote, Yates (convicted of criminal libel in 1885, by reason of a paragraph in the *World*, January 1883), and now W. T. Stead, imprisoned for a technical offence committed in the course of his "Maiden Tribute of Modern Babylon" crusade.

I have myself seen some of the evidence (*a priori* evidence, but to me absolutely conclusive) that was laid before the Mansion House Committee, and anything more ghastly mind cannot conceive. . . .

From GEORGE BERNARD SHAW

[Archer had induced Shaw to help him, with notes on picture-galleries, in the composition of his unwillingly undertaken *World* art-criticisms. The letter which follows forms part of a correspondence arising out of his attempt to induce his friend to accept a half-share of the proceeds of the articles. The controversy soon settled itself by Shaw's appointment as art critic *en titre*.]

14th December, 1885

I re-return the cheque, and if you re-re-return it, I will re-re-re-return it again ("again" being here, as you justly observe, tautological). The considerations which induce me to do so follow in no particular order.

1. The idea of one man sucking another's brains is a depraved individualistic idea. No man has a right of property in the ideas of which he is the mouthpiece. The law does not permit a man to patent a discovery, but only an invention concreted as a machine. The ideas of your criticism are mere natural raw material which neither of us is entitled to monopolize. You have only to imagine Norman, Morley, Lowe, Robertson, Dibdin and myself sending in our claims whenever we detect in your writings an idea to which our conversation with you led up (and which therefore would never have occurred to you without us) to perceive the frightful and anarchial

impossibilism to which your proposition of private property in ideas—especially critical ideas—must lead in practice. If I am to be paid for what I suggested to you, for example, the painters must clearly be paid for what they suggested to me. This is the *reductio ad absurdum.* The devil has presented you with a depraved conception disguised as conscientiousness. . . .

As it is, I have the advantage of seeing the galleries for nothing without the drudgery of writing the articles. I do not like to lose the record of contemporary art life, and yet going to a gallery by myself bores me so much that I let the Academy itself slip last year, and should have done so this year but for your bearing me thither one day. (I perceive your manly form stooping at the catalogue desk, and moving along as if your hat had blown off and were making three or four knots before a gentle breeze.) If you decline to utilize your complimentary tickets in future for my benefit, you will be perpetrating an act—or series of acts—of wanton and fiendish malignity. Pray observe that I am not actuated by motives of generosity. You are much better off than I am, and any pecuniary consideration on my part for you would be senseless. I perceive the proposed arrangement to be unjust, and therefore I am proof against your special pleading that you are placed in "an unpleasant hole" by my obduracy. Were you to be placed naked in a blast furnace, my decision would be the same. Fiat justitia: ruat cœlum. (Latin!)

Here you approach in person, evidently resolved to confer—at least it is like your footstep and shadow. "Hallo, etc."

G. B. S.

From Robert Louis Stevenson *and* Mrs. Stevenson

[The letter below from R. L. S. has reference to the imputation of "aggressive optimism" contained in W. A.'s *Time* article on "Robert Louis Stevenson: His Style and His Thought"; and forms a characteristic pendant to the letters of October 28 and 30, and November 1, 1885, printed in *The Letters of Robert Louis Stevenson.* Doubtless, too, the subject had been freely debated in the interim, during Archer's visits to Skerryvore.]

[*February,* 1887]

Dear Archer.

The other day, in the midst of my pangs, I remembered, with a smile, that you must be informed of my malady: a sub-acute threatening of rheumatic fever. You were right; I felt damned second-hand. Pray invoke no more diseases on my head; I have enough of my own, and your invocations carry. A thousand thanks for all you did to amuse Mrs. Stevenson; she had a capital time.

I am still but shaky and sweaty, and feel unfit for any strain, however trifling; but I continue to keep her nose to the wind.

Yours sincerely,
R. L. S.

My dear Mrs. Archer,

I am ashamed that I have not written to you before to thank you for sending my old hat. I have also been suffering from rheumatism, and have fallen into a most feeble state—I mean so far as regards will power, as it is called. I have absolutely none. I could not, a few nights ago, get to bed, simply from vagueness of mind, and so sat up until morning broke. I had a dismal dream of you last night. I thought you gave me your baby, which from politeness I could not refuse, and when I got to my own place it had become twins. I have hardly yet recovered from the shock. I have had another. Have you or Mr. Archer seen the portrait of Louis (not the "pen picture" in the Pall Mall) but the dreadful thing on a whole page of an almost unknown (thank God) journal? I can only say, as the man did who saw Mr. Hyde trample over the child, "it was hellish to see". Louis has been very ill indeed with a complication of disorders, but really seems to be over the worst. I wish he had another "Shaw" to read. Nobody writes amusing books now. There is nowhere gaiety. All is serious and more or less dull. . . . I send kindest regards to you all, even including Master Baby who so sadly embarrassed me in my dream.

Sincerely Yours,
FANNY V. DE G. STEVENSON

To ROBERT LOUIS STEVENSON

10 *Feb.* 87

MY DEAR STEVENSON,

I am more than sorry to hear that you have had even a threatening of rheumatic fever; but I cannot reproach myself in the matter. It was not on you that I imprecated a chastening bout, but on the aggressive hero of sundry romantic works of fiction such as "Virginibus Puerisque" and "Familiar Studies of Men and Books". You may assert as much as you like that you and he are the same man—I shan't believe it. The powers above have been playing a comedy of errors in sending *you* the corrective I ordered for *him*—or rather a tragedy of errors, you will say. . . .

Please tell Mrs. Stevenson that she couldn't possibly be more shocked than we were at the idea of baby turning into twins. It takes three people most of their time to keep him out of mischief as it is. "Mrs. Stevenson" has now become in baby's mind a sort of mythical heroine—I think he conceives her as a mighty huntress, for he asks every now and then to have a ride on his rocking-horse "like Mrs. 'Tevenson". My wife joins me in kindest regards.

Yours ever,
W. ARCHER

We have seen the *Court and Society* portrait—we now require a photograph as an antidote.

[To the *Contemporary Review* of April 1887 Stevenson had contributed an article entitled "The Day after Tomorrow", in which, assuming the establishment of a successful and economically sound socialist polity, he pointed out how devoid of "danger, enterprise, hope, the novel, the aleatory", and therefore how dull and uninteresting, life would be under such conditions. "Our race", he says, "has not been strained for all these ages through that sieve of dangers which we call Natural Selection, to sit down with patience in the tedium of safety. . . . If Mr. Mallock, on his way to the publishers, should have his skirts pinned to the wall by a javelin, it would not occur to him—at least for several hours—to ask if life were worth living. . . ."

A "mildly jocose" notice of this article, by W. A. ("Mr. Stevenson Among the Pessimists"), appeared in the *Scottish Leader* of April 16th.]

From Mrs. R. L. Stevenson

Skerryvore
[*April* 30(?), 1887]

Dear Mr. Archer,

That deadly thing, the conscience, has been crushing me like a boa constrictor. In consequence I have been looking up my correspondence and answering all my letters in rotation—not in alphabetical order, or yours should have come first—and now I am reduced to simple ill-nature. I find that conscience always produces that effect in time, so beware. I have a fine malicious opening in being able to say truthfully that in your article upon Louis' "Day After Tomorrow" you seem nowhere to have grasped his meaning: however, you made it amusing, and that is something in these dull days. When I began writing this letter the tea-tray was brought in; I filled a cup for everybody, and have just discovered that I have drunk them all successively. You see what one is capable of in a conscientious fit: again I say, beware! With this I enclose two photographs. I found I had no others. I fear they are but a sorry exchange for the one you gave me. Use them as you please; to kindle the fire with, or to frighten Tom Archer to bed with when he is refractory. I think mine specially suited to the latter purpose.

Mr. Sargent has just been here, and has painted a really good portrait of Louis. I understand that the standing figure where I play the part of an East Indian ghost is to be published by the Pall Mall. I stipulated that the ghost be left out. It seems a pity that it should not have been this new one, though for some inscrutable reason, conscientious probably, Mr. Sargent prefers the first. The last one is at Mr. Sargent's studio, where he told me he should be glad to show it to any friends of mine. If you feel inclined to look at it, the studio is 13 Tite Street, Chelsea, not far from the dingy lodgings where you saw me. I should like to know your opinion of it. Also I should extremely like to know whether "The Red Lamp" was really a failure or not. I cannot make out from the reviews. I hope not. I cannot bear to have people fail in anything. I wish that nothing but success were possible.

Thank you very, very much, you and Mrs. Archer, for the Spanish information. I shall send it to my sister. She, my sister, has just sent me a photograph of my boy who died some ten years ago. I had not been able to look at it before, and can hardly do so now. After all, there is nothing terrible in life but death. It seems almost impossible that the child of a mother can die.

We shall be drifting through London before long on our way to Aix les Bains, being only detained by the non-advent of some friends from Rome. I trust that the German measles has run its course and left no evil behind. If the baby has it, take great care of his eyes. With kindest regards from us all, from us three to you three, believe me,

Yours most sincerely,

FANNY V. DE G. STEVENSON

To MRS. R. L. STEVENSON

2 May, '87

MY DEAR MRS. STEVENSON,

Many thanks for the photos. We hope to have better ones some day, but in the mean time it is pleasant to have these. Your husband looks rather too troubadourish to be quite himself—indeed the whole picture conveys a certain suggestion of an American hero named Buffalo Bill who is being extensively displayed on the hoardings just now—but the likeness, I think, is nevertheless good. Why don't you have Mr. Sargent's picture photographed? My wife and I went down to see it this afternoon (Sargent was out), and are delighted with it. It is living to the tip of the cigarette. I should have thought the face wanted a little more work; the side on which the light falls seems a little flat; but these are technical matters I don't understand.

Talking of understanding, I may or may not have understood "The Day After Tomorrow", but in any case my article referred only to one paragraph of it, and was meant to be mildly jocose, not seriously critical. I thought to add a little zest to life (to mine if not to Louis's) by pinning his skirt to the wall with a javelin. I daresay the missile wasn't of the sharpest, but I think the aim was fair. Had I "gone for" a vital part, I should have taken three words for my text: "Of those who fail I say nothing, for *despair is sacred.*" This is the gist of the sentence, and the three words are exact. Have they any meaning? To me they sound like gibberish, and only one remove from cant. (Forgive me—we went on from Tite Street to Carlyle's house, and the *genius loci* seems to have possessed me.) It is just because despair is *not* sacred but damnable, and because people are beginning to find that out, that the present order of things is doomed. What is to follow no man knoweth—neither Mr. Hyndman nor Mr. Stevenson, neither Stepniak nor Bismarck—but for my part I suspect some form of Socialism is the *least evil* we can look forward to; and before it comes we (or our children) will have our fill of aleatory enjoyments in some great Armageddon compared with which the little squabbles of 1789–1815 will seem child's play.

You see I too had a Scotch grandfather who preached, and I believe the Apocalypse was his special province—so there is another case of heredity for you.

We look forward to seeing you on your way to Aix les Bains. Our measles are entirely over now, and I promise to gag my Scotch grandfather. How go the dramas?

Yours very truly,

WILLIAM ARCHER

[The summer holiday of 1887 was spent by Archer, with his wife and little son, at the old home in Norway. Happening, when he was on the point of returning, to see in the Norwegian papers that Ibsen was summering at the village of Saeby, on the coast of Jutland, he telegraphed asking for leave to visit him *en route*, and, receiving a cordial invitation to do so, braved the terrors of a rough crossing of the Skager Rack, and arrived at Frederikshavn without catastrophe. A letter, of July 25–28, 1887, describes the visit.]

... I found at the hotel in Frederikshavn a Norwegian business man, a very decent old fellow, who was going to drive to Saeby. I proposed to share the conveyance, the more so as I had a Huntley and Palmer biscuit tin full of roses from A—— J—— for Fru Ibsen. The old boy consented with alacrity, and away we drove at the rate of about five miles an hour in the rummiest old trap you ever saw. It was a delightful drive—a perfect summer day, the corn ripe all round, the wild flowers brilliant, and the Cattegat dancing in the sunlight. All the way we could see

Saeby Church straight ahead, and at last we rattled over a bridge, past a lovely old watermill, and into the quaint old main street of Saeby—one-storey houses, with great high gables, and all brightly painted or at the very least whitewashed. The moment we were over the bridge, I saw a short, broad figure ahead in an enormously long surtout and a tall hat made of silk looking far too small for the immense head. It was Ibsen, evidently on the lookout for me. I stopped the trap, we greeted each other with effusion, and then he insisted that I should remain in the trap and drive on to the Hotel Harmonien, where he was stopping, he following on foot. This scene proceeded to the [immense astonishment] of my fellow-traveller, whom I had found to be a fine old stock-conservative, and had therefore not informed of my object in visiting Saeby. Ibsen looked for all the world like a most respectable parson, but I am sure my old friend looked at his boots to see if they were normal, and would not have been surprised if he had produced a torpedo from his tail-pocket and had proceeded to set it under the ark in which we were travelling.[1]

We drove into the courtyard of Hotel Harmonien, and by the time I had settled with my fellow-traveller Ibsen had arrived. He took me up into an enormous, barely-furnished, uncarpeted room on the first floor, with four if not five windows, and two bedrooms opening off it at the back. This formed his apparte-ment, and here we sat and talked for about an hour, until Fru Ibsen came in from a walk in Saeby forest, of which more anon. I presented the flowers, which she promptly rescued from the biscuit-box and was

[1] "You arrange for a Flood to o'erwhelm the Earth,—
And I'll gladly set a torpedo to the Ark."
Ibsen, *To My Friend the Revolution-Talker.*

[exceedingly enthusiastic about]—indeed they made a splendid show, and she was evidently immensely touched by their being a [greeting from Norway]. After about another hour we had dinner, then coffee and cigars (I smoked half of one without fatal results—there are no such things as cigarettes in Saeby). Then I thought the old min would be wanting to have his siesta, so I proposed to go and take a walk in Saeby wood, and return in an hour or two. So said, so done. [In Saeby forest he loses himself, and does not get back till past six.] Then we had tea, or rather supper, and at eight I set off to walk back to Frederikshavn. . . .

Now for a few Ibseniana. I must say in the first place that the old min was really charming throughout—perfectly frank and friendly, without the least assumption or affectation or stiffness of any sort. If I only had the art of drawing people out I could have got any amount of ideas out of him. Unfortunately I haven't the art—on the contrary I have a morbid shrinking from talking to people about their own works; so that our conversation was, on the whole, far too much devoted to mere small talk, and (strange to say) politics, Norwegian, Danish and Irish. However, I shall jot down a few of the things that turned up in the course of our talk. He said that Fru Ibsen and he had first come to Frederikshavn, which he himself liked very much—he could knock about all day among the shipping, talking to the sailors and so forth; and besides he found the neighbourhood of the sea favourable to contemplation and constructive thought. Here at Saeby the sea wasn't so come-at-able, but Fru Ibsen didn't like Frederikshavn because of the absence of pleasant walks about it: so Saeby was a sort of compromise between him and her. Fru Ibsen afterwards added that the Norwegian steamers at Frederikshavn were a source of perpetual temptation to her. For the present Ibsen is not writing anything, and hasn't been all last winter, because his time has been greatly taken up with business connected with the production of his plays in Germany. . . . Meanwhile the old min is revolving plans, and hopes to have "noget galskab faerdigt til naeste aar".[1]

I tried to get at the genesis of a piece in his head, but the fear of seeming to cross-examine him prevented me from getting at anything very explicit. [However] it seems that the idea of a piece generally presents itself before the characters and incidents, though when I put this to him flatly he denied it. It seems to follow, however, from his saying that there is a certain stage in the incubation of a play when it might as easily turn into an essay as a drama; and he has to incarnate the ideas, as it were, in character and incident, before the actual work of creation can be said to have fairly commenced. Different plans and ideas, he admits, often flow together, and the play he ultimately produces is often very different from the intention with which he started. He writes, and re-writes, scribbles and destroys an enormous amount before he makes the exquisite fair copy he sends to Copenhagen. As to symbolism, he says that life is full of it, and that therefore his plays are full of it, though critics insist on discovering all sorts of esoteric meanings in his work of which he is entirely innocent. He was particularly amused by a sapient person . . . who had discovered that Manders in *Gjengangere* was a symbol for mankind in general, *l'homme moyen* (not especially *sensuel*), and therefore called *Man*ders. . . .

1 "Some tomfoolery ready for next year." The "tomfoolery" proved to be *The Lady From the Sea*.

In politics he came out very strong against the "compact majority", but on this point his thinking is scarcely less crude than U. D.'s for example. This may seem a hard saying, but the fact is I am becoming more and more convinced that as a many-sided thinker, or rather a systematic thinker, Ibsen is nowhere. He is essentially a kindred spirit with Shaw—a paradoxist, a sort of Devil's Advocate, who goes about picking holes in every "well-known fact" as J. would say; or, as Ibsen himself would put it, looking at the teeth of every "normally built truth" and proclaiming it too old to pass any longer. And Ibsen is even worse than Shaw, who (in the main) knows himself for what he is and remembers that the exception proves the rule. To Ibsen, on the other hand, his paradoxes are apt to present themselves as the whole truth, and his general idea is that the exception destroys the rule. To say that the minority is always right, as Ibsen did in so many words, is at least as unphilosophical as to proclaim the infallibility of the majority. But this question of Majority v. Minority is really one which can only be treated thoroughly in a scientific, one might almost say in a mathematical, essay; whereas the minority-paradox is the very thing for enforcement in dramatic form. The upshot of all this is that if Ibsen were not a great poet he would be a rather poor philosopher—but that is in fact what you can say of all the leading spirits of this century; for example of Carlyle and Ruskin; George Eliot is the one exception that occurs to me at the moment. But then Ibsen *is* Ibsen, and I am the last to complain that he is *not* Herbert Spencer. Of course even as a thinker he is on a totally different plane from men like Tennyson and Browning, who only pretend to think and never get any forra'der.

Altogether my day at Saeby was an unforgettable experience. You'd better preserve this letter—it may be useful sometime. Perhaps Tomarcher (as he calls himself) will some day come across it and say:

> Ah, did you once see Ibsen plain,
> And did he stop and speak to you,
> And did you speak to him again?
> How strange it seems and new!

It is "Shelley" in the original—but a greater than Shelley is here; at least a greater than Shelley ever *was*, though it is hard to say what he might have been but for that white squall in the Gulf of Spezzia. It gives one a strange sensation to sit at a man's table and eat and drink and talk with him on equal terms, and then to think every now and then: This is the man who wrote *Peer Gynt* and the 4th act of *Brand*, and *Et Dukkehjem* and *Gjengangere*. Except Shakespeare, whom I would give a year of my life to interview (whether as his shoe-black or otherwise), I don't know that there is anyone in all literature whom I would care so much to know as Ibsen. Of course one would like to have seen Goethe or Thackeray or George Eliot, but they have not the enigmatic attraction of Ibsen.

By the way, before starting for Saeby I also read Björnson's *Over Aevne* [Beyond Human Power]. It is a very remarkable play, which I had not done justice to before, having read it in manuscript. Old B. B. is a great poet too, and I was glad to find Ibsen and his wife warm in praise of *Over Aevne*, though there is a suggestion of *Brand* about it which a small-minded man, with any ungenerous sense of rivalry, might have turned to Björnson's disadvantage. . . .

Yours,
W. A.

To CHARLES ARCHER

19 *August*, 1887

Having just finished a short and stupid letter to the *Pioneer*[1] (there will be blasphemy in Allahabad) I must find time to give you a scart o' the pen. Scotch is running in my head, thanks to Stevenson's *Underwoods*, which I was reviewing all yesterday. . . . He's really a great being, is R. L. S., and I feel jolly remorseful for ever having written anything that gave him a moment's—not pain, but dissatisfaction. I went down to Bournemouth for a day last week and had a long yarn with him. He was up to his eyes in old papers which he was destroying in preparation for a start to America. I wish I could remember a tithe of our talk. I had it out with him about *The Egoist*, but without coming to any very definite result. By the by, he is one of the heretics who depreciate George Eliot. Of course it is natural that the leader of the narrative-at-any-price school should have a certain down on her methods, and I knew already that he had; but I was rather taken aback to hear him say that, if Mrs. Oliphant had only husbanded her strength, he thought she had more genius than George Eliot. He found far more "geniality" in Mrs. O. than in George Eliot. He says he knows as a literal fact that Mrs. Oliphant writes at her meals—but for my part I shouldn't be surprised to learn that she wrote in her sleep. . . .

R. L. S.'s mother told me a story of him when he was a child. His nurse used to be very pious, and was always saying: "If I'm spared". One day he was walking in the street with his father, and was explaining to him some new phenomenon he had observed

[1] For several years W. A. contributed a weekly letter on The Theatre to the Allahabad *Pioneer*.

in the construction of the street lamps. "I'll show you it when we come to the next lamp-post", he said, "if I'm spared". . . .

Addio,

Yours,

W. A.

8 *Sept.* 1887

. . . . .

I see the *Times* in a long article echoes my *P.M.G.* review [of *Underwoods*], which gratifies me a good deal; not that I had any doubt of the merit of the book, but because I was rather afraid that a glowing notice in the *Gutter Gazette* would set the other papers against it. I forget whether I told you of my last interview with R. L. S. at an hotel in South Place, Finsbury ("I call it Todgers's for short," he said), and how I tore half over London at 10 p.m. one Saturday night to find a lawyer to help him to draft a codicil to his will, at which operation I subsequently assisted. On reflection, I don't think I can have told you this. He was in bed when I went, being much exhausted with his journey from Bournemouth; but my *P.M.G.* notice of *Underwoods* had just appeared that day, and he insisted on seeing me to tell me that he was delighted with the review, for, as in the case of the *Child's Garden*, I had accurately hit his intention, which was to react against the hysterical school of poetry. He agreed with me that it might possibly do the book harm with other reviewers, but he said he didn't care—he naturally would say so, but I believe he thought so too. He said, too, that he shared my opinion as to the blank verse being the best [thing] in the book, and was also very glad that I had said a word for the "Requiem", which a lot of people had told him was nonsense and advised him not to print.

They have set up at Skerryvore a huge sort of visitor-book album, simply inscribed "Skerryvore" on the cover, and to this they asked me to contribute the last time I was there. I said I would "next time", thinking within myself that very likely I should never see its face again—but after reading *Underwoods* the spirit moved me, and I wrote the enclosed seven stanzas, which, if they ask me again, I shall put in the book. There is one thing that pleases me a good deal in it:

There shall we find the landlocked estuary,
The harbor there.

I think these are very pretty lines, and I say it without prejudice, for the thing that is pretty about them, the dying fall of "estuary" at the end of the line, is prigged direct from Rossetti. . . .

A white-robed, star-crowned harbinger of rest
To storm-tossed wanderers hungering for the shore,
Moveless amid wild waters of the west
Stands Skerryvore.

The sailor, seeing, knows his haven near,
Foretastes his wife's content, his children's joy,
Or scents the tavern with its reeking cheer
And maids not coy.

So from our second, southern Skerryvore
Benignant streamers flash athwart the surge—
Flash to the far horizon—aye, and o'er
Its utmost verge.

We mark them and take courage—"Treacherous sea",
We cry, "where now thy might and our despair?
There shall we find the landlocked estuary,
The harbour there!"

Alas! not so!—we tack and tack again,
Now scud before the blast, now stem its rage—
No roadstead opens from that shoreless main,
No anchorage;

But still the cheerful light beams forth above,
Half solacing, half mocking our distress—
We marvel at its splendour, and we love
Its loveliness.

And when o'er us the gulfs of rest shall close,
The mariners that follow, more and more,
Shall bless the fount of light and strength that flows
From Skerryvore.

[In the autumn of 1887, when the Stevensons were on their way to America, Archer had painfully compounded, at W. E. Henley's suggestion, what he himself called "a long George-Robins-cum-Paul-Pry article", entitled "Robert Louis Stevenson at Skerryvore", which appeared in the *New York Critic* of November 5, 1887. The article, though written much against the grain, was not unhappy—Mrs. Stevenson found it "admirably done, and in perfect taste". But it provoked from Stevenson one of those outbursts of sheer, irresponsible high spirits which helped to make him so irresistible as man and as letter-writer:]

William Archer, Esq.

Sir,

You have done the deed. You have confused the Blue Room with the Red in Skerryvore: a fault for which pardon is impossible. God, sir, do you suppose me so impotent a workman that I should say a mirror faced the fire when in truth it only faced a window? No, Mr. Archer; blood is what I require. Besides, sir, I play with more than one finger on the piano; the difficulty about my playing is that I cannot go quicker than—say—adagio assai; but that is a different matter; and I can use any number of fingers (and hands, sir) if you let me go at my own pace.

We feel your reference to the food keenly; your devotion to heavy meals sounds strangely, let me tell you, in a pessimist; Captain's Biscuit should be good enough—is too good—for a pessimist.

And then, Mr. Archer, I had always heard you were so incorruptible; and I find you, in your reference to my moustache, lending yourself to a low private vengeance on the part of Henley. And what, sir, if I have but little? If my moustaches reached from pole to pole, they could not rescue my Immortial Soul.

Much you know of Mrs. Stevenson's strength of character; but you may have an opportunity of learning more. A woman who feeds her friends on Captain's Biscuit!

No, sir, the whole thing cries to Heaven for vengeance: therefore tremble, for illness has neither tamed the mind nor aged the body of Yours

R. L. S.

P.S. My entrance Hall is no narrower than your own —Sneck up!

P.P.S. My wife is not so graphic a narrator as her husband—this is to sow wanton discord in a quiet family.

P.P.P.S. My house is not unpretending: I give you the lie, sir.

P.P.P.P.S. My sanctum is NOT cheerful:—it is as dreary as a boot-jack.

P.P.P.P.P.P P P P P my limp fingers!—how about goes slavering mad. your limp nose?

From Robert Louis Stevenson

[Addressed, on envelope]

The Reverend
William *Archer*
care of *Tom Archer*
in his new house of
26 Gordon Square,
London, W.C.
England. [1888]

My dear Archer,

I sail for the South Seas from San Francisco June 15th: seven months gone, after health, sport and bankruptcy. How my wife is, I cannot say; she is further from me than I am from you—in San Francisco, where she has engineered this dashing cruise. All luck be with you, and the Mistress and Tomarcher. We calculate we shall have three mails during the 7 months, let us hear from you. Scribners will know where to send.

I am Blooming Alone.

Yours sincerely
Robert Louis Stevenson
Pirate Captain
(for seven months)
of another man's yacht
R.C.S.I., K.O.P.P.
E.R.B.O.T.T.O.M., etc.

IX

1889–1892

THE COMING OF IBSEN—*MACREADY*—THE INDEPENDENT THEATRE—THE CENSORSHIP

"THEREFORE I would say to the budding critic: Think, think, think! When you blame, blame with a reason; when you praise, praise with a difference. There is one sort of praise for the harmlessly trivial, another for the strenuous and the noble; forget this, and you debase the critical currency. Keep your mental plate ever 'sensitized'. Do not reject and deny an impression because it comes to you from an unexpected quarter, and upsets your preconceptions as to how you *ought* to be impressed. Approach a work of art always with the *desire,* never with the *determination,* to find in it a masterpiece. . . . When you *must* condemn, do so in such a way as to make your victim *think,* rather than merely writhe and swear. Be helpful if you can, 'and let who will be clever'. Deal tenderly with the susceptibilities of actors and actresses, whose marble and canvas are their own flesh and blood. And, finally, do not be so impolite and illogical as to inquire whether I, who thus preach to you, act up to my precepts."[1]

For five years now, week in week out, following these precepts so far as in him lay, Archer had upheld in the *World* his standards of drama, and preached, whenever occasion served, his gospel: Back to life.

[1] "Mr. Pinero as Polonius," *Pall Mall Gazette,* February 1, 1894. The reference is to an address by the dramatist, in which he urged the importance of praise in criticism, and would have had young critics make their motto: Praise, praise, praise!

In this time he had made himself something of an oracle to the small but growing public which would fain have taken the drama seriously, and had begun to count as a power in the inner circle, "the unassembled parliament", as Mr. Granville-Barker has called it, of the theatrical world, respected even by the section of that body least in sympathy with his views and aims. He had not always been able to carry out his own precepts to the extent of making his "victims" think rather than swear; but some who began by swearing went on to think; and that, on the whole, he practised the style of helpful criticism which he preached is shown by very many letters from budding dramatists thanking him for help and encouragement, and by the fact that the men who held the future of the drama in their hands were, without exception, his friends then and throughout his career. "His object", says one of the chief of them, Sir Arthur Pinero, "was so transparently one of encouragement, that it was impossible, I believe, for the most thin-skinned of authors to feel more than a passing hurt at anything he wrote in disapproval."[1] And again: "His aim, as I have said—the main purpose of his life—was to get the best out of a writer that was in him, and not to be satisfied till he got it."

The position he had attained and his character for sincerity were to stand him and the "new drama" in good stead in the time of storm and stress that was at hand, when the theatrical world was "swept with confused alarms of struggle and fight", and he was in the thickest of a fray in which the combatants were not overnice in their choice of weapons.

The descent of Ibsen—a visitant, in the eyes of

1 "I'd far rather be rib-roasted by you", Henley wrote to him, some years later, "than praised by —— and Co."

many, the reverse of celestial—to trouble the theatrical waters, found the native English drama, to all appearance, but little advanced from the point it had reached in 1886, when *About the Theatre* appeared. If, in the spring of 1889, Archer had reviewed the productions of the past three years, it might have taxed his faith to discern any very definite signs of progress. No new playwright of distinct promise had appeared; while of the three dramatists who, in 1886, had seemed to be coming men, only one had since then made any distinct advance. Apart from Gilbert and Sullivan opera, the only work of the period which might have seemed to possess enduring vitality had come from Pinero, to whose credit there stood two brilliant farces—*The Schoolmistress* and *Dandy Dick*—and a "fresh, honest, amiable, irresistible, preposterous"[1] comedy of sentiment—*Sweet Lavender*. And these were essentially fantastic works —in his more serious and ambitious attempts even Pinero had as yet achieved no striking success.

But beneath the surface things had been moving. A public had grown up which wanted a drama bearing some recognizable relation to the realities of life, and was prepared to accept the serious treatment of themes which, a few years before, would have been taboo. And it was Pinero who, when the feet of Ibsen were already on the threshold, demonstrated this fact. His *Profligate*, produced on April 24, 1889, proved to be one of those epoch-marking plays which have an importance in theatrical history out of proportion to their intrinsic merits. With all its faults, it was a vigorous attempt to "get back to life", and its success proved, once for all, that the English dramatist need no longer be entirely dominated in his choice of themes by the fear of "the

[1] W. A. in the *World*, March 28, 1888.

young lady in the dress circle". It proves, too, in the retrospect, if proof were needed, that the coming of Ibsen must be considered as a symptom of a movement already under way, rather than as the efficient cause of the marked advance of the next few years.

The thoughts of the new public had naturally turned to the Norwegian dramatist, whose merits others besides Archer had been proclaiming for years past, and several of whose modern plays were now accessible in English. In the spring of 1889 a scheme was started for a subscription performance of *A Doll's House,* the most famous and successful of the modern prose plays. The scheme came to nothing for the time; but a young actress of high talent and ambition, Janet Achurch, and her husband, Charles Charrington, stepped into the breach. Determined to produce the play, and finding the existing translation hopeless for stage purposes, they applied to Archer for a playable text, and found him more than willing not only to supply what they wanted, but also to stand by them with rede and deed in the staging and production of the piece. On May 31st he writes: "Though I am so busy I scarcely know whether I am standing on my heels or my head, I must send you a line to tell you how *Et Dukkehjem* is getting on. I am wasting any amount of time over the rehearsals; but there are always little things in which I can put them straight, and I want to give the production as much chance as possible. The first night is this day week; so two mails from this you may expect a budget of notices—and pretty things they'll be, I've no doubt."

Pretty things a good many of them were. Compared with the storm that greeted the production of *Ghosts* two years later, the reception of *A Doll's House* seems now almost calm and reasonable, but at the time it appeared as though party spirit could hardly go much farther in obscuring counsel on an æsthetic issue. The controversy which the play had provoked nine years before in the North was transplanted to England, and took root and flourished rankly; the voices of Ibsenite and anti-Ibsenite were, for the first time, heard in the land; and here, even more than in Scandinavia, the disputants were mainly concerned to exalt or condemn the tendency of the play—its "gospel"—their view of which determined, in the main, their opinion of its merits as drama. Ibsen had struck a great blow for the emancipation of women, and for true morality, in a drama of rare force—or he had produced a dreary and grossly immoral work, which cut at the very roots of family life. Nora was a thoroughly sympathetic and heroic heroine—or, in the words of the influential critic of the *Daily Telegraph*, she was "the socialistic Nora", "a mass of aggregate conceit and self-sufficiency". Much criticism, of course, was more relevant and less hysterical than this, but the greater part was tinged with partisanship of one complexion or the other.

There was general agreement, however, as to the merit of the production and the acting; Miss Achurch's Nora placed her at a stroke in the front rank of rising actresses; and the play must clearly have appealed to a substantial number of people outside the small group specially interested in Ibsen and his ideas, for the venture was much more successful than had been expected—at least by Archer; the anti-Ibsenite vituperation no doubt contributing to this result. Instead of the week originally intended, the production ran for three weeks (twenty-four performances), and when the Charringtons, in accordance with arrangements previously made, left for Australia, the receipts had very nearly covered the considerable expenses.

"It was this production", Archer wrote long after, "that really made Ibsen known to the English-speaking peoples. In other words, it marked his second stride towards world-wide, as distinct from merely national, renown—if we reckon as the first stride the success of *Pillars of Society* in Germany. Mr. and Mrs. Charrington took *A Doll's House* with them on a long Australian tour; Miss Beatrice Cameron (Mrs. Richard Mansfield) was encouraged by the success of the London production to present the play in New York, whence it soon spread to other American cities; while in London itself it was frequently revived and vehemently discussed. The Ibsen controversy, indeed, did not break out in its full virulence until 1891, when *Ghosts* and *Hedda Gabler* were produced in London; but from the date of the Novelty production onwards, Ibsen was generally recognized as a potent factor in the intellectual and artistic life of the day."

The air was soon full of projects for fresh Ibsen translations. Naturally enough it was the "social dramas" that mainly attracted translators, as more easily dealt with, and more likely to appeal to the public, than the earlier plays from saga and history. But Archer felt that the time was now ripe for a complete English version of the poet's works, including all the mature prose dramas at the least. By November, a publisher (Mr. Walter Scott) had been converted to this view, Archer contracting to "supply competent translations of eleven plays of Ibsen" to be issued in four volumes;[1] Ibsen's sanction had been obtained; and Archer was plunged in the work of translation, revision, and editing which was to occupy so great a share of his time and thought for the next sixteen

[1] Eventually thirteen plays in five volumes: *Emperor and Galilaean* and *Hedda Gabler* being included.

years. Since Ibsen could grant no copyright, early publication was essential in order to forestall possible competition; and within a year, by November 1890, the first four volumes had appeared, Archer having in this time translated four plays (including the massive *Emperor and Galilaean*),[1] and thoroughly revised his own and his collaborators' versions of the remaining six, besides supplying introductions for the whole ten. And though he held that in translation two heads are better than one, and valued highly the help received from his collaborators, "revision", as he understood the word, was such a drastic process that the amount of time and labour expended on it often fell but little short of that required by original translation.

While the work was still proceeding, another meeting with Ibsen confirmed the good understanding that had existed from the first between the poet and his interpreter. An old enthusiasm for the Wagnerian music-dramas (whose combination of great music with grandiose poetry had always appealed to him) took Archer with Shaw and Dibdin to Bayreuth in the summer of 1889; and the next summer he was again in Bavaria, the attraction this time being nominally the Ober-Ammergau Passion Play, but actually, we may suspect, the Ibsen household at Munich. Here he received a cordial welcome from the poet ("His notoriety in England and America is, as he says, 'a fairy-tale' to him, and he is—for him—profuse in his acknowledgments of my share in bringing it about"); spent a pleasant day[2] with him and his family; and (sacrificing for the purpose, without much regret, a couple of hours of the Passion

[1] In translating this play he was enabled (by arrangement) to make occasional use of Miss Catherine Ray's version, published in 1876.
[2] Described in "Ibsen As I Knew Him," *Monthly Review*, June 1906.

Play) had, at the Residenz Theater, his first view of *An Enemy of the People* on the stage. "It was vilely staged", he remarks "—if they'd have let me direct a couple of rehearsals, I'd have made a different play of it—but it was fairly played, and went like wild-fire with the house."

All through these busy and eventful times Archer had been wrestling with a monograph on William Charles Macready, the first volume of a projected "Eminent Actors" series[1] which was to be published under his editorship. The book, which appeared in the early summer of 1890, had cost him much labour. "This Macready", he had written to Brander Matthews in December 1888, "has turned out a gigantic piece of work, simply on account of the wilderness of material. I hope to make a tolerable job of it, but the boiling-down is heartrending." The outcome was a book which is a model of the art of compression—brief, yet comprehensive; packed with matter, yet easy and pleasant to read; accurate in statements of fact, and clear and impartial in its treatment of matters of opinion. Of the sketch of the Macready-Forrest quarrel, for instance, with its tragic climax in the Astor Place riots, Professor Matthews writes: "Nothing could be more accurate, more disinterested, or in better taste, than W. A.'s account." And the last chapter, "Art and Character", is a summing up at once entertaining and judicial.

In the summer of this year a plan, long meditated, of removal to the country in the interests of health was at length carried out. A small cottage near Ockham in Surrey, christened Walden after Thoreau's

[1] The series ended prematurely after the appearance of two more volumes—*Betterton*, by R. W. Lowe, and *Macklin*, by E. A. Parry.

retreat, was the family's home for the next five years, though rooms in London had to be retained, and the father had perforce to spend many of his days and nights in them. The move was a fortunate one for the health of all three, and in that beautiful countryside, then unspoiled by jerry-building and motor-cars, William Archer could indulge to the full his love of long walks and talks with friends—Pinero, Shaw, Walkley (then living hard by), Lowe, Dibdin, and many others. Sometimes in later years these excursions, extended by rail, would take him to George Meredith's house at Boxhill, or even as far as the little cottage over the Kent border where a young writer named Edward Verrall Lucas had made his nest.

Archer's review of the native drama at the end of 1889 had left him, on the whole, in a "depressed and pessimistic mood". He finds it difficult to discover any "slightest stirring of rebellion against Mammon and Mrs. Grundy". *The Profligate,* however, is a point of light, and we have a first mention of a scheme set on foot by Messrs. Grein and Jarvis for the establishment of an Independent Theatre on the lines of Antoine's Théâtre Libre—a scheme of which more was to be heard.

Eighteen hundred and ninety, on the other hand, was a year of good promise. Looking back, in his annual review, at its events, which included the appearance of Henry Arthur Jones's *Judah* and *The Pharisee,* and Pinero's *Cabinet Minister,* and the production at the Haymarket of Henley and Stevenson's *Beau Austin,* Archer confessed to a feeling that theatrical life at large was becoming more and more worth living. And, though big with troubles to come, the year had been in itself a quiet one, the Ibsen controversy having temporarily gone to sleep.

But with 1891 there set in a period of storm. Before the year had gone far, the Ibsen battle had been joined again with redoubled fury, to last, with occasional lulls, for half a decade; the Independent Theatre had reared its head, to be greeted, as something new and strange, with a shower of half-bricks; while the next year witnessed the first important move in the long siege operations against the Censorship. As his "Roseate Retrospect" of January 1891 shows, it was mainly a prevision of stirring events to come that inspired Archer's optimistic view.

Ibsen performances began straightway, with a production of *A Doll's House* in January, a young American actress named Elizabeth Robins making a success in the part of Mrs. Linden. *Rosmersholm* followed in February, and, being ill produced and on the whole poorly acted, gave the anti-Ibsenites a plausible excuse to say Aha! The mildest of the adverse notices spoke of "the utter preposterousness of those portions of the play that are comprehensible" —the tone of the more severe may be judged from *London's* description of the play as "this cancerous production".

But worse by far was to come. Owing mainly to Mr. J. T. Grein's enthusiasm and tenacity, the Independent Theatre Society, for which he and others had been working for more than a year, had at length come into being. It was a modest organization of most slender resources, intended to give the non-commercial drama, both native and foreign, a chance upon the stage, by means of occasional subscription performances in theatres hired for the purpose. Since no money was to be taken at the doors, the performances would be technically private, and it was believed that plays which, for one reason or another, the Censor could not be expected to pass for public performance, could be given without licence, as *The Cenci* had been given in 1886 under the auspices of the Shelley Society.

Greatly daring, the Independent Theatre Society opened its first season, on March 13th, at the Royalty Theatre, with a performance of Ibsen's *Ghosts*. Immediately an incredible hubbub went up to heaven. The majority of the newspapers broke out into wild and whirling cries, and vied with each other in hurling the most offensive epithets ingenuity could devise at the play, its author, the promoters of the production, and its audiences. There were clamours for the intervention of the police, or the Lord Chamberlain, or both; and, though no official action appears to have been taken, lessees and managers were so intimidated that thenceforth, before letting their theatres to the Society, they insisted that the play to be produced must be previously passed by the Censor.

It is needless, and it would be unedifying, even in these days of plain speaking, to give samples of the deposit left by this torrent of abuse. Some of the gems are well known, and the historian of the stage will find a fairly representative collection in the studies made by Archer for his projected *Ibsen Schimpf-Lexikon*, or *Anthology of Abuse*.[1] The flood was soon swelled by the new freshet of vituperation raised by the production of *Hedda Gabler*.

The new play had appeared in Copenhagen in December 1890. Ibsen had now become "a commercial proposition", and, the fact being established that his work had a certain market value, it was not long before the discovery was made that copyright in his plays could be secured as they appeared by

[1] "Ghosts and Gibberings", *Pall Mall Gazette*, April 8, 1891. "The Mausoleum of Ibsen", *Fortnightly Review*, August 1893. See also G. Bernard Shaw's *Quintessence of Ibsenism*, p. 89.

the publication of the Norwegian text in England. Mr. W. Heinemann, the publisher to whom this discovery was due, made arrangements with the poet for the publication of the new play in an English version by E. W. Gosse. A misunderstanding, natural enough in a complicated negotiation in which five parties were concerned, arose as to the effect of Mr. Heinemann's acquisition of the play on the arrangements previously made by Archer for its inclusion in Walter Scott's edition. The matter, however, was amicably adjusted, and the incident had the happy result of bringing Archer into relations with the firm which was eventually to publish, under his editorship, the complete standard edition of the poet's works.

No sooner had the play appeared in English than the great opportunities offered by the rôles of Hedda and Thea seized upon the imagination of two young American actresses, Miss Elizabeth Robins (the Mrs. Linden of the recent *Doll's House* production) and Miss Marion Lea; and they determined to stake everything to make the parts their own. Their enthusiasm carried all before it; a theatre was secured and an efficient company organized, and Archer, delighted to further the good work, was soon busy in helping to fit the published version for the theatre, and in the staging and production of the piece. The performance took place at the Vaudeville Theatre on April 20th, and the trenchant power of the drama, and the strong, sinister attraction of the chief character, brilliantly presented by Miss Robins, made a deep impression. The comparative absence of an atmosphere of symbolism and poetry, too, contributed to the immediate success. The anti-Ibsenites stuck stoutly to their guns; some of the criticisms, indeed, were among the most delectably wrong-headed produced by the whole controversy; but it was plainly to be seen that they were not a little staggered, if only by the sheer theatrical effectiveness of the piece.[1] Even those who waved it aside as intolerable were forced to allow it some negative merits, in comparison with the other plays. After a series of matinées, the play went into the evening bill, and in the event Miss Robins and Miss Lea had no reason, even from the pecuniary point of view, to regret their gallant venture.

Lectures on contemporary poetry, which led on to further lectures and articles in the late nineties, and, in the fullness of time, to *Poets of the Younger Generation*, and a series on "Four Stages of Stage-History" (under the headings: Betterton, Cibber, Garrick, and Kemble) at the Royal Institution in May and June, cost Archer a good deal of time and trouble; for lecturing, at that period at least, was by no means congenial to him. An easier and pleasanter by-employment was the translation of a few of A. L. Kjelland's charming novelettes, which appeared this year under the title of *Tales of Two Countries*.

These tasks disposed of, and the fifth volume of the Walter Scott *Ibsen's Prose Dramas* safely out of hand, he was free to devote such leisure as he could command to "cutting into lengths"[2] his brother's prose translation of *Peer Gynt*, which had now reached him from India—Ibsen having definitely refused to

[1] The effect produced bordered on hallucination in some cases; the critic of the most prominent theatrical daily, for instance, wrote: ". . . It was like a visit to the Morgue. . . . There they all lay on their copper couches, fronting us, and waiting to be owned. . . . There they all were, false men, wicked women, deceitful friends, sensualists, egotists, piled up in a heap behind the screen of glass which we were thankful for. . . ."

[2] Such was his own description of what was really a pretty thorough re-shaping.

let the poem be put before the English public in prose, but having accepted Archer's amended proposal for an unrhymed version following the metres of the original. The leisure was not abundant, for the season was a full one, and throughout the autumn the Press war between the old drama and the new went on merrily, the Independent Theatre production of *Thérèse Raquin* in October adding fuel to the flames. Feeling ran so high that the Press controversy had reactions in private life, as characteristic letters[1] of this time show.

The year had been a notable one in home-made as well as in foreign drama, for, besides the Independent Theatre and Ibsen productions, it had seen the appearance of Jones's *Dancing Girl* and *Crusaders*, Pinero's *Lady Bountiful* and *The Times*—a dramatic crop distinctly superior to that of any recent year. Eighteen hundred and ninety-two had a quieter record, but one, in its way, yet more encouraging, for it produced what was of even greater importance than mature plays: the prentice works of three new and notable dramatists. In February a talent full of brilliancy and promise, though time was to prove it orchid-like, rootless, made its first dazzling essay in drama in *Lady Windermere's Fan*; in March a quieter, saner genius, deep-rooted in its homely mother-soil, showed modestly forth in J. M. Barrie's *Walker, London*; and December saw the stormy Independent Theatre production of *Widowers' Houses*, at the end of which George Bernard Shaw made his first bow to an incensed theatrical audience, and in three minutes had stilled the raging waters by the magic of his Irish speech. "Even the most obstinate disparager of that institution" [the Independent Theatre], said Archer in his candidly

[1] Pp. 193–195.

critical notice (which drew from the new dramatist the characteristic post-card reproduced below[1]), "must admit that in this case, if in no other, it proved its utility and justified its existence." Verily, a true remark—even truer than its maker could at the time foresee.

The controversy between the old dispensation and the new was diverted for a time into a fresh channel by the appointment in March 1892 of a Select Committee "to inquire into the operation of the Acts of Parliament relating to the licensing and regulating of Theatres and Places of Public Entertainment, and to consider and report any alterations in the Law which may appear desirable". The terms of reference covered a consideration of the operation of the Censorship, and Archer sprang into the lists, a solitary challenger, and was examined, as the sole advocate of abolition, at some length. He was a good deal hampered in his assault by his inability to point to any actual instances of the strangling of works of genius by the Censorship, and his studiously moderate and cautiously worded evidence seems to the reader of to-day scarcely as damaging as the Censor's own defence of his office, in the course of which occur Mr. Pigott's appreciation of Ibsen's plays,[2] and his yet more remarkable declaration of indifference to public opinion: "The only opinion I care for is the opinion of the people I am immediately concerned with, that is the managers." That this state of insensibility was not absolute, however, would

[1] P. 196.

[2] "I have studied Ibsen's plays pretty carefully, and all the characters appear to me to be morally deranged. All the heroines are dissatisfied spinsters who look on marriage as a monopoly, or dissatisfied married women in a chronic state of rebellion . . .; and as for the men, they are all rascals or imbeciles."

appear from his fortifying himself in the face of Archer's attack by the reflection that Mr. Clement Scott (of the *Daily Telegraph*) is on his side, "and for every reader Mr. Archer represents he represents a thousand". With the managers solid in favour of the Censorship, and no voice lifted against it from the ranks of the dramatists, the result of the Committee's deliberations was a foregone conclusion: the report simply repeated the finding of the Committee of 1866: "That the censorship of plays has worked satisfactorily, and that it is not desirable that it should be discontinued; on the contrary, that it should be extended, as far as practicable, to the performances in music-halls and other places of public entertainment." Seventeen years later, when a native drama had arisen that was worth fighting for, and that could be and had actually been injured by the Censorship, the battle was to be renewed on somewhat more even terms.

The translation of *Peer Gynt* appeared in the summer. It had no great immediate success with the public, but it at once impressed many lovers of poetry whom the prose dramas had left cold, and it has made itself felt ever since, both in England and America. In spite of the enormous loss of power and beauty entailed by the sacrifice of the rhymes and by other shortcomings, its appearance probably did more than any other stroke in the Ibsen campaign to dispel the grotesque anti-Ibsenite vision of the poet as a prosaic and humourless hot-gospeller.

Another blow to this conception was impending. As the year drew towards a close, Archer was devouring Ibsen's new play,[1] sent over in sheets, and noting (he admits) with a sinking heart, as he glanced ahead

[1] *Bygmester Solness* (*The Master Builder*).

down the sheets, how for many pages on end the play seemed a mere duologue, with "Solness—Hilda, Solness—Hilda" endlessly repeated.

The sale of the *Pall Mall Gazette*, with the resulting change in its politics, disconcerting as it was at the moment, turned out, in Archer's case, to be a piece of good fortune. The *Westminster Gazette*, promptly founded to carry on the Liberal tradition, naturally commanded his allegiance, and he worked for it from the beginning. But it was not long before he had, in addition, re-established a footing in the camp he had left. For George Halkett, the illustrator of *The Fashionable Tragedian*, who had since become well-known in art circles, and had, as a caricaturist, proved a tower of strength to Conservatism in Scotland, settled in London at this juncture, and joined the editorial staff of the *Pall Mall*. The kindest of hearts and the gayest of spirits, he doubtless wore his Conservatism lightly; and, at all events, the friendship between the two men went much deeper than did their politics. It was not in the nature of things that the two should be working in one city and not be helping each other in some fashion. Consequently, from the first, we find in Archer's collections occasional white *Pall Mall* articles variegating the green of the *Westminster* reviews; and later, Halkett's elevation to be Art Editor, and then Editor, of the *Pall Mall Magazine* led to W. A.'s becoming a frequent contributor, and finally to his receiving the commission which took him to America for the second time and launched him on his work as a publicist.

IXa
LETTERS OF 1889–1892

[Considerations of space make it impossible to include more than one or two of many letters dealing minutely with the performances of Ibsen's plays. Those relating to the historic first productions of *A Doll's House* and *Hedda Gabler* have been chosen as samples.]

To Charles Archer

13 *June*, '89

We have fought a good fight for the Old Min, and have won a really glorious victory. It would take me a day's hard writing to give you full details, but I shall send along with this a budget of press notices. Of course most of them are silliness itself; but still the play has been the great event of the week—almost of the season. It has been more talked about and written about than even *The Profligate*. It holds the B.P. like a vice—and what's more, they pay to see it. The receipts are not large—between £35 and £45 a performance—but that, for an out-of-the-way house, is by no means bad, especially as it is scarcely advertised at all. Of course Miss Achurch has the lioness's share in the success. She is really a delightful Nora—not ideal; her voice and tricks of utterance forbid that—but she *feels* the part right through, and is often very fine and even noble. In short she is *a* Nora and a very beautiful one, though not quite *the* Nora. It is by far the biggest thing she has ever done; compliments and offers of engagements have poured in upon her; no actress for years has made such a success. She varies rather from night to night.

I always go to see the last scene, which is to me *the* great thing of the piece and one of the Old Min's biggest achievements; and once or twice I have seen her play it *perfectly*. At other times she goes in for motiveless *fortes* and *pianos* which mar the smoothness of it. On the first night Waring (Helmer) got a little wrong in his lines and didn't say the speech: "I would work for you, etc.; but no man sacrifices his honour even for one he loves"—so that of course she couldn't get in her *Millions of women have done that.* I was mad at that, for she speaks it beautifully—it was almost the one misfortune of a glorious evening. Since then we have of course got the passage put right, and the B.P. now rises to the occasion unfailingly. . . . But *what* a scene that is! Every speech in it rings like a clarion. They may call it pure logic if they like, but it is logic saturated with emotion. I cry over it every night. It's very curious, the first time I saw Miss A. rehearse it she was deadly—querulous, whimpering, wretched. I arranged to meet her half an hour before the next rehearsal and go through the scene with her; but that day she was ill and didn't come to rehearsal at all; so I told Charrington what I thought was wrong, and he said he would go through it with her. The next rehearsal I sat in the stalls and listened to it—the thing was totally different. It gripped me line by line and simply thrilled me with intellectual pleasure and intense emotion. At the end she came to the footlights and said: "How was that?" I said: "If that scene moves the audience half as much as it has moved me to-day, the play's all right"—and it was! There was another rather amusing thing about that scene. X. Y., the acting manager, a Philistine of the Philistines, happened to see it one day at rehearsal. At the end he said: "You'll excuse me, Miss Achurch, it's no business of mine, but I can't help saying that that scene's splendid—most interesting—certain to go." She rushed across the stage and almost embraced him, and we were all delighted to have conquered the doughty Y. But next day he came to me and said: "It was rather good, my going into raptures over that scene. *I* had no idea it was the last act. *I* thought it was the first act, and it was all going to be cleared up. . . ."

Fru Gundersen of the Xiania Theatre, who is over here just now, told me Miss A. was the best Nora she had ever seen, and she had no reason to put it as strongly as that if she didn't think so. In short we have had a splendid week, and whatever else comes of it, Ibsen has triumphed. I only wish you had been here to see. By the by, I mustn't forget to say that we have got up a really charming little scene—an ideal *Dukkehjem*. Some day I shall tell you of the manifold adventures and labours I went through in mounting it. Now I have got to finish my *Pioneer* letter.

[Extract]

30th June, 1889

. . . Talking of photos, the Old Min has (at my suggestion) sent Miss Achurch a leonine head of himself (not a favourable likeness) inscribed: ["To Miss Janet Achurch, with hearty thanks from Henrik Ibsen"]—and along with it he sent a card to me, which I copy, as it is not long:

[Translation]

d. 26.6.89

"DEAR MR. ARCHER,

Accept my heartiest thanks also for your last letter, and for all your good and joyful tidings! I shall owe you a debt of gratitude all my life long. The movement in London marks a shining epoch in my life, and far surpasses anything I had ever dreamed of.

And may my wife and I offer our respectful greetings to Mrs. Archer?

Your affectionate and obliged,

HENRIK IBSEN."

So you see the Old Min's friendly this time at any rate.

From HENRIK IBSEN

[Translation]

MUNICH, 3 *November*, 1889

DEAR MR. W. ARCHER,

It is with exceedingly great pleasure that I have this moment received your kind letter of the 1st inst., and I make haste to answer it at once.

For all you have done in the past and are still doing to win admission for my works in England I shall ever feel that I owe you a deep debt of gratitude.

Of course I give my sanction with the greatest willingness and pleasure in regard to those plays of mine which you propose to translate and publish through Mr. Scott's publishing house; and I am particularly obliged to you for the terms offered in regard to the author's fee.

Your splendid and valuable édition de luxe of *A Doll's House* has arrived in good condition. For this beautiful gift, too, I send you my most hearty thanks. I should have done so long ago. I have the book always lying on my table, and it is highly admired by all who see it and who are in any degree judges of artistic typography. I cannot deny that I

From the drawing by] [*George R. Halkett*

By permission of the British Drama League

HENRIK IBSEN IN 1891

take a good deal of pride in the thought that a work of mine has attained to publication in mighty England in such a handsome dress.

With very cordial greetings to Mrs. Archer from my wife and from myself, I subscribe myself

Most sincerely yours,
HENRIK IBSEN

[A visit to Copenhagen in the spring of 1890, with a view to an article[1] on the Royal Theatre, gave Archer an opportunity of comparing the great Danish actress, Fru Hennings, with Miss Achurch in the part of Nora. After giving a list of plays seen at the Royal Theatre—Molière, Holberg, Heiberg, etc., etc. —he goes on:]

. . . Then (specially for my benefit) *Et Dukkehjem*. In all the lighter scenes Fru Hennings not only beat Miss Achurch but played with an astonishing mastery—one of the most wonderfully finished performances I ever saw. When the plot began to thicken, Miss Achurch, as it were, gradually pulled up. Unquestionably, I think, Miss Achurch at her best got the pathos of the part much better than Fru Hennings; still her [Fru H.'s] performance was exceedingly fine —[finished to the highest degree]. But in the last scene she broke down entirely. Miss Achurch was incomparably finer—or rather Miss Achurch was right and Fru Hennings wrong. She simply scolded Helmer, and became in reality the objectionable person of Clement Scott's imagination. It is a great pity—I mean to speak or write to Fru Hennings about it, for I find that other people here (Edvard Brandes for instance) feel vaguely that the last scene is wrong, though they don't seem to know precisely

[1] *Harper's Magazine*, February 1892.

what is wrong with it. E. Poulsen's Helmer is excellent; but the truth is, Helmer's a bad part. I find on speaking to Poulsen about it that he wanted to play Rank, but there was no one else to play Helmer. Jendorff an excellent Rank—Krogstad very good—it was curious to note that here, as in London, Krogstad got a round of applause at each of his exits. . . .

To Charles Archer

8 July, 1891

. . . . .

I have just been correcting the proofs of the last act of *Hedda*—the last pages of Scott's edition—I feel a little like Gibbon in the famous summer-house at Lausanne. Those five volumes will be on the whole the most satisfactory job of my life, even with all their imperfections on their heads. And some day, perhaps, we shall get some of the imperfections ridded out—don't omit, every time you take one of the volumes up, to mark emendations on the margin. The last act of *Hedda* quite thrilled me as it acted itself before me in the proofs. Miss Robins was really fine in it—she had moments of inspiration. I must tell you what poor old Joe Knight said to me one day. We were talking about Barrie's *Ibsen's Ghost*, which was produced on the afternoon before the last performance of *Hedda*. I said it was rather funny. He said: "Well yes—but I assure you, Archer, at the point where Miss Vanbrugh changed from Thea into Hedda, and I saw the black figure and the long white arms glimmering through the darkness of the stage, the feeling of the real thing gripped me and thrilled me, and I could hardly resist going back that night and seeing it once more." Certainly it was a big thing, that last act, and how it held even the densest audiences! They used always to hiss Hedda at the lines: "I did it for your sake, George", and "I couldn't bear that anyone should throw *you* into the shade"—and certainly Miss R. was diabolically feline in those lines. What always fetched me most in her performance was a point in which she departed from Ibsen's strict intention. It is where Hedda is sitting by the stove, absorbed in the contemplation of Lövborg's having "had the will and the courage to turn away from the banquet of life—so early". Instead of starting, where Brack says he must dispel her pleasant illusion, Miss R. used to speak three speeches: "Illusion?" "What do you mean?" and "Not voluntarily?"—quite absently, looking straight in front of her, and evidently not taking in what Brack was saying. She used to draw deep breaths of relief ("befrielse"), quite intent on her vision of Eilert lying "i skönhed", and only waken up at her fourth speech: "Have you concealed something?" Now the old min evidently didn't intend this, but it is one of those things I'm sure he would be grateful for, it was so beautiful. I shall never forget her saying of "Not voluntarily?" with a sort of dreamy surprise, not in the least realizing what Brack's words implied, yet beginning to wake up, as when a persistent external sound forces itself into a dream, and you are just awake enough to wonder vaguely what it can be. If the other acts had all been as good as the last, it would have been a creation indeed—and many scenes in them were always excellent. Miss Robins would be the ideal Rebecca (a much more perfect Rebecca than Hedda, I think) but there seems to be a sort of etiquette forbidding her to play it for some time at least after poor ——'s attempt. . . .

I have been reading the *Tour to the Hebrides*—

surely the most entertaining book ever written. And how well Bozzy writes! He's really a master of easy, gentlemanly prose.

No more at present, from

Yours,

W. A.

From WILLIAM DEAN HOWELLS

Sept. 17, 1890

MY DEAR SIR,

I should feel myself as graceless as some people seem to think me if I failed to thank you for the kind expressions concerning myself in your paper in the *New York Dramatic Mirror* of September 13th. But the personal matter is of little importance compared with the æsthetic question, and I thank you even more for the expressions not concerning me. I read a paper of yours in the *New York Review* last year, which I was tempted to make a joyful noise over in the "Study", but somehow refrained, and so spared you the infamy of my praise in public. But you shall not escape it in private. A few more such papers as that, and the light which everyone else sees will begin to pierce the skulls of even Anglo-Saxon dramatic critics. The poor fellows are not to blame for their stupidity; God made them stupid, but unless He has been greatly misunderstood He did not make them proud of their stupidity. What I am trying to teach them in this country, where the theatres are to the dramas as the religions are to the gravies—a hundred to one—is that if we are ever to have American plays they must come out of American life, and they cannot naturally appear with a Parisian trousseau. This appears to vex them, and so they call names. I expected something of the sort. Of course the things here that I have praised with many reservations are "poor things but our own". They are poor in trying to be like the old stage-plays, but the worst of them have interesting gleams of truth in them, and so I try to make people believe that so far as they *are* our own they are good. It is "hard sledding". Still, there is some little response. The public and the managers are more intelligent, I think, than the critics.

Yours very truly,
W. D. HOWELLS

WM. ARCHER, ESQ.

From BRANDER MATTHEWS

Sept. 10th, 1890

DEAR ARCHER,

I have just read your paper in the *Mirror*, and I am moved to make a suggestion. Howells (as interpreted by you) is right—character is, of course, of far greater consequence than action. But Howells despises the art of the playwright; he thinks that the "tricks of the trade" are not worth learning and that there is no need to "know the ropes". Now, I find that the men who write *successful* plays in which action is subordinated to character are "old stagers" —*vieux routiers* Sarcey would call them. Ibsen is no novice in stage-craft. Nor are the authors of "Paris Fin de Siècle" and of "Jed Prouty" and "The Old Homestead" which Howells praises. To my mind the art of playmaking must be mastered first: and Scribe, Sardou and the two Dumas are the best teachers I know. Having once acquired the grammar of the art, the dramatist may simplify his rhetoric at will.

And the pupil need not imitate the teacher:

Gérome—hard, dry, and no colorist—is a great teacher; and his pupils are often colorists and impressionists and *pleinairistes* and what not. Mais il faut de l'école! How does this strike you?

Yours truly,

BRANDER MATTHEWS

To BRANDER MATTHEWS

WALDEN, COBHAM, SURREY,
28 *Sept.*, '90

MY DEAR MATTHEWS,

. . . . .

As to the question raised in my *Mirror* article —of course you are quite right in this sense: that there is a peculiar theatrical technique which the playwright must not and cannot neglect—in other words, the stage is a medium just like marble or pigments, and like them, is subject to its own peculiar conditions. But I don't think the French, or any other people, have exhausted the study of these conditions. Indeed they cannot in the nature of things be studied once for all; for they change with every nation and every generation. The great dramatist will make his own technique, will study the conditions of his art for himself, and, by gradually dominating his public, modify his conditions to suit his own needs of utterance. So it seems to me what we critics have got to do is to clear our mind of rules which, from Aristotle downwards, have only been generalizations from the practice of dramatists. Of course, where a playwright is obviously trying to conform to a particular set of canons and fails, we have to point out his failure and the reasons of it; but that is a different thing from dropping on vigorous and vital work because the playwright is a law unto himself.

Remember, I don't mean to say that there isn't force and justice in Sarcey's position—it would be a preternaturally bad case that hadn't a leg to stand on; nor do I mean that Howells and I are altogether right; but I think we err on the side of life and progress, while the conventional criticism errs on the side of stagnation. I suppose your position is the *juste milieu*—but I'm an incorrigible Radical in the drama as in other things.

. . . .

Yours very truly,
W. ARCHER

To CHARLES ARCHER

20 *Nov.* 90

. . . I'm sorry to say I haven't even looked at your *Peer Gynt* yet. You can't conceive how I'm beset with work. It is a case of ["Forward and back, and it's just as far"]—I begin to feel that the only way to call my soul my own again will be to ["go round about"]—to Italy or somewhere—possibly to Samoa, whither the Stevensons are trying to lure us. Of course when Ibsen is cleared off there *should* be a certain relief—but it will only be a vacuum for more work to rush into. If you come to think of it, four volumes of Ibsen in exactly a year is no child's play—I wonder how many hours the mere proof-reading has taken. . . .

F. is, I think, really better under her new regimen, and Tom[1] is flourishing but naughty. He is much interested in Orpheus and Eurydice, apropos of Glück's *Orfeo,* which is the most beautiful thing I ever heard, by the way. He got me to translate *Che farò* to him, and then inquired: "What *did* Orpheus

[1] Æt. 5.

do without Eurydice? Hadn't he any servant? Hadn't he anyone to cook his meals for him?" . . .

To CHARLES ARCHER

7 September, 1891

. . . Before I forget it, let me put on record a conversation I had with Tom[1] the other day, in which he floored me more completely than he has ever done hitherto, which is saying a good deal. I came home one evening and found him just gone to bed. I inquired whether he had been a good boy, and learned that he had a confession to make. He put it in this form: "Beatrix (Walkley) stole one of my dollies, so I had to prick her in the knee." The "had to" rather upset my gravity . . . but nevertheless I tried to improve the occasion. Presently a sense of injury overcame him, and he burst into tears and said: "When people do anything to hurt me, I'm not allowed to do *anything* to hurt them back again—everything's either rude or naughty." I represented that supposing people did hurt him it didn't make the hurt any better to hurt them. By this time he had stopped crying, and he replied with the utmost promptitude and conviction: "No, but you *feel* better"—and the truth was so evident that I felt hypocrisy was useless, and there was nothing for it but to change the subject. However, he himself went on: "Now Rose (the servant) doesn't exactly *hurt* me, but she hurts my feelings." I pointed out to him that the best plan was not to have any feelings to

[1] Æt. 6. It must have been about this time, when Irving's Lear was being much discussed, that the following dialogue took place: *Tomarcher*: "What did King Lear die of, father?" *W. A.*: "Well you see, he was a very old man—and his daughters had been very cruel to him—and he had been out all night in a terrible storm——" *T.A.*: "That's the worst of old people—the least thing upsets them!"

be hurt; on which he replied: "But I'm made that way! I can't make a hole in myself and let my feelings run out, for then I should be dead!" Whereupon I told him to go to sleep, and retired routed. I daresay you have heard of his remark to F. when she had offended him in some way—"I wish I had as kind a mammy as Horace" (one of his friends); "I wish I had as kind a mammy as *any* little boy—but you're not even an *average* mother!" The other evening I came home and heard pitiful wails going on upstairs; it appeared that one of his front teeth had come out, and he was inconsolable because he could not comfortably suck his thumb. In the course of a long argument, F. suggested to him that she was sure Achilles did not cry when he lost his first teeth; upon which Tom replied, still weeping bitterly: "They didn't suck their thumbs in those days—that *proves* it."

[Mr. Clement Scott, one of the leading champions of the old order of things, and vituperators of Ibsen, the "Ibsenites", and the Independent Theatre, had written complaining of the substance and the tone of a controversial article by Mr. Y., a prominent supporter of the Independent Theatre movement. Archer replies:]

15 *Oct.*, '91

MY DEAR SCOTT,

I am glad that your letter affords me an opportunity of assuring you that I had nothing to do with Y.'s needlessly offensive article. He told me that he was writing it, and gave me an outline of what he proposed to say. I spent some hours in trying to persuade him that his accusations of corruption were all nonsense, and that he was to all intents and purposes ignorant of the subject he was dealing with. As you see, I failed to convince him, but I did my best. I was sincerely sorry that he should spoil his excellent case by gross exaggerations and misrepresentations.

On the general question of courtesy and discourtesy, controversial fairness and unfairness, I fear you and I differ too fundamentally to arrive at anything like an understanding. No doubt we are both working out our destiny, and both subject to illusions. You have called me and those who share my literary tastes a number of more or less unsavoury names, and have accused me, personally, of feigning enthusiasm for Ibsen in order to "boom" my own translations.[1] Of course you know me well enough to know that that is all nonsense—that I am neither a "muck-ferreting dog" nor a mercenary charlatan. You say these things in the ardour of controversy, in the rapture of rhetoric, sincerely believing, I don't doubt, that you are thereby promoting the cause of good art and good morals. I naturally differ from you. I don't think you will help the Old Drama, any more than Y. will help the New, by such methods. On my side, I don't think I have called you any names, or assigned you any base motives; but perhaps I have taken too little trouble to find the least offensive method of expressing my too frequent dissent from you on questions of literature, of morals, and of taste.

Yours truly,
W. ARCHER

[1] In the stage-productions of Ibsen's plays (after the single performance of *The Pillars of Society* in 1880) Archer had, so long as he remained a theatrical critic, no pecuniary interest whatever, except in so far as the productions might stimulate the sale of his translations, from which he derived a modest royalty.

[Archer had evidently written privately to G. R. Sims, taking somewhat strong exception to a newspaper article by the dramatist. In answer to a short but courteous reply from Mr. Sims, dated October 19, 1891, he writes:]

DEAR MR. SIMS,

I regret and apologize for the last sentence of my letter, which must have seemed ill-tempered, and discourteous to other dramatists as well as to you. I don't quite know why I wrote it. There are playwrights, I fear, who do bear resentment for criticism, but I have never had any reason to class you among them. Perhaps I was a little annoyed by the reappearance of an old innuendo which I had contradicted years ago, to the effect that I had hawked plays about from theatre to theatre. Not that I should be particularly ashamed of having done so had it been the case; but as a matter of fact I never had energy enough, or belief enough in my own plays, to make any serious effort to get them produced. Perhaps, too, the old cry of "Physician, heal thyself" irritated me a little—the very natural, but not very just, notion that a critic should himself excel in the art he criticizes. Clearly, if he had it in his power to be an artist, he wouldn't be a critic; but it is not very generous of you artists to twit us critics with the fact, especially as it has no real bearing on the merits or demerits of our criticism. But all this does not excuse the snappish tone of my letter, which I sincerely regret.

Yours truly,
WILLIAM ARCHER

From GEORGE BERNARD SHAW
[Postcard]

14th December, 1892

I have come to the conclusion that Moy Thomas (who sat it[1] out again yesterday, every line) is the greatest critic of the age, and that Massingham is entirely right in his estimate of you and Walkley. A more amazing exposition of your Shaw theory even I have never encountered than that World article. Here am I, who have collected slum rents weekly with these hands, and for 4½ years been behind the scenes of the middle-class landowner—who have philandered with women of all sorts and sizes—and I am told gravely to go to nature and give up apriorizing about such matters, by you, you sentimental Sweet Lavendery recluse.

G. B. S.

[1] *Widowers' Houses.*

X

1893–1899

THE THEATRICAL "WORLD"—STUDY AND STAGE

THE five years 1893–97, the mid-'nineties, form in a sense a culminating period in Archer's life-work as a theatrical critic. He had attained to maturity and authority of style,[1] and was reaching the height of his influence, while his zest for the theatre was unblunted, and he had not yet begun to feel the world of criticism too narrow for him, and to look round for fresh worlds to explore. Appropriately, he has left a full and easily accessible record of his dealings with the drama and of the annals of the London stage in those years, in the five volumes[2] of his collected *World* criticisms, published annually from 1894 to 1898.

It was the exceptional quality of the theatrical harvest of 1893 that gave the impulse for the series, making it seem to Archer worth while to collect and republish his criticisms. It appeared as though the long labour of hoeing and trenching and weeding was at last beginning to justify itself by its fruits. "Never within my memory", he wrote, "—not often, surely, in the annals of the English theatre—has the student of the stage had so much to 'break his mind upon' in a single season." Tennyson's *Becket* was produced in February, with great success; and in the same month the enthusiasm of Miss Elizabeth Robins carried *The Master Builder*[3] on to the stage—

[1] "You have acquired", wrote Stevenson of *The Theatrical "World"* for 1893, "a manner that I can only call august; otherwise I should have to call it such amazing impudence."

[2] *The Theatrical "World"* of 1893, 1894, 1895, 1896, 1897.

[3] Translated by Archer and E. W. Gosse in collaboration.

against Archer's advice (for he feared that the play, though a masterpiece, was so strange and unusual a masterpiece that it would be caviare to the British public), but with his whole-hearted and effective co-operation. The piece had indeed a somewhat mixed reception. It cut across the Ibsenite and anti-Ibsenite ranks, disconcerting some adherents (Walkley among others[1]), while it made a number of influential converts. But, being admirably acted by Miss Robins as Hilda and Mr. Waring as Solness, it had a real success, as success went in such special productions, and the interest aroused by it led to a series of subscription performances in June—the plays given being *Hedda Gabler*, *Rosmersholm*, *The Master Builder*, and the 4th Act of *Brand*. *Rosmersholm* for the first time produced its due effect, Miss Robins's Rebecca West being finely tragic, and Lewis Waller's Rosmer having the one indispensable quality of distinction. Archer was, of course, in the thick of the work of staging and rehearsing the series. Less adequate and successful, though important as a sign of the times, was Tree's production at the Haymarket of *An Enemy of the People*.

In May came Pinero's *The Second Mrs. Tanqueray*, to show that the native English drama could now measure itself with all but the very greatest achievements of contemporary dramatic literature; while the year was rich in important work by other established British dramatists—Jones, Oscar Wilde, Grundy, and Parker—and the Independent Theatre produced interesting prentice works by George Moore and Dr. Todhunter, and a little tragedy of common life,

[1] Archer made Walkley's defection the occasion for one of his best pieces of expository criticism: "The Melody of *The Master Builder*; an Open Letter to Mr. A. B. Walkley", attached to the single-volume edition of the play.

Alan's Wife, which aroused much controversy, and at least did something to vindicate the right of the dramatist to take all life to be his province.

Productions from beyond the seas, too, were of rare interest. The whole company, and practically the whole repertory, of the Théâtre Français were passed in review—the performance of *Œdipe Roi* being specially memorable, and calling forth a memorable *World* notice. And the English critics and public had their first taste of the consummate art of Eleanora Duse.

The years that followed were less heartening in respect of home-grown drama. Though Pinero continued to advance in his art, and Jones to produce ambitious and often successful work, and though promising first attempts were made by new-comers, such as Esmond, no play of the calibre of *Mrs. Tanqueray* attained striking success with the public. In 1895, shortly after the production of *The Importance of Being Ernest*, the most artistically satisfying, though the slightest, of Oscar Wilde's pieces, the meteoric course of that ill-fated genius ended in darkness. The two most cheering events of the period, as we can now discern, were Shaw's only moderately successful début on the regular stage with *Arms and the Man* (1894), and the great success of *The Little Minister* in 1897, which established Barrie as a dramatist. But the full significance of these events was not yet apparent; and meantime the great and almost exclusive vogue of harmless but empty cape-and-sword drama (such as *The Prisoner of Zenda* and *The Red Robe*), and of musical comedy sometimes worse than empty, tended to block the way against more ambitious and less immediately profitable work. It was borne in upon Archer that, if progress was to continue, some special agency must be devised for bringing serious and artistic work before the public capable of appreciating it, a public small in comparison with the mass of theatre-goers, but no longer inconsiderable, even in numbers. In the Epilogue to the volume for 1896 he urges the remedy which he had had at heart from boyhood—the establishment of one or more Repertory Theatres, made independent by endowment of the necessity for making immediate appeal in every production to the sheeplike multitude. A tentative attempt towards such an organization, in which Archer took an active part, was started in 1896 under the name of the New Century Theatre; yet even this, as will be seen, had to import most of its wares.

Thus, in the later volumes of *The Theatrical "World"* series, most of the criticism of plays which has retained its interest deals with the classic or with the imported drama. For, while the native drama seemed to be marking time, the progressive leavening of the public taste by wider acquaintance with the English drama of the past and with foreign masterpieces of the present did not cease. In 1894 the Independent Theatre production of *The Wild Duck* threw light on a new facet of Ibsen's genius for all who had eyes to see—including Archer himself. Seeing the play on the stage for the first time, he recognized for the first time its extraordinary scenic qualities. The performance, except in the case of Miss Winifred Fraser's Hedvig, did little justice to the play. "It was certainly", he wrote, "not the brilliancy of the interpretation that dazzled me. Yet, as the tragedy of the House of Ekdal unfolded itself, with that smooth, unhasting, unresting movement which is Ibsen's greatest invention in the technical sphere—every word at once displaying a soul-facet and developing the dramatic situation—despite my long familarity with the play, I felt almost as if a new planet had swum into my ken."

In 1896 the First Part of *King Henry the IV* was restored to the London stage by Beerbohm Tree's courage and enterprise; and later in the same year there was another welcome extension of the field of acted Shakespearean drama in Irving's production of *Cymbeline*. Ibsen's *Little Eyolf*, which had appeared at the end of 1894, was produced in November of 1896, with remarkable success—due in part to the attraction of "three of the ablest actresses in London" (Miss Robins, Miss Achurch, and Mrs. Patrick Campbell) "playing their best", but partly also to the grim power of the drama. This, the début of the New Century Theatre, was also its most successful production; but Echegaray's *Mariana,* Ibsen's *John Gabriel Borkman,* and Henley and Stevenson's *Admiral Guinea,* produced in 1897, were at least successes of esteem, and the interest of helping to stage and rehearse them and the pleasure of seeing them on the stage were some compensation to Archer for his otherwise unremunerated labours in the enterprise.

Both Archer himself and others have spoken of the comparative uncertainty of his judgment in questions of acting. Yet in these volumes, as throughout his work, the pages dealing with acting are among the most interesting. It was, indeed, only as to performances in modern prose drama that he confessed to feeling some infirmity of judgment. As regards Shakespearean acting, and "poetic" acting in general, no critic ever held stronger views or could give clearer reasons for them. "This is the branch of histrionics", he wrote, "that I love most, have studied most, and in my own esteem know most about." The differentia of his criticism, that which tinged it throughout, and distinguished him, as a critic of acting, from most of his contemporaries, was its tendency to lay greater stress on sound impressions than on those of sight. This was an inborn, inherited disposition. It was through sound, through the rhythms of music, of verse or of exquisite prose, that his emotions were most directly and unfailingly reached. His ear for such rhythms and cadences was abnormally keen. Life had few greater pleasures for him than listening to beautiful speech beautifully spoken on the stage, and few greater torments than to hear such speech mangled and distorted. Thus, whatever its other merits, a performance, and above all a Shakespearean performance, that had not correctness, fluency, and beauty of diction, could never really satisfy him, far less arouse his enthusiasm. In rehearsing Ibsen's plays, and any others with which he was concerned, it was his practice, as each scene went on, to make a note, in the little note-book that was his constant companion, of all deviations, even the smallest, from correctness of emphasis and cadence, and to make suggestions for their amendment at the first pause.[1] Instances innumerable might be quoted of his insistence on accuracy, impetus, and beauty of diction as the one thing needful above all others. Thus, of Irving's Becket: "There is much more than his mere personality in Mr. Irving's Becket; there is imagination, there is composition, there is—pray, Mr. Printer, indulge me with characters adequate to so startling an averment—there is DICTION! . . . Oh, the

[1] "Nothing escaped him", writes Miss Elizabeth Robins, "from the slightest inflection of voice, the significance of the smallest gesture or most fleeting expression, up to the crescendo of a climax, or the capital crime of the smallest alteration of the text—nothing escaped that note-book." (*Ibsen and the Actress.*)

difference between his diction in *Becket* and in *Lear!* . . . Many of his lines and sequences were a joy to the ear—one regretted the evanescence of their charm. . . . If Mr. Irving had *spoken* Lear, especially in the later scenes, as beautifully as he speaks Becket, we—well, we might have had longer to wait for this production." Again, of Tree's Falstaff: "Falstaff is a part in which the actor must be not only letter-perfect but comma-perfect, if he is to play it with full effect. . . . It suffers cruelly from paraphrases and approximations. Falstaff always puts the right word in the right place; you can no more improve the rhythm of his speeches than you can their meaning. . . ." Even slight false emphases, which scarcely one hearer in a thousand would notice, or, noticing, would deem of any importance, were not trifles to him. Thus, of Ada Rehan's Maid Marian in *The Foresters*: "Unfortunately she is not so careful either of metre or emphasis as she ought to be. In more than one place she murdered the verse by inserting small words not in the poet's text; and she made several slips of accent, such as this: 'We leave but happy *memories* to the forest', whereas the emphasis should clearly be on the 'happy'."

Of his nice appreciation and intense enjoyment of great acting there is a good example in the series of criticisms of Bernhardt and Duse, when, in 1894 and again in 1895, "The Rival Queens" gave London such an opportunity as it had not enjoyed for half a century and more of comparing two great artists in similar, sometimes in the same, parts, and forming itself into two camps to debate their merits. In this inevitable controversy, Archer, while admitting Bernhardt's advantages in range of talent, in physical endowment, and in her "incomparable art of poetic diction", was, on the whole, in the camp of

Italy,[1] holding that Sarah's world-wide exploitation of her powers in showy, violent, and sanguinary parts, such as those written to her measure by Sardou, had gone far to ruin her art, and convert it into "a marvellous, monotonous, and often vulgar virtuosity".

Duse, on the other hand, unlike Sarah in such characters, "does not act merely with a set of surface nerves which long habit has dissociated, or, so to speak, insulated, from the real centres of sensation. She throws her very being into her task. . . . She is more completely *alive* on the stage than anyone else I remember to have seen. Even to the very finger-tips, she lives the life of the character. Compare her Santuzza in *Cavalleria Rusticana* with her Mirandolina, and you will find that she has not only changed her costume, her voice and her accent, but her very temperament. This is acting, this is great art; and what a delight it is to see and recognize it! . . ."

Yet his admiration for the great French actress in parts worthy of her, particularly those of the classical repertory, was undiminished. "In the languishing passages so frequent in Phèdre", he says, "she was nothing less than divine. You do not realize the possibilities of beauty in human speech if you have not heard her exhale these four lines:

> Noble et brillant auteur d'une triste famille,
> Toi, dont ma mère osait se vanter d'être fille,
> Qui peut-être rougis du trouble où tu me vois,
> Soleil, je te viens voir pour la dernière fois!

I am not ashamed to confess that the sheer exquisite-

[1] "The Rival Queens", *The Theatrical "World"* of 1895, pp. 202 seq. See also the admirable study of Duse's Santuzza, *The Theatrical "World"* of 1894, p. 163.

ness of her delivery of these lines brought the tears to my eyes, which had remained dry as the desert throughout her Marguerite Gautier." And when Bernhardt in 1895 tried London with *La Princesse Lointaine,* which had been coldly received by the Parisian critics, his love of lovely words and of high imaginings inspired him to a criticism which made some amends to the poet[1] for the lack of appreciation in his own country, and which Archer himself looked back upon with some complacency a few years later, when Paris and most of the world had recognized Rostand's powers and gone wild over *Cyrano de Bergerac.*

Much characteristic self-revelation is to be found in the series. The Epistle Dedicatory to the 1893 volume has already been quoted. Not less interesting is the Epilogue to the volume for 1894, which ends with a passage that might stand as a statement of the spirit informing, not these volumes alone, but the whole body of Archer's dramatic criticism. "The faculty for making the best of the actual without losing sight of the ideal", he says, "lies at the root of the policy enforced in the foregoing pages." Such a policy, he goes on, is with him, "not a matter of choice, but of irresistible tendency."

"I was born with an instinctive, unreasoning, unreasonable love for the theatre, simply *as* the theatre, the place of light and sound, of mystery and magic, where, at the stroke of the prompter's bell, a new world is revealed to the delighted sense. That unreasoning love is still strong within me. If all the germs of progress were stamped out, and the stage declined entirely upon spectacle and buffoonery, I should still, I believe, find a melancholy fascination in the glare of the footlights. But close upon the

[1] See Rostand's letter of thanks below.

heels of this mania for the theatre came another and still more absorbing passion—the passion for high thoughts and beautiful words, for things delicately seen, and subtly felt, and marvellously imagined—in short, for that divinest emanation of the human spirit which we call literature. These two things have I loved, sometimes blindly and foolishly, sometimes, I hope, with understanding; and it has been the instinctive, inevitable effort of my life to make these two one flesh. Literature in the theatre—great inventions greatly realized, beautiful words beautifully spoken—such literature as can attain its highest potency only in this most fascinating, because most complex and human, of artistic mediums—that has been the whole yearning of my conscious life. Where I have found it, I have rejoiced with a great joy; wherever I have seen or imagined any movement, any endeavour, towards it, I have proclaimed the fact with an eagerness (I doubt not) often fanatical and disproportionate. That the drama should once more take rank among the highest expressions of English creative genius, and that the theatre, not as a place of mere pastime, should once more become a preponderant interest and influence in the lives of thinking men and women—that is the end to which, like all the rest, this year of my life-work is dedicated."

To the mass of miscellaneous work detailed in the Bibliographic Appendix—magazine articles, editorial work,[1] translations, etc.—which in these years helped to fill up any vacuum in Archer's time left by theatrical criticism, only the merest reference can here be made. But to it must be added a large amount of

[1] Including the selection and editing, in collaboration with R. W. Lowe, of three volumes of *Dramatic Essays*, by the foremost critics of the early nineteenth century.

reviewing. In particular, at this time and for years to come, his book reviews were a feature of the literary page of the *Daily Chronicle*. Being anonymous, they were of more service to the paper than to the critic's reputation with the general public; he remarks in a letter that he is getting tired of hearing his reviews attributed to nearly everybody else in London. But they brought him not seldom into pleasant and sometimes fruitful relations with authors of distinction—such men as Thomas Hardy, Francis Thompson, William Watson—who before long came to recognize his hand, and were grateful for criticism at once careful, penetrating, and kind. Many of them, too, furnished matter for major works soon to come.

The first of these, *Study and Stage*, was a "Yearbook of Criticism" on a new plan. The completeness of record aimed at in *The Theatrical "World"* had rather hindered than helped its success in the book-market. The general reader, wrote Archer himself, "didn't care two raps for theatrical history", and, seeing that at least half the book was given up to matter that was of value only from the antiquarian point of view, did not buy or read it. "I regret to announce", he writes to a friend in January 1899, "the decease, at the early age of five, of *The Theatrical "World"*—totally unlamented." In *Study and Stage* ephemeral matter was discarded, and only the most important *World* criticisms of 1898, along with the cream of his *Daily Chronicle* reviews, were included. The book was much praised; and it contains, indeed—in such papers as the notices of Tree's *Julius Cæsar* production and of Mrs. Craigie's *The Ambassador*, the reviews of Henley's and of Hardy's poems, and the paper on "Carlyle and Burns"—some memorable criticism. But, since the experiment was not repeated, we may assume that the success of the volume was one of esteem only. The attempt to influence directly a wider public than that reached, week by week, by his *World* articles had to be given up as commercially unprofitable. But the steady pressure exerted by those articles towards the reunion of literature and the theatre still went on.

Friends had departed and new friendships taken root and grown during these years. In 1894 Edmund Yates's death made the "expectation of life" of the *World* and consequently of its dramatic critic's post seem for a time uncertain; and Archer received tempting offers to induce him to join, as dramatic critic, the *Saturday Review* (which had just come under Mr. Frank Harris's editorship). But the end of the *World* was not yet come, and the new proprietors willingly agreed to such an increase of salary as justified Archer in resisting the temptation to change. None the less did a second heavy loss befall Edmund Yates's paper; for its musical critic, feeling within him an increasing purpose towards drama, accepted the vacant post on the *Saturday Review*, and the columns of the *World* knew the initials G. B. S. no more.

In December of the same year came the news of Stevenson's death—the blow that had so often appeared imminent fell at last, just when there seemed reason to hope that it might yet be long deferred. "It would be presumption in me", wrote Archer, "to rank myself among his friends; for I held a very small space in his life." But in his own life his affection for Stevenson held to the end a very special place—since he had never been disposed to canonize R. L. S., but had merely loved him, the later efforts of the Devil's Advocates left his feeling untouched. It is probably no accident that, among the great masses of literary papers, printed and manuscript, left behind by Archer, there is only one packet for the safe custody of which he seems to have taken special thought—the large envelope marked: "Stevenson papers—Preserve these carefully."

The next year saw the beginning of a longer and closer friendship—a benefaction sent by fortune, it might seem, as an indirect reward for Archer's eagerness to foster all new stirrings of life in drama. In March 1895 he receives from Charles Charrington the manuscript of a remarkable play by an author unknown to the stage, and at once writes, in considerable excitement: "I have read *Carlyon Sahib*, and am exceedingly interested in it—so much so that if you can possibly put me in communication with the author I should like to write him in detail about it, or still better to see him. . . . It is the most original and powerful play I have ever come across in manuscript, to my recollection; and I should very much like to see it brought to perfection. I almost despair, however, of conveying my meaning, except in conversation, and a long conversation, with the author. Do you think that would be possible? I think you said he was a Professor in Glasgow." The author chose the better part, and a meeting soon took place. It was written that the chief fame of Gilbert Murray was to be won in other fields than that of the native English drama. But the long conversations and the correspondence that ensued, if they did not bring the play to perfection, had a yet happier result, in laying the foundation of an almost brotherly friendship of thirty years.

A notice[1] of *Power Through Repose*, the treatise in which an American lady, Miss Annie Payson Call, set forth her system of nerve training, marks the begin-

1 "The Gospel of Repose", *Illustrated London News*, April 11, 1891.

ning of a friendship which, growing and strengthening with the years, was to be a momentous one for Archer and his family. His lack of aptitude for and interest in bodily exercises made him an unsatisfactory pupil. But his wife, among others, benefited much by the "nerve training", and, deeply interested in its possibilities as a preventive and curative method, she set herself to master it, and in course of time became qualified to instruct others, and to apply the treatment in cases within her own circle in which it was indicated. The field of these activities gradually widened as the years went on and the beneficial effects of the treatment became known, and accommodation was soon required for patients.

Thus, by 1895, the smallness of the Walden cottage and its distance from London had begun to be felt as inconveniences. Tom Archer, too, had exhausted the educational resources of the neighbourhood, and it became clear that a move must be made. The boy was slight and delicate, and his parents might well have hesitated to expose him to the rough and tumble of a public boarding-school, even had they had a higher opinion, on general grounds, of that system of education. The family accordingly flitted to Dulwich, and Tom was entered as a day-boy at Alleyn's College of God's Gift, where several of his connections had preceded him. At Dulwich the family were in the midst of relations and friends—and this remained their headquarters for ten years, though rooms had, of course, to be kept up in London. From 1896 for some years the rooms were in Great Ormond Street, where Graham Wallas, another much-valued friend acquired about this time, was Archer's next-door neighbour.

Xa

LETTERS OF 1892–1897

From Thomas Hardy

16th October, 1892

Dear Mr. Archer,

I am glad the *Tess* reached you. I have been so drawn to your writings by their accord with my views that I have often thought of testifying to that agreement by sending a book: but I have hitherto been deterred by a fear lest you might have the same volume to review. I am relieved to know that you had written your remarks first: though I do not think I should have ventured to send it yet if I had suspected that the reviewing had not yet finished.

Yours sincerely,

Thomas Hardy

Max Gate, Dorchester

To Charles Archer

Xmas Day [1894]

. . . . .

Of course you've heard by this time that Stevenson is dead. I didn't write you last week, for just at mail-time we were beginning to think it doubtful after all. But there's no doubt about it now, though it's still hard to believe it. He was the most beautifully *live* creature in the world. I went into town rather late on Monday of last week, got to Holborn at 11.30, and there saw on the evening-paper bills "Death of R. L. Stevenson". I bought the *Star*, and thought the telegram looked fatally genuine. On my way to Queen Square I made up my mind that I wouldn't write about him—it was all very well for people who hadn't known him to do the ordinary critical estimates, or for people who had known him well, his acknowledged friends as it were, to write their tributes to him; but I fell between the two classes—I couldn't write as if I hadn't known him, and to write my "reminiscences" would seem like bragging of his friendship and making copy of it. But when I got to Queen Square, instead of the telegram I expected from the *Chronicle,* there was a telegram from Henley, who has just become editor of the *New Review,* asking me to do a memorial article for his first number. It touched me very much that R. L. S.'s oldest and most intimate friend should apply to me; but still I felt as if I couldn't say anything to the purpose but "Ave atque vale!", and actually wrote a telegram to that effect. However, on thinking it over, I saw that this was precisely the one opportunity, as it were—that Henley was the one man for whom I could write—so, on condition that he would tell me frankly if he didn't like what I wrote, I promised to try. Then the other applications came pouring in—four of them, *Chronicle, Saturday Review, Illustrated News, Manchester Guardian,* all of which I refused. It took me two whole days and a half to screw out an In Memoriam (in prose, of course)—commonplace and laboured, I'm afraid, but still I'm glad I did it. You will receive it probably by next mail. Henley added the very appropriate motto from *Aes Triplex.*[1] Then came doubts as to the genuineness of the news. . . .[2] So my article was to be held over, in the hope that it would never appear. But on Sunday morning came the confirmation from San Francisco, and on Sunday evening I went over to Henley's at Barnes, to see if

[1] "In the hot fit of life, etc."
[2] See letters from W. E. H. below.

the article couldn't be got into the January number after all, feeling that it was so high-pitched it would be almost indecent in February. It was a strange scene, in Henley's gloomy house by the river. You know his only child, an exceedingly clever and beautiful little girl of 8 or so, died last spring; so he and his wife are not too cheerful at the best of times. . . . Francis Watt and Henley's brother Anthony were there at supper—also a pair of saturnine beings. However Henley was very nice, and talked very freely about Louis—reminiscences of their very rackety times in Edinr. before Stevenson had done anything except a few Cornhill articles—before the Inland Voy age orthe Donkey. You know there has been a coolness between them of late, which was just, I fancy, passing over. Henley admitted that those verses: "Oh Time and Change, they range and range" were written about Louis. . . . He said Louis had never taken any notice of them, which confirmed my idea that the offence was on Henley's side, and that Stevenson simply lay low and let Henley's wrath burn itself out. I don't think R. L. S. had it in him to sulk or cherish a grudge.

It's a terrible loss; but after all that people had published about him—about his fear of failing powers and of brain trouble—it was almost a relief to find it true that he had died "i skönhed" . . . .

I was looking over some of his letters the other day, and found a very characteristic phrase. He had had a threatening of rheumatic fever, and was pretty low—"but", he ends up, "I still keep her nose to the wind". He was a rare and radiant creature. . . .

Din,

W. A.

From W. E. HENLEY

21/12/94

DEAR ARCHER,

My mind misgave me so last night and to-day that I went to town expressly to withdraw the obituary. When I got there, I found that Heinemann had anticipated me; so there you are.

I believe—now—that *nobody's* dead; but that the thing is a daring and devilish plant: the same in kind, but far worse in degree, than those reports of serious illness which used to come suddenly, every now and again, from overseas. If I had kept my head, I should have saved you a bucketing, at least. But a general delusion is hard to withstand; and so you had your pains, as I hope and believe, in vain.

If the thing's true, your work will not, of course, be lost. And if it's not, then none, I believe, will so rejoice and be so exceeding glad as yourself.

In either case you have made me your debtor by yet another good stroke at a pinch; I thank you with all my heart. . . .

And now, dear Archer, hope and believe with me; and you shall see that you have done neither in vain.

Yours always,

W. E. H.

[NO DATE]

MY DEAR ARCHER,

I was wrong; and I ask your pardon. After these Frisco telegrams I abandon hope.

I have written to Heinemann to say that, if it's practicable, I think you should appear in January: . . . we shall see what we shall see—that is, what the Practical Man thinks possible. It is steep on you,—

this chopping and changing; but it is also steep on *me*. So you must do your best to forgive me the pass to which I've brought you.

Today I have felt it more than ever before. I have hitherto hoped and believed that we had but to meet for the wrong to be made right. And now that's impossible; and there is nothing for us but, as I wrote of and to him langsyne, for us to

"Lie in the Peace of the Great Release
As once in the grass together".

Well, well——

W. E. H.

To CHARLES ARCHER

1 *May*, '95

. . . . . .

Things are jogging on much as usual here, except for this infernal Oscar Wilde business, which by the way will be over today. I'm afraid Oscar hasn't the ghost of a chance, and of course even if the jury acquitted him he's practically a dead man on his own admissions in the previous trial. It's a loathsome and unthinkable business, but certainly Oscar's madness is not inconsistent with an extraordinary courage and nerve. It appears that yesterday in the witness-box he made a sort of speech of such beauty and power that the people in court applauded him loudly, though of course the feeling is intense against him. Really the luck is against the poor British drama—the man who has more brains in his little finger than all the rest of them in their whole body goes and commits worse than suicide in this way. However, it shows that what I hoped for in Oscar could never have come about—I thought he might get rid of his tomfoolery and affectation and do something really fine—but . . . I intended to add substantially to this, but haven't a moment, and it must go as it is. . . .

From Edmond Rostand

[1895]

Monsieur et cher confrère,

Je viens de recevoir le journal dans lequel vous avez si longuement et si sympathiquement parlé de la *Princesse Lointaine.* Ai-je besoin de vous dire que votre article m'a ravi?

Eh, quoi! cet article, qu'on dirait écrit par l'ami le plus intime, par le plus cher confident de ma pensée, je le dois à un inconnu de moi? Cette défense si fine et si spirituelle de ma pièce, ce commentaire délicat de mes plus secrètes intentions, cette analyse qui est assurément la plus complète qui ait été faite de mon œuvre, je la dois à un étranger? Comment avez vous fait, Anglais, pour comprendre des choses que tant de Français n'ont pas comprises? Et pouvais-je m'attendre de trouver à Londres le plus ingénieux réfutateur de M. Francisque Sarcey? Rien qu'au début de votre article, qui est délicieux, j'ai vu que j'avais affaire à un admirable lettré, à un poète. Et la suite m'a prouvé que ce lettré devait être initié a la langue française mieux que beaucoup des nôtres! Car rien ne vous a échappé. Et vous êtes le seul ayant compris ce que j'ai voulu faire, ce *déguisement d'une action morale, psychologique, sous les formes d'un conte de fées.* Je trouve, dites-vous, cette combinaison singulièrement piquante. C'est l'éloge qui m'est le plus sensible. Car cela, en effet, était nouveau, et il n'y a guère que des poètes qui l'aient senti. Les autres m'ont reproché de donner des sentiments humains à des personnages de tapisserie! sans comprendre que c'était de cela qu'il fallait justement me louer! Vous avez admirablement analysé Mélisinde, et son caractère, et personne que vous n'a remarqué l'ironie secrète que l'on aurait dû sentir en plus d'un endroit.

Je vous suis très reconnaissant de vôtre article, et vous prie de croire à ma désormais vive amitié. J'ai bien ri de vos pointes à cet autre critique, dont j'oublie le nom,[1] et dont l'article, d'après ce que vous dites, devait être considérable de sottise, délicieux à lire à force d'incompréhension. Merci au nom de tous les poètes de défendre la cause de la fantaisie et du rêve contre la pesante, ignorante et hippopotamesque critique.

Très cordialement vôtre,

EDMOND ROSTAND

From HENRIK IBSEN

[Translation]

CHRISTIANIA, *the 27th June*, 1895

DEAR MR. WILLIAM ARCHER,

[The beginning of the letter deals with business matters and with W. A.'s correction of a mistake of Jules Lemaître's regarding the relationship of Asta and Alfred Allmers in *Little Eyolf*. The letter goes on:]

More and more do I feel it as a painful deficiency that I did not learn to speak English while there was yet time. Now, of course, it is too late. Had I mastered the language I should now pay a visit to London straightway. Or, rather, I should doubtless have done so long ago. I have been thinking over many things in these latter days, and have come to feel a strong conviction that my Scottish

[1] The initials were G. B. S.

ancestry has left very deep traces in me. But these, of course, are only feelings—perhaps only wishes that such should be the case. I lack the experience and the knowledge which would enable me to judge.

With respectful greetings to Mrs. Archer, I subscribe myself,

Most sincerely yours,

HENRIK IBSEN

From J. M. BARRIE

[1896]

AN OPEN LETTER TO MR. WILLIAM ARCHER

My dear Archer (or perhaps better, Dear Sir, or simply Sir), I have read with attention your letters in the *Daily Chronicle* (or shall we say in a contemporary?) to Mr. Herbert Beerbohm Tree (but suppose we cut the Herbert as not really essential) on his forthcoming production of *Henry IV*, and as a dramatist who has already bored you considerably I should like (pending the production of my new play) to bore you a little further with my reflections thereon. Not that they will be about Mr. Herbert Beerbohm Tree's coming production (I hope you will agree with me that as he is now going off we should restore the full name on this occasion—it makes such an admirable mouthful to exit on). No, I would draw your attention to advisable cuts in front. In your own part, dear W. A. I mean on the first night of my pieces. I watch you, Sir, through the hole in the author's box.

Your first entrance. It is too conventional—always the same. Why look so apologetic—why so fearful of being seen by anyone who respects you? You drop into your seat and stare at your boots. The boots business might be cut altogether. It would probably be more effective to look up at the author's box and smile pleasantly.

Your first exit. I think you might put more life into this. I am far from asking you to rush out, but what happens is this (I was sitting behind you the other night and watched—but I also notice it from my box). Your mouth opens wide and you quickly put your hand over it. Then you think you may as well sit down again. Then you think you will go out, then you think what's the good? Then you go. You don't really exit. You put your back against the first wall and stand up stage, as it were, talking to two bearded ruffians disguised in initials.[1] You have not the appearance of one talking about the good things that have been said during the act.

The second act. Much of your business seems unnecessary. Such expectation as was in your face in Act I has now passed away. In its place are several lines that might be omitted. You have the appearance of a man who, for some reason of his own, is counting a hundred many times.

Want of facial expression. This indeed is your greatest want. You must guard against it. You get worse and worse. I am thinking particularly of your laugh, which you seem to have cut out in the long ago. Restore it. My characters have said and done the wittiest things, but you don't rise to them. The other night at the Garrick, when someone said he was to make a common or garden speech, a ripple of laughter ran along the stalls till it reached you. It cd. not even jump you and proceed. You are like the ground that is cleared in a forest when a fire is ap-

[1] Archer, Walkley, and Shaw, the Three Musketeers of dramatic criticism as someone called them, were at this period constantly to be seen together at all important theatrical functions.

proaching. When in my box I look at you only—fascinated. At first I had a consuming pity for you. You can't think how sorry I felt for you. My one excitement was not the play, but curiosity as to whether you would last to the end. But that feeling has passed. My grand ambition now is to make you laugh—just once. Then I shall write plays no more. You think I have never succeeded. *I am not so sure.* Do you remember cherchez la femme?[1] You do. (You will never forget it.) You upbraided me, you said it was a popular appeal. My dear W. A., it was put in absolutely for you. When the time drew nigh I sat glaring at you. I leant forward in the box. You did not know what was coming. Suddenly you got it in the face. The house roared, and I glanced away—only a second, but it had done for me. When I looked again you were no longer there. You had got beneath the seat—ostensibly to tie a bootlace (confound your boots), but I think—I sometimes think—to laugh. I believe—I sometimes believe—you were holding your sides and guffawing. When you reappeared you were counting hundreds again. But I shall have you yet. *You shave.* I like this. I can see what you are up to so much better. As for the beards of your initialled pair of friends, they don't give me a fair chance. I beg you to cut them entirely. Let A. B. W. and G. B. S. shave their beards and come out into the open.

I am, Sir,

With hopes that I shall do you yet,

ANON

[1] "... For instance Mr. Barrie must needs drag in ... from some Christy Minstrel patter (I should imagine) the lugubrious *cherchez la femme* wheeze." W. A.'s notice of *The Professor's Love Story*.

From FRANCIS THOMPSON

May 31, 1897

MY DEAR ARCHER,

I surmised from the beginning, from internal evidence, that it was to you I owed the kind article on my new book in the Chronicle. Now my belief is confirmed by my publisher, and I hasten to thank you, with an emotion which I have very little power to express. Four years ago your article would not have drawn from me this acknowledgment. I had then no enemies: I had a good "lead off", and to praise me was the fashion. Independence was shown by attack; and the common critic, who loves to be, like the god of battles, with the big battalions, followed in the wake of praise, according to his sheep-like nature; carefully saying over again what his brethren-sheep had said before him. To-day all is changed. My chief supporter (Coventry Patmore) is dead; the few who really admired me are no longer in a position to make their voices heard: while I have enemies on every hand, raised by the mere fact of my first success. . . . And this moment you have chosen to strike by my side with a whole-heartedness you have not before displayed. Nay, if I do not read ill between the lines, you have been gentler to my faults than you would otherwise have been, because you saw that they would find abundant censors; while my merits there would be "none to love, and very few to praise",—besides yourself.

In all this there is a courage, an independence, a chivalry, for which I thank you indeed much; but for which I admire you yet more. It is a brave act, when the cry is against me, and to support needs more independence than formerly to oppose. And I am the prouder of it, because I am so all but unknown to you that no one can say (as they are accustomed to say) that you have supported me out of private friendship. If I have not hitherto known you, I feel that now I *do* know you—at least I know "the better part of you", your spirit. I have no hope that my book and name, that sinking ship which the many are deserting, will survive the organized attack on me. But at least you have made a gallant last stand for me, and I shall not be smothered out of existence without a struggle. I never knew until late years how powerfully people's views (theological, philosophical or otherwise) influenced their attitude towards contemporary poetry. But I found that my friend, Patmore, depreciated writers solely or chiefly because he hated their philosophy. I have found that George Meredith's admiration for my work falls off as he recognizes the opposition between my philosophy and his. He may allege other reasons, but I am convinced that is the basic reason. Yet I myself can admire *his* poetry, though I am in fundamental antagonism to his philosophy. And so with others. Beauty is beauty, though it may be inspired in defence of what I hold to be more or less untrue.

As to the substance of your Article: I am very pleased to find you upholding the *Anthem of Earth*, which a former supporter has described as more like highly figurative prose than poetry. It is not surprising, since he holds my namesake Jimmy (of *The Seasons*) to be a master of blank verse. You are quite right as to the derivation of the form in many passages. It is from the later Shakespeare. Unlike most critics, I have always considered Shakespeare's late blank verse to be his greatest and most characteristic. But it needs an understanding, as well as an ear, to appreciate it; while the more smoothly *linear* versification of his earlier periods can be followed by the ear alone. I deliberately took it as a model; thinking that my lifelong study would enable me to do what critics have pronounced impossible, what even Coleridge confessed he had tried to do and failed—i.e. catch the rhythm of Shakespeare's verse. I have not merely read it constantly, but I have analysed its principles. When I was a child of seven, standing in my nightgown before the fire, and chattering to my mother, I remember her pulling me up for using a certain word. "That is not used nowadays", she said; "that is one of Shakespeare's words." "Is it, Mamma?" I said, staring at her doubtfully. "But I didn't know it was one of Shakespeare's words!" "That is just it", she answered. "You have read Shakespeare so much that you are beginning to talk Shakespeare without knowing it. You must take care, or people will think you odd." She was a prophetess. Now everybody is thinking me "odd", and that I do on purpose what is often as unconscious as that childish Elizabethanism uttered in my little nightgown before the fire.

Will you pardon me for so long and egotistic a letter? The main thing is, that I thank you most warmly for an article the insight of which is rendered the more remarkable by your lack of any personal sympathy with my views; and the courage of which, at this juncture, is beyond all praise. . . .

Thanking you again with all my heart,

I remain,

Yours very sincerely,

FRANCIS THOMPSON

To FRANCIS THOMPSON

June 7, 1897

. . . I simply expressed (very inadequately) the pleasure your work has given me, without the least thought as to what anyone else thought or might think. That, however, is not strictly true. Your letter reminds me that I read some extracts to a friend, and then said: "This is not work which can possibly be *popular* in the wide sense; but it is work that will be read and treasured centuries hence by those who really care for poetry." This comes back to me as you speak of the reaction. I assure you no conceivable reaction can wipe out or overlay such work as yours. It is firm based on the rock of absolute beauty; and this I say all the more confidently because it does not happen to appeal to my own speculative, or even my own literary, prejudices.

Yours very truly,

WILLIAM ARCHER

To G. G. A. MURRAY

24 *July*/97

MY DEAR MURRAY,

I send you today two copies of the *Speaker*, with a modest request that you will tear out the pages containing the article "Ibsen in Translation" and my reply, and return them (the pages) to me when next you write. Because a gentleman is ungrateful enough to go for me as a translator,[1] I don't see why I should impoverish myself, and create a fictitious sense of prosperity in Sir Wemyss Reid,[2] by squandering my hard-earned sixpences on the *Speaker*—yet the transaction is one of which I ought to keep a record. If you had been anywhere within call, I should have inflicted my letter on you before sending it, and taken your sense as to the advisa-

[1] The gist of the criticism—the *Speaker*, July 10, 1897—is contained in the sentence: "Ibsen's beautifully polished style is hastily thrown into the rough and ready 'dialogue' of the English stage."

[2] Proprietor of the *Speaker*.

bility of saying anything at all. I read it to Wallas, and he said "Send it"—but I'm not quite sure it was the wisest course.

Yours,

W. A.

From G. G. A. Murray

July 26, 1897

My dear Archer,

The two Speakers have just come. I think the man is probably unaccustomed to translation, and thus falls into two mistakes.

(1) He finds certain particular effects, word by word, in the original, and expects to find *the same* in a translation; whereas the utmost conceivably possible would be something equivalent. As to "nok", "jo" and "vel" he drivels. His principles would lead to something like the practice of a historical Cambridge scholar who always translated σοὶ "Sir, to you", and τρῶές ρα "The Trojans, God help them!"

(2) Not realizing this, he aims at a translation which shall, as exactly as possible, *recall to him* the original as he remembers or reconstructs it; whereas the real business of the translator is to produce on people who don't know the original an effect as nearly as possible equivalent. . . .

The only point in which I thought he was at all right was the charge of using Americanisms; I remember noticing "right upstairs", and I think there was some other trivial thing. . . . I wonder at his not feeling the beauty of language in your translation. Parts of the Master-Builder and, say, the last Act of Borkman—to take merely what comes first into my mind—seem to me extraordinarily beautiful as mere language. I believe that that sort of union of beauty with naturalness is the true ideal of Language, and much more imperatively so in an acting play than in other forms of high literature. To object to "don't" and "won't" in dialogue is the part of a loon, as the Latin grammar says.

However, I think your letter is entirely convincing to anyone who knows your work and has had experience of translation. *I* can't think of any modern translation into English which I have read with as much satisfaction—so much feeling of ease and fulness and freedom—as yours of Ibsen. . . .

Yours ever,

G. G. A. M.

To G. G. A. MURRAY

28 *July*/97

MY DEAR MURRAY,

. . . . .

I fancy "right upstairs" must be a Scotticism —I distinctly remember Miss Robins (an American) protesting against it. You don't take it as analogous to "Right here" and "Right there", do you? It is "right" in the Latin sense—"a right line". What would you say? "Go straight upstairs"? To me, that is not quite the same thing—it is what one would say to a naughty child, meaning "Do anything else at your peril!" Whereas "Go right upstairs" means (to my mind) "Don't trouble to pay your respects to Mrs. Borkman, or any thing of that sort—stand not upon the order of your going, but go at once." That seems to verge towards the American "right here" and "right now", I admit. Anyhow, there seems to be a cloud of witnesses against "right upstairs", so when the time comes it shall go. Let us hope something worse won't take its place. It's a point of patriotism—Pan-Anglican patriotism—with me to use *good* Americanisms, but I don't do so consciously and voluntarily in Ibsen. . . .

Off to Switzerland on Friday—wish I were back again. And yet I don't know—I mean to take my cycle with me and try to get over the St. Bernard to Aosta, and hear Italian again before I die. And if once I'm in Gallia Cisalpina, why shouldn't I cross the Rubicon? I once started for the Matterhorn and ended on the Pincian, which is a mountain I greatly prefer; but dio mio! I was young then, and comparatively wealthy. . . .

Yours ever,

W. A.

To G. G. A. MURRAY

DULWICH,
23 Nov. '97

MY DEAR MURRAY,

I have been using you abominably, and am at once contrite and impenitent—I really couldn't and can't help it until *Admiral Guinea* is fairly off the stocks. You can't conceive what a hole this makes in my time, and how I have to fit in other things with it like the pieces of a Chinese puzzle. Today, for instance, I have been permeating the East End—Ratcliff Highway, Limehouse, Stepney, the Ghetto—in search of a model brig to represent the *Arethusa*; and after walking seven miles or thereabouts came back brigless. It was fun, however, and took me into some queer quarters. I could have had a fleet of full-rigged ships (I came across fourteen in different pawnshops and other repositories) but nary brig was to be found. The wonder is that I got back with my watch—not that the population was predatory to any great extent, but simply that, after having made the plunge into a pawnshop, it seemed a pity not to go the whole hog and "pop my ticker" while I was about it. If ever you write a nautical drama, I adjure you to make your *Arethusa* a full-rigged ship, or a barque at the very least.

The upshot is, I haven't had a moment to give to *Andromache*[1]—and even if I have had (literally) a moment, I couldn't in that moment throw myself into an antikisirende frame of mind—I should have felt it unnatural that Alcimedon should not say to the priest: "Stash your patter", like Mr. David Pew. . . . But the Admiral will be launched on Monday—and then——!

I forget whether you and I have ever discussed *Admiral Guinea,* or whether you have read it. The play has always been a little mania of mine—Pew seems to me such a refreshing scoundrel, and the dialogue of the other characters exquisitely written. I declare it's a pleasure simply to hear the lines spoken at rehearsal. . . .

By the by, there is a fair probability of my getting Scott to bring out a revised edition of Ibsen's prose plays in single volumes. So any time you are looking into any of them you might mark the points that seem to you particularly intolerable and send me a note of them. Did you see a rabidly Jingo article of mine in to-day's *Chronicle* about Newbolt's naval songs? I can't help it—the fellow writes well. I hope Lady Mary doesn't know it was mine. If you have not already divined and betrayed me, I beg you will respect the sacred anonymity of journalism.

Yours,

W. A.

[1] Professor Murray's play, on which W. A. was advising him.

From HENRY JAMES

[Henry James, with whom Archer had for some time been on cordial terms, seemed marked out by his literary eminence and his theatrical leanings as a potential supporter of the New Century Theatre. To a letter inviting him to join the Committee, he replies:]

29th March, 1897

MY DEAR ARCHER,

I feel that I ought to have written to you before; but I delayed first—for a number of days—in order to have seen Miss Robins; then because I had the sense, in a deterrent degree, of what I had *not* to say; and first and last because I am crippled, and obliged, each day, to squeeze all dictating into a narrow compass of time. Besides, I have been taking for granted you would have seen Miss Robins and gathered from her that I have succumbed to two or three simplifying reflections. I won't trouble you with them here, for it is their upshot that essentially matters; and some day I shall have a chance, face to face, to express them better. Their upshot is, at any rate, that I haven't seen my way to embark. Perhaps a comprehensive mention, in three words, of my grounds of backwardness is that forwardness can only put me in a "false position". I am turned another way, and should appear, by figuring in your scheme as one of so small a cluster of supports, to commit myself to an attitude, an activity and an anxiety not corresponding to my real preoccupations—that is, to what I want especially to do and dare. I don't mind adding that this impracticability might have to some extent a shifting scale, and that to appear as one of a greater number of participants, a prop in a larger group, would represent more, to my own sense, the measure of the sympathy I have at your disposal and which I should be sorry to see you undervalue. I do hope still to be able to testify to it in some artful way, and I am

Yours most truly,

HENRY JAMES

XI

1898–1900

POETS OF THE YOUNGER GENERATION—AMERICA TODAY—FAREWELL TO IBSEN

THROUGH the whole of 1898 and far into the next year Archer was much burdened with a piece of work undertaken, probably, without clear prevision of its magnitude. We have seen that he had already, in 1891, begun to take a benevolent interest in the best of the contemporary verse that came before him in masses for review. This interest had grown in the intervening years. In January 1898 he writes: "I have been writhing for weeks past under the incubus of a lecture[1] to be prepared for a Society of Women Journalists, with whom may the Devil fly away. It is now off my hands (not yet off my tongue unfortunately) and I have a moment's leisure." There were further similar lectures, and in August there appeared a *Fortnightly Review* article on "A Shropshire Poet"—one of the first critical utterances in which the terse Muse of A. E. Housman was recognized and appraised. These were preliminary studies for a book, to be called *Living Poets of the Younger Generation*, contracted for with one of the chief poetry publishing houses of the time, John Lane. There are repeated references in Archer's letters of the period to this seemingly endless task, always waiting, as it were, at his elbow, when not actually on the anvil. Thus already in the summer of 1898: "My poets weigh on me like a pyramid of Old Men of the Sea." In January 1899: "I am as usual up to the ears in work—haven't touched the POETS for

[1] On "Some Living Poets".

weeks. The Younger Generation will be grey-headed before my laurels are woven for them." The spring, as we shall see, brought a further interruption due to his visit to America. It is not till August 1899 that he can write: "Am very busy, trying at last to get the confounded poets book off my hands." The stars were evidently inauspicious; even after the book was ready there came a further pause of more than two years; for, owing to the outbreak of the Boer War, publication was delayed till the end of 1901.[1]

Poets of the Younger Generation—the "Living" had to be dropped, for one of the poets had in the meantime departed without waiting for his wreath—is a formidable-looking volume of 560 pages, containing appreciations of the work of no less than thirty-three singers, and illustrated with copious selections and quotations. Some of the poets dealt with were, and have remained, obscure, and the reader is tempted at first to think that the critic must have woven the meshes of his net too fine, and made with it too wide a cast. Yet he had, in fact, adhered strictly to his announced principle of including only those poets whose work, or some substantial portion of it, gave him genuine pleasure, and had resisted firmly suggestions for the inclusion of yet other singers, in whose verse he could find no savour. "The one merit I claim for my criticism", he writes, "is sincerity. The things I praise are the things I genuinely enjoy; and I could not if I would simulate such enjoyment. Everyone, I presume, is subject to these personal limitations of taste; at any rate, when I find a man who professes to enjoy everything in literature, I am apt to doubt whether he really enjoys anything." A critic who does equal justice to such diverse talents

[1] The delay had one happy result—it rendered possible the inclusion of a study of George Santayana's slender volume of highly-wrought verse.

as A. E. Housman and W. B. Yeats, Francis Thompson and William Watson, Kipling and Santayana, can hardly be held to lack catholicity of taste, and we can see now that he erred rather on the side of over-hospitality than of fastidiousness. But the result of his strict adherence to his personal taste as the standard of selection is that the genuine enjoyment which informs the criticism communicates itself to the reader; and though the flowers of the anthology naturally differ widely in magnitude and beauty, there are surprisingly few which do not possess some charm, of colour, form, or fragrance, even for us today. When the revolt against the nineteenth century has run its course, and readers again begin to take interest in the poetry of the end of Victoria's reign, they will find it keenly appraised and charmingly illustrated in this large but by no means heavy volume.

"It has been literally the dream of my life", wrote Archer,[1] "to revisit the United States. Not once, but fifty times, have I dreamed that the ocean . . . was comfortably crossed, and I was landing in New York. I can clearly recall at this moment some of the fantastic shapes the city put on in my dreams—utterly different, of course, from my actual recollections of it." The dream was now to come true. By George Halkett's friendly offices, a proposal to furnish a series of articles on the American Stage for the *Pall Mall Magazine* was laid before the proprietor and virtual editor, the Hon. W. W. Astor (afterwards Lord Astor). It was favourably received; but Mr. Astor, having a low opinion of the state of drama in America, and probably no very high one of the importance of drama in general, deemed it a matter

[1] *America Today*, Letter I.

of too little moment to be the sole object of such a mission, and suggested an enlargement of the scheme to include a study of the social and political situation, with special reference to the effect of the Spanish-American War on the relations between North and South and between England and the United States. The inspiration was a fortunate one, for it provided the opportunity for widening the range of his interests and activities which Archer had been seeking half-consciously for some time past. Yet, with the diffidence as to his own powers which throughout consorted so oddly with his unshakable confidence in his ideas and ideals, he felt grave misgivings as to his fitness for the enlarged commission. "Warmly as I would wish", he wrote to George Halkett, "to carry out the enlarged scheme which he (Mr. Astor) was good enough to suggest, I do not feel *confident* of my power to do so." And when actually embarked on the emprise he writes: "It is rather a wild-goose venture I am on here. . . . I have been cursing my folly for undertaking it ever since I signed the agreement with the Hon. W. W. Astor. . . . As they say on this side of the world, 'I've bitten off more than I can chew'. However, I shall try to have a good time while I am about it; but oh! I shrink from the social circus in which I expect to find myself willy-nilly a performer." The prospect of seeing the States once more, after twenty-two years' absence, of meeting on their own soil the American friends he had made "on the other side", of establishing personal contact with the civilization the growth of which interested him so intensely, and of trying his hand at work outside the rut into which he felt himself slipping, was a temptation he had been unable to resist, and as he wrote the above words, on March 4, 1899, he was within sight of the lights of New York harbour, on the threshold of a visit which was to be followed by many others and to influence deeply all the rest of his life.

Eight weeks spent (mainly in New York, but with excursions to Philadelphia, Washington, Boston, and Chicago) in a pleasant but bewildering whirl of hospitable entertainment, theatre-going, and intercourse with men of light and leading, produced as their immediate fruit a series of letters—"American Jottings"—published in the *Pall Mall Gazette* and the *New York Times*, and the materials for three papers on politico-social topics and three on the American Stage, which appeared in due course in the *Pall Mall Magazine*. And, early in 1900, the non-theatrical letters and articles were reprinted in the volume entitled *America Today*. The "Jottings" were the record of what was necessarily but a hasty and superficial survey of one corner, though an important one, of a vast and varied civilization; but the politico-social papers—particularly the first and second, "North and South" and "Republic and Empire"—are on a different plane, and proved at once, even to himself, the baselessness of his misgivings as to his powers as a publicist. They form an early and striking example of their author's faculty for going straight, as by intuition, to the root of any matter which interested him, and grasping its essentials. They met with much appreciation in America,[1] and the second paper was in its day an important contribution to the cause of Anglo-American friendship—indeed, in spite of the enormous changes in the circumstances, its statement of the conditions on which alone that friendship can be maintained and drawn closer has much relevance even at the present day.

[1] See letter (p. 246) from Theodore Roosevelt, then Governor of New York State.

One of those conditions—the conciliation of Ireland—was fulfilled, we may hope finally, (after what welter of tragic crimes and blunders it boots not to remember) before Archer's death; of another, the complete equalization of the status of all citizens of the British Empire, we have only recently seen the consummation.

But a still more important result of this adventure to Archer personally was the multiplication and strengthening of his own ties with America. Brander Matthews's hospitable house was only the chief of many the doors of which were thrown wide to him; wherever he went he made friendships and acquaintanceships that were to be of value, both spiritual and material, in future days; and he returned home with the "Anglo-American patriotism" which had hitherto perhaps been something of a youthful dream, developed and rationalized by fuller knowledge.

In these last years of the dying century the apparent stagnation in the theatrical world—broken though it was by signs of life such as Tree's restoration of *Julius Cæsar* to the stage, and the appearance of Pinero's delightful *Trelawney of the Wells*—had bred in Archer, as his letters of the time show, occasional moods of discouragement. But one event of great promise there had been, though it had taken place not on the stage but in the book-world—the publication (1898) of the first-fruits of Bernard Shaw's work for the theatre, in the two volumes *Plays: Pleasant and Unpleasant*. It was very many years since a publisher had found it worth while to place the works of a contemporary English dramatist in the hands of the public in a seemly and readable form. The new departure was in itself of the happiest omen. And the contents of the volumes, whatever their merits or demerits as drama, had plainly the breath of life in them. Though Archer's criticism[1] of the plays was candid to, or beyond, the verge of severity, he did not fail to recognize their importance. The appearance of the book, he wrote, "is an event, literary and theatrical, of the first magnitude".

As a new dramatist came on the scene, the career of an old one was drawing to a close. Ibsen's seventieth birthday, falling in March 1898, had been widely celebrated in the northern kingdoms and Germany by banquets and festal performances of the dramas. England was not yet ready to come into line, but the tone of the Press on the occasion showed that the Ibsen battle had been virtually won; that ignorant and contemptuous prejudice had given place to respect, tempered though it might sometimes be with a good deal of aversion; and the presentation (organized by Archer and Edmund Gosse) of a handsome set of silver subscribed for by English admirers delighted the old poet perhaps as much as any of the more elaborate tokens of homage.

That summer, obeying an urgent appeal from his relations at Tolderodden, where he had not been able to set foot for many years past, Archer joined his brother there, and with him returned to England by way of Christiania, Denmark, and Germany. Ibsen met the travellers with true Norwegian hospitality, and with the courtesy and cordiality he never failed to show where Archer was concerned. He was even, for him, communicative: telling, amidst much other talk, of his journey through Norway in the fifties, when commissioned by the Government to collect folk-songs, on which he collected no folk-songs, but did collect the legends

[1] Mr. Bernard Shaw's Plays, *Study and Stage*, pp. 1-22.

and impressions which helped to inspire *Brand* and *Peer Gynt*; of his state of nervous overstrain when these poems were on the anvil, a state in which he would go on composing verses all the time, even when asleep or half awake, to find, when he tried to write them down, that they were "utter rubbish"; of his reluctance to see his own plays performed, because the personalities of the actors were apt to come between him and his conceptions, and permanently to distort his idea of his own work; even of his love (unusual in Norway, where Johnson's view of oatmeal prevails) of oatmeal porridge "with a lump of butter in it", a taste he attributed to the Scottish strain in his ancestry.

After seeing all that was to be seen at the theatres of Copenhagen, Berlin, and Vienna, the travellers reached Munich, and there, on a sweltering Sunday of September, had an unforgettable meeting with the second of the Great Twin Brethren of Norwegian literature, Björnstjerne Björnson. "Never", wrote Archer,[1] "have I spent a more interesting hour. . . . My long admiration for the poet would have made it interesting to me even if the man himself had been less impressive. . . . But had I been ignorant of his writings, and even of his name, I could not have been ten minutes in his company without recognizing in him a man of genius. . . . Without declaiming, without orating, without even monopolizing the conversation, he struck me as the most eloquent man I had ever encountered." Indeed, Björnson's personality recalled irresistibly Johnson's saying of another great orator: "If a man were to go by chance at the same time with Burke under a shed, to shun a shower, he would say: 'This is an extraordinary man'." Nothing could have contrasted more

[1] "Björnson's New Play", *Daily Chronicle*, February 2, 1899.

strongly with Ibsen's close-lipped, somewhat formal courtesy, than the buoyant, flashing geniality—geniality in both the German and the English sense—of this old man eloquent of the North. The ugly terms "introvert" and "extravert" might have been specially coined to describe the two men. And if, as is possible, Björnson shared with some of his admirers the view that Archer had shown too exclusive a devotion to the theatre of Ibsen, and had done less than justice to his own dramatic works, there was no sign of such a feeling in his manner, or in the copious stream of talk, political, literary, and personal, which sent the two Englishmen away in a glow of admiration and delight.

A flying visit to Christiania the following autumn for the opening, on September 1st, of the new National Theatre, brought Archer once more, and for the last time, face to face with the two chieftains. In the *Daily Chronicle* of September 6th and 8th he describes the three festal evenings, devoted to Holberg, Ibsen, and Björnson in order of seniority: the tremendous reception given to the two living poets, the careful arrangements made to hold the balance even between the two, and the immense enthusiasm which greeted the performance of *An Enemy of the People* on the Ibsen night, and of *Sigurd the Crusader* on the evening devoted to Björnson. Of the second (Ibsen) evening he says: "The enthusiasm at the close of the evening was even greater than at the opening, the cheering louder and more prolonged. The one person in the theatre who was entirely calm and collected was Henrik Ibsen. I met him in the corridor as we were going out, and stammered my congratulations. 'Don't you think it went very well?' was all he said."

Not many times more were the two to meet. "A

few days later", Archer writes,[1] "I parted from Ibsen for the last time, at his house in Arbins Gade. Punctilious as ever in his courtesy, he accompanied me to the outer door, and we shook hands on the threshold. Nearly twenty years had passed since I first saw him in the dim old Roman salon; and in all that time, whether in speech or writing (though we had had business relations not quite without complexity) I had met with nothing but kindness, consideration, and cordiality at his hands. What I said I do not remember, but doubtless it was not the right thing. The right thing to have said was very plain. Thinking of all that I owed to the poet and the man, I should have used the simplest and most comprehensive of the formulas of gratitude in which Norwegian abounds, and said to him: 'Tak for alt'—'Thanks for all'."

[1] "Ibsen As I Knew Him", *Monthly Review*, June 1906.

XIa

LETTERS, ETC., OF 1898–1899

From George Bernard Shaw

26th April, 1898

My dear Archer,

I wrote you a long letter about your Chronicle review [reproduced in *Study and Stage*—"Mr. Bernard Shaw's Plays"], but on looking over it I see nothing in it that would interest you except the postscript,[1] which contains simple information, and an explanation of "the poet's secret" in *Candida*, which will dry your tears.

I knew that the book would simply mow down the critics. I pick my way daily through their corpses. I have to hop, by the way, because I have hurt my left—oh, I forgot: you saw my condition at the Globe.

You really are the very blamedest dunderhead—explaining all the most exciting social phenomena of your time as mere aberrations of Shaw.

I have just begun a new play—*Cæsar and Cleopatra*. The Queen's bodyguard, discoursing in the first act in the manner of Sardou's butler and housemaid, have already given the most unexpected touches of local color to the scene.

G. B. S.

To George Bernard Shaw

30th April, 1898

My dear Shaw,

If you really want to "mow down" the critics, write a few more *Candidas*—that's the way to do it.

[1] The postscript, besides an interesting analysis of the conclusion of *Candida*, contains a list of persons who had served as models for prominent characters in the Shaw drama.

Anyone can achieve the triumph of being misunderstood; it is only the bungler (sometimes, no doubt, a bungler of genius) who makes a virtue of his limitations and pretends to aim at and rejoice in "mowing down" people. I ask for nothing better than to have it proved that my analysis of your limitations is wrong, imperfect, founded on insufficient or misread evidence. It will cost me nothing, less than nothing to confess it. But the evidence I want is good plays, not expositions of the excellence of your sociology (which I don't doubt), or assertions that such and such a character is taken from such and such a real person. That I don't doubt either; but the merit of a likeness depends, not on whom it is meant for, but on whether it is like; and furthermore, a likeness may be very like, and yet a shocking work of art, and especially out of place in a given dramatic picture.

W. A.

From GEORGE BERNARD SHAW

29 FITZROY SQUARE,
2nd May, 1898

Well I am DAMNED! Your *analysis* of my limitations! Why, you stupendous ass, you draw a line through my plays which represents your own limitations in your most fatuously lazy mood; and you then proceed to explain that everything outside that line is mere Shawism (which doesn't in the least account for it), and everything inside it is heaven-born genius. You are getting a great deal worse than Clement Scott: everything that is not a stagily sentimental *coup de théâtre* makes you simply petulant. . . . .

I have just begun *Cæsar and Cleopatra*. The psychological woman-tamer, at 50, operating on an

Egyptian girl of 16, will require at least 30 columns of the Chronicle for adequate denunciation.

G. B. S.

[The dedicatory verse below, evidently written to accompany the presentation to Ibsen on his seventieth birthday, seems to have been laid aside unused. Probably Archer felt it to be too high-sounding to fit the modest "memorial", and he may have thought, also, that an English prose address, such as that actually sent, would go better with an English gift.]

Se! af Dumhed's Hær beleiret,
Tænker, Digter, Du har seiret!
Vi, som kjæmped' for at bane
Vei for Din og Lysets Fane,
Byder Hövdingen, hin Stærke,
Dette Seirens Mindesmærke.

[Lo! by Dulness' hosts beleaguered,
Thinker, Poet, thou hast conquered!
We, who fought to cleave a passage
For thy lightward-beckoning banner,
Lay before thee, Chieftain mighty!
This memorial of thy triumph.]

From THOMAS HARDY

21.12.98

MY DEAR ARCHER,

Just a line to thank you for your generous criticism. If I had known that you were to review the book[1] I should not have had the temerity to send a copy till later.

[1] Wessex Poems.

Your happy phrase,[1] "seeing all the words of the dictionary on one plane" (anent the Peasant's Confession) touches, curiously enough, what I had thought over. Concluding that the tale must be regarded as a translation of the original utterance of the peasant, I thought an impersonal wording admissible.

Always yours,

T. H.

To CHARLES ARCHER

THE PLAYERS,
16 GRAMERCY PARK,
NEW YORK,
19 *March*, 1899

You see I have followed on your heels closer than either you or I anticipated the night I saw you off at Euston![2] Of course I can't begin to tell you a quarter of what I have seen and done during the fortnight I have been here. By the by, I narrowly escaped roasting, or at any rate losing all my goods and chattels, in the Windsor Hotel fire. . . .

By way of being near the aristocracy, my friends, and at the same time having a number I can remember in this city of numbers, I have taken a room at 234 Fifth Avenue (2345 you see), 32 dollars a month. I am a member pro tem of 7 clubs. . . . Of course American hospitality is simply overwhelming. Was at a luncheon party at Matthews' yesterday—Howells, Bronson Howard, Augustus Thomas (*Alabama*), Norman Hapgood (young critic, a good

[1] "There are times when Mr. Hardy seems to lose all sense of local and historical perspective in language, seeing all the words in the dictionary on one plane, so to speak, and regarding them all as equally available and appropriate for any and every literary purpose."

[2] His correspondent had returned to India via America and Japan.

fellow and frightfully in earnest) and two other men. I *never* heard such a running fire of stories, and almost every one of them good. . . . It was my first meeting with Howells, a charming old fellow. . . . In the theatrical way, by far the most interesting thing I have seen is *Griffith Davenport*, by James A. Herne, quite the best popular play I ever saw; no psychology, but any amount of quite poetic feeling; as much above *Secret Service* as S.S. is above the ordinary Adelphi melodrama. And *perfectly* acted—a huge cast, and every one as good as he or she could be. Mrs. Herne's performance was probably the best piece of absolute untheatrical nature I ever saw. . . .

I am more than ever charmed with America. The people are simply delightful, and I am convinced that twenty years hence New York will be one of the most beautiful cities in the world. They are going ahead gigantically in architecture and art in general. Even the rottenness of their municipal politics is a temporary condition, I feel sure. There are all the elements of good in this strange seething cauldron, and I believe they're coming to the top. . . .

To G. G. A. MURRAY

2 August, 1899

MY DEAR MURRAY,

I was wondering what had come over you, and am glad to hear it is only Churt. I wish I could run down and see you, but am very busy trying at last to get the confounded poets book off my hands—am struggling with John Davidson at the present moment—a dour subject to tackle. I have got Shaw's *Cæsar and Cleopatra,* which he says I am to send to you. But I am minded to keep it and read it to you; it is not a thing that one can appreciate alone. You don't want to read Pickwick to yourself—you lose half the fun of the thing. I expected to be infuriated by the thing, much as one resents a "Comic History of Rome" or of England. But really there is amazing cleverness in it, though it is outrageously long, and tedious at some points. I think Shaw has invented a new genre in this sort of historic extravaganza, though fortunately no one but he is likely to practise it. . . . .

Are you adscriptus glebæ, or do you ever come up to town? If so, drop me a card a day in advance and come and look me up. On Friday I dine with Colvin at the B.M. to hear Stephen Phillips read Francesca—rather an ordeal! Remember me very kindly to Lady Mary and believe me

Yours ever,

W. A.

From THEODORE ROOSEVELT

Aug. 31st, 1899

MY DEAR MR. ARCHER,

I cannot deny myself the pleasure of writing to compliment you upon your altogether excellent articles on the conditions of affairs in America, both as to the relations between the North and the South and between America and England. What I especially liked about your article was that it was so eminently sane and moderate. Indeed, I think that if there was any error at all, it was in the direction of not giving quite enough weight to the change of feeling towards England. Your division of the American sentiment into three classes is exactly right, and also your sense of the relative importance of these three classes. But I think, in the first place, that the great mass of Americans—those who know the least about England and foreign nations—have been rather more stirred than you suppose to kindliness for her; and in the second place, I hardly think you lay enough weight upon the fact that, in two or three generations, the great bulk of the descendants of the immigrants of non-English origin become absolutely indistinguishable from other Americans and share their feelings. This is markedly so with the Scandinavians and most of the Germans of the second, and all of the Germans of the third generation, who practically all during 1898 felt toward Germany and England just exactly as other Americans did. . . . Twice recently I have addressed huge Methodist meetings of eight or ten thousand people, each drawn as regards the enormous majority from exactly that class which you pointed out as standing between the two extremes. In each case the men who introduced me dwelt upon the increased good feeling between the English-speaking peoples, and every complimentary allusion to England was received with great applause.

Of course, to gush, or be hysterical or over-effusive about the matter would defeat its own ends, and what you say about the Irish business is perfectly true. I became a Homeruler in consequence of reading Lecky, and have continued so partly because I have thought it would be a good thing for Ireland, and partly because I should like to see the removal of the one great obstacle to friendship among the people who speak English all over the world. As you know, the Canadians and the Australians have always taken exactly the attitude towards Home Rule that the Americans have.

. . . . .

As I have been one of the people who have experienced a change of heart, I have some right to speak for them. I should not republish my Venezuela article now. I have exactly the feeling about Americanism that you describe. Most important of all is it for this country to treat an American on his worth as a man, and to disregard absolutely whether he be of English, German, Irish or any other origin, whether he be of Catholic or Protestant faith; but fundamentally I feel that all the English-speaking peoples come much nearer to one another in political and social ideals, in their culture and systems of government and of civic and domestic morality, than any of them do to any other peoples. I want to get along well with everybody (for instance, I have a great regard for the Germans: I wish them well where they do not conflict with the English-speaking peoples, and earnestly hope there will be no rupture with them); but most of all, I earnestly hope that there will not be the slightest rift between the English-speaking peoples themselves.

. . . . .

Very sincerely yours,
THEODORE ROOSEVELT

XII

1900–1905

THE SOUTH AFRICAN WAR—*REAL CONVERSATIONS*—THE DRAMATIC REVIVAL—THE END OF THE *WORLD*

THE outbreak of the Boer War in October 1899 forced upon Archer, as on thousands of other Liberals, a difficult choice of paths. And the choice he made was surprising, not only to many of his closest friends, but also in some degree to himself. His hatred of war was sincere and unswerving, and, while the parleyings dragged on through the summer and autumn, the idea of England's going to war on the questions at issue had been repugnant to him. But the opening phases of the campaign, by showing the offensive strength of the Boer Republics and their aggressive spirit, and calling forth the dangerously hostile feeling of Europe, wrought in him a change of heart. Rightly or wrongly, he came to regard the war as a deplorable necessity, an ordeal which, as matters stood, could not have been avoided without allowing the coherence of the British Commonwealth of Nations to be seriously endangered, if not destroyed. And since in his view the best hopes of the world lay in the co-operation of the English-speaking peoples, of which the consolidation of that Commonwealth was a necessary condition, he was compelled, both by reason[1] and feeling, for once to take his stand with the majority and in opposition to many of his most valued friends.

The acceptance of the war as a necessity, however

[1] His reasons are set forth in "A Plain Man's Politics" (*Monthly Review,* November 1901); his feelings in various *Morning Leader* articles, notably in "The Lesson of the Mauser", February 5, 1900,

abhorred, carried with it, to his mind, the obligation to do all that lay in the power of a private individual to help; and when the call came for volunteers for home defence, he at once joined the Inns of Court Rifles. Writing to an anti-war friend on February 5, 1900, he says: "Talking of [Empires], I don't know whether you will be glad or sorry to hear that the British Empire has taken a new lease of life—I have joined the volunteers! My military experience has not yet got beyond being bully-ragged by a solicitor's clerk for not knowing my right hand from my left; but when I have mastered that useful branch of education, I shall no doubt make as good a mark for a French bullet as anybody else. . . . It is not bad fun, and relieves nervous tension." A week later he reports: "I am beginning to know my right hand from my left, but cannot yet distinguish between my front and my rear—a matter of considerable moment, else you might find yourself winning the Victoria Cross when your intention was to run away." Once more, in giving reasons for his action (reasons summed up in the sentence: "It is in the hope of saving my son from being a conscript that I have become a volunteer"), he confesses that not reason but feeling is, ultimately, at the root of the matter. "And now", he says, "let me own to a strain of hypocrisy running through this article. All the reasoning in it is sincere enough, and yet I am well aware that it is not reasoning, but instinct, that has led me, the most unwarlike of men, to shoulder a Lee-Metford. As I lay 'slimly' ensconced the other day, behind a furze-clump on a windy upland, waiting for a word of command, and looking down upon a grey cathedral city among the green water-meads of the valley below, I realized clearly that it was no process of political thought that had brought me there, but sheer unreasoning love for this beautiful, this reverend, this illustrious land, mother of nations, and fountain-head of that speech which, ennobled by a peerless company of poets, is to-day on the lips of freemen all around the globe."

In the years that followed, till his resignation a year after the close of the war, his letters contain frequent descriptions, often scribbled in pencil in railway trains, of experiences in camps of exercise and at manœuvres—experiences health-bringing, in spite of discomforts and hardships, and made pleasant by the spirit, almost universal in his Corps, of good humour and mutual helpfulness, and by the realization that he was still young enough to "rough it" with enjoyment. "Of course", he writes in August 1902, "it's a great farce my sticking to the Corps, and I don't know that I mayn't resign next spring—I am the worst possible soldier, both mentally and physically. Yet I am very loth to give it up—it will be like bidding a last good-bye to youth. And, except for the sense of inefficiency, I really enjoy it. . . . One thing I know—if I was to do any soldiering at all, the Inns of Court was the Corps of all others for me. They are extraordinarily good fellows take them all round; and I must say they make me feel as if England had some kick left in her after all."

Differences of feeling are often less disastrous to friendship than differences in speculative opinion, and the fact that Archer's attitude on the burning question of the time, though it may have temporarily strained his relations with some of his intimates, did not in any instance lead to permanent estrangement, may have been partly due to his candid admission that he was moved in the matter as much by irresistible instinct as by reason. It is significant that these very confessions were made in the journal founded to represent the views of the so-called pro-Boers, when the *Daily Chronicle* went over to the camp of the majority. "The Lesson of the Mauser" was the first of a series of weekly articles contributed to the *Morning Leader* and to its successor the *Daily News and Leader*, which, under the general title, first of "Study and Stage" and later of "Things in General", was continued, almost without a break, for seventeen years. It came to be something like a point of honour with him to keep the series unbroken, even when, as often happened, he was beyond the seas or on the other side of the globe; but the articles never became a mechanical task—on the contrary, he kept up the weekly column mainly because it served as an outlet for the thoughts and feelings *de omnibus rebus et quibusdam aliis* which constantly pressed for utterance.

From some of these weekly discourses we have already had occasion to quote, others will be referred to hereafter. Not a few, of which "The Origin of Good" and the quaintly named "Our Babu Speech"[1] may be taken as typical, strike a very deep note, giving utterance to the creed which warmed and inspired their author throughout his life. But they ranged over a multitude of subjects, great and small, from the destiny of man to the philosophy of fashions,[2] and they included (for he was too true a Scot not to love a debate) innumerable tilts with Bernard Shaw, Walkley, Robertson, and others over most questions in literature, in the drama, in sociology, even in politics.

Meanwhile, at the turn of the century, we find him busied with a very thorough revision of the Ibsen prose dramas (in which he enlists the critical

[1] *Morning Leader*, November 23, 1907, and March 21, 1908.
[2] "Modes et Robes", *Morning Leader*, January 23, 1914.

assistance of Gilbert Murray) for a "one play a volume" edition issued by Walter Scott; with the polishing off of his *Poets* volume; and with a series of "Real Conversations" with celebrities which, originally suggested by George Halkett, appeared in the *Pall Mall Magazine* from 1901 onwards, and were published in book form in 1904. "I cannot but believe", he says, at the close of the "Imaginary Conversation with the Courteous Reader" which forms a preface to the book, "that, for many a day to come, someone here and there will be found to value these unvarnished jottings of what, at certain moments of the first years of the twentieth century, certain men and women of the time were thinking, feeling and saying.

Courteous Reader: You appeal to posterity then?

W.A.: In right of my interlocutors, I do."

Since the list of interlocutors included such names of abiding interest as Pinero, Hardy, W. S. Gilbert, David Masson, and George Moore, the anticipation was a not unnatural one. But the reader who, "here and there", may be attracted to the book by these names will, I think, find the pages devoted to less prominent people—such, for instance, as the two women novelists, Mrs. Craigie and "Lucas Malet"—at least as interesting as any in the volume.

"Italy", he wrote at this time, "is the only country that never disappoints you. It is more wonderful than your hope; it is lovelier than your memory." Thrice in these years—in the first three winters of the century—he was able to put his hopes and memories to the test. The first visit, made partly with a view to a "Real Conversation" with Mr. W. Heinemann, then living in Italy, was the occasion of his coming under fire for the first and last time; when, during a walk along the sands on the Volscian seaboard, his party found themselves involuntarily personating the "unseen enemy" at which the guns of the neighbouring artillery school were practising with shrapnel. Fortunately a proportion of the shells failed to burst, and the possible tragedy ended in gaiety. "My host", wrote Archer, "an old friend of the colonel of the regiment, told him the story of our ten minutes under fire, and I heard something of a non-commissioned officer having been put under arrest—no doubt for having missed us." "This three weeks' tour," he says in a letter, ". . . has been an extraordinary success in point of enjoyment, though not quite so great, I fear, in point of business. In weather, I have had the luck of the old 'un—exquisite days in Rome, exquisite days by the Mediterranean, exquisite days in the Alban and Sabine hills. . . . And then, I've had all manner of diversions—I've been bombarded with shrapnel by the esercito Italiano, and enjoyed it immensely (especially seeing Heinemann skip like a young goat, as indeed we all did, only I couldn't see myself)—I've had my first experience of table-turning and spirit-rapping . . .; and then, for a final diversion, I have assisted at the baptism of fire of the new Italian drama, and a very fiery baptism it was—the Teatro Costanzi that night did a great deal to reconcile me to English theatrical conditions. But there is a lot of fine work in the play.[1] I wouldn't at all swear that D'Annunzio mayn't become a great dramatist, though in that case he'll have to tame himself a bit. A great poet he undoubtedly is—and he knows it, if ever man did."

The early years of the new century had seen a quickening of the progressive movement in things

[1] D'Annunzio's *Francesca da Rimini*.

theatrical,[1] which, under the pressure of the long-run system and of other unfavourable conditions, had been so greatly hampered during the late nineties as to seem at times to have come to a standstill. The Stage Society, an organization founded, at the very end of the departing century, on a broader and firmer basis than the previous enterprises of the kind, took up with energy the work of producing at special performances plays of merit which were unsuited, either in fact or in the view of short-sighted managers, for the ordinary commercial stage. The Society's productions included, besides foreign plays, several pieces by untried authors who afterwards made their mark. But its chief achievements were to make it clear that Bernard Shaw's plays were not only brilliant as literature, but also, when adequately produced, highly effective on the stage; and to bring to light, in a young actor, Harley Granville-Barker, the talent of a heaven-born producer and the promise of a remarkable dramatist.

One of the early productions of the Society had been Gilbert Murray's *Andromache,* a saga-play which owed its origin in part to Archer's suggestion, and which had given rise during its composition to much discussion between the author and his friend. In May 1904 a yet more ambitious experiment was made, on Archer's initiative, by the New Century Theatre, in staging, with Granville-Barker as producer, Professor Murray's fine version of the *Hippolytus* of Euripides. The experiment was a notable success. "Whatever the villainous critics may say", wrote Archer to the scholar-poet after the first performance, "I think we may congratulate ourselves on having done a really beautiful thing, and made a

[1] Archer, at about this time, contributed an account of the movement to the *Encyclopædia Britannica.*

deep impression on everyone who is capable of being impressed by great literature on the stage. I think future performances will be better, when the people are less afraid of it. It will stand keying up at some points. . . . But the main point is that the thing was noble and beautiful, and all the critics in the world can't alter that." Criticism was more favourable than could have been expected. In some cases, indeed, it was enthusiastic; and the impression made was so marked that when, in October of the same year, Granville-Barker and J. E. Vedrenne began their memorable management at the Court Theatre, the *Hippolytus* was the first play produced.

In default of the resources in space and capital required for a true repertory theatre, this management adopted the "short-run" system, and was thereby enabled to gain a hearing, under favourable conditions, for several new dramatists—among others John Galsworthy and Granville-Barker himself (whose *Voysey Inheritance* gave, for the first time, full assurance of his powers), and for a number of foreign masterpieces, including *The Trojan Women*, the *Electra*, and the *Medea*, *The Wild Duck* and Hauptmann's *Der Biberpelz*. But the plays, new and old, of Bernard Shaw formed the mainstay of the enterprise, and their great attractiveness proved once for all what Archer had long been dinning into the ears of managers (and what, indeed, had already been demonstrated in America and Germany[1]), namely, that the dramatic work of this humorist-philosopher

[1] The seed of the Continental vogue had been planted in 1900, when Archer recommended an Austrian visitor, Herr Siegfried Trebitsch, to read the *Plays: Pleasant and Unpleasant*, and the *Plays for Puritans*, as the most notable things in the English drama of the time—thereby kindling in the fervid Teuton an enthusiasm which led to the production in Vienna of *The Devil's Disciple*, the first step in the conquest of Germany.

"BREAKING A BUTTERFLY"

(*Max's rejoinder to the "World" criticism of "The Happy Hypocrite," December* 1900)

had only to be given a fair chance on the stage in order to be widely popular.

There was unmistakable progress, too, on the "regular stage". Pinero had entered on his period of greatest mastery with *Iris* and *Letty*; Jones's admirable gift of dramatic story-telling was seen at its best in *Mrs. Dane's Defence*; and Barrie, with *Quality Street* and *The Admirable Crichton*, showed that he had mastered the art of giving dramatic expression to his delightful humour and fantasy. It seemed for a time as though "poetical drama" might come alive again in the plays of Stephen Phillips. And the appreciation of Shakespearean drama, now that managers had ventured to vary the beaten round of familiar tragedies and comedies with productions of the long-neglected histories and Roman plays, and had begun to pay somewhat less attention to magnificence of mounting and more to diction and all-round acting, had become more widely diffused and more genuine. Such productions as Forbes Robertson's *Hamlet* and Lewis Waller's *Henry V* were much more truly revivals than most of the Shakespearean solemnities of the eighties and nineties. In July of 1905, the last year of his connection with the *World*, reviewing the stage-history of the past year, Archer remarks on the noteworthy fact that the two most popular authors of the season have been William Shakespeare and George Bernard Shaw.

Even if we allow for a touch of humorous exaggeration in this estimate, the remark is significant of the change that had come over the scene during the twenty-odd years of Archer's work on the *World*. In a review of the year 1884 he would have had to note as the chief successes *The Private Secretary* and *The Ironmaster*—adaptations of a German farce and a third-rate French drama—while Shakespeare would have been represented by moderately praiseworthy productions of two stock plays, *Twelfth Night* and *Romeo and Juliet,* and a poor one of *Hamlet.* A comparison between single years is, of course, apt to be misleading, but if a series of years of the new century were set against a similar series in the eighties, the contrast would be no less striking.[1] To this change many causes had contributed. But if, on leaving the paper which he had served, and which had served him, so long and well, Archer cast a look backward over these twenty years, he can hardly have failed to realize that his hope of bearing a hand in the rescue of the drama from the slough of the mid-nineteenth century had not proved vain.

But to consolidate the position, to guard against relapse, and to make further progress possible, it was, he held, more than ever necessary that Matthew Arnold's demand: "Organize the theatre!" should at last be heeded. Before ever Matthew Arnold had spoken, he had set before him the same ideal. A repertory theatre, or theatres, placed by one form of endowment or another above the necessity of catering for the million in all productions, and thus able to maintain a reasonably high standard in its productions of contemporary drama and to keep truly alive the best drama of the past—this, we have seen, was the remedy for the chaos of our theatrical conditions which he had constantly advocated whenever he saw, or thought he saw, an opportunity. The time seemed now to have come for concerted, constructive effort towards the realization of this ideal. Early in the new century we read of a Committee

[1] The movement continued throughout the decade. Five years later Archer could write: "For the first time for two centuries, to put it briefly, we have some of the best and most brilliant minds in England or in Europe working, and working successfully, for the stage."

established to further the cause, and find Archer busily engaged, with Granville-Barker as an untiring ally, in working out concrete proposals. The results of much careful thought, based on a comprehensive study by the collaborators of National, Municipal, and other Endowed theatres in every country where such institutions already existed, were embodied in a "Blue-Book"—*Scheme and Estimates for a National Theatre*—which, printed by subscription in 1904 for private circulation, and thereupon subjected to exhaustive criticism and amendment, was finally submitted to a number of the leaders of the theatrical and literary world, and was very generally approved by them. From these proposals, as a point of departure, proceeded the further efforts of the National Theatre Committee, which. as we shall see, occupied a great share of Archer's attention and energy during the rest of his life.

The *World* phase of his long campaign was now drawing to a close. During 1905 there were signs of change ahead in the management; before the year was out the paper had changed hands, and, feeling no confidence in the stability of his position under the new régime, Archer considered the proposals of the new Liberal daily paper, the *Tribune*, that he should go over to them. "I offered to do so" [on certain terms] "nearly a fortnight ago", he writes, "and I have had no reply. . . . I don't care the toss of a coin how it turns out—I don't really feel the energy to undertake what would practically be the dramatic management of the new paper (it is to appear on January 15) and have only faced the idea because I felt there was a possibility of gaining (what I had always lacked on the *World*), to wit, influence. I felt I *oughtn't* to funk it; but I do, and shall need no consoling if the whole thing falls through. I am heartily sick of dramatic criticism altogether; but no doubt I shall have to stick to it so long as it sticks to me."

The transfer took place in due course. *Hamlet* had been, in a double sense, his "first footing" on the London Press; in his first article for the *World* he had dealt with Salvini's Othello and Lear; he now began his third venture, in the first number of the new paper, with a notice of *As You Like It*, his favourite among Shakespearean comedies. His last *World* article appeared the next day.

XIIa

LETTERS OF 1899–1904

To Charles Archer

Thursday, 14th Dec., '99

(Position—Methuen repulsed at Magersfontein and Gatacre smashed at Stormberg.)

Well, here's a cheerful end to the century! And to cheer you up a little more, I send a hurried line to say that at last the Old Man *is* an old man, and the new play is a sad fiasco. It is a mere hash up of fifty old ideas (going as far back as Peer Gynt and Den Grönklaedte) and is utterly without dramatic fibre. Furthermore it is scabrous to a degree—if it weren't like deserting the Old Man, 'pon my soul I'd let some one else translate it. Of course it is not at all wonderful that a man of 71 should write such a piece, but it is wonderful that the man who wrote this should have written *Borkman* only three years earlier. The first act disappointed me greatly, though, on a second reading, I thought rather better of it. There are flashes of the old fire in it, though scarcely any new material, and no dramatic action even foreshadowed. But the second act merely repeats the first (almost word for word in long passages), and the third is wild without being effective. It is a caricature of Ibsen, and a triumph for the heathen, who will declare (wrongly) that it is indecent, and (rightly) that it is mad. The N.C.T. can't possibly touch it, and I can scarcely believe that anyone else will—though it is on the cards that Shaw may declare it his masterpiece, and the Charringtons do it on a Sunday evening. Good Lord! how I wish I either had it translated or hadn't to translate it. So the old man goes out with the century! It is sörgeligt; but, after all, how many men have had such an innings! . . .

[NOTE—The letter that follows was probably the last received by William Archer from Henrik Ibsen. The kindly consideration shown in it both for his Danish publisher and his English interpreter, and the eagerness of the old poet, then upon the verge of his last illness, to see his last work in English dress while there was yet time, give it a special and somewhat pathetic interest.]

[Translation]

CHRISTIANIA, *the* 28.1.1900

DEAR MR. WILLIAM ARCHER,

I am very grateful to you for your letter to my son, which he has shown me.

[The next paragraph conveys Ibsen's acceptance ("Since it is of great consequence to me that your translation should be published as soon as possible") of a reduction in the author's fee on account of *When We Dead Awaken,* owing to the sheets not having been sent over by the Danish publisher to England in time to secure the American copyright. The letter goes on:]

The Gyldendal Publishing Company still consider that they are in no wise to blame for the difficulties which have arisen. It would therefore be painful both for Hegel [the head of the Danish firm and Ibsen's old friend] and for his manager if they learned that I have been obliged to accept a reduced payment for the English and American edition. To avoid this, I beg that this time Mr. Heinemann's cheque may be sent to me personally here in Christiania, and not, as on previous occasions, to the Gyldendal Company; so that there will be no need for them, in Copenhagen, to know anything of the alteration in the terms.

Dear Mr. Archer—I am truly much concerned at the thought of all the trouble this matter has caused you. Fortunately it is now happily at an end, and I look forward with much eagerness to seeing these my latest creations in English dress.

To Mrs. Archer and to yourself I send my warmest and most thankful greetings, and remain now as ever,

Your most obliged and affectionate,

HENRIK IBSEN

To GEORGE BERNARD SHAW

[To the suggestion referred to in para. 2 of this letter, Mr. Shaw had replied in a long letter in pencil. W. A. rejoins:]

Feb. 1*st*, 1900

MY DEAR SHAW,

As the man says in Stevenson, "Golly, what a letter!"

I write to you suggesting that the N.C.T. might do one of your plays; you haven't a play that we want free for us to do; one would think nothing could be simpler. But somehow a "position" is set up, which has got to be "worked out" laboriously, with tons of black lead lavished upon it. There is no "position" whatever. We have never agreed about plays, and we never will. There is not the least reason why we should. I have never given a red cent for the ideas in plays. You and other people have had to point out to me the ideas in Ibsen's plays. Some of them I see, some of them I don't (nor, I believe, does Ibsen). But the play has always been the first thing to me; it is the last thing to you.

Never was black lead more hopelessly wasted than in this letter. You haven't even persuaded me that I ought to be ashamed of myself for admiring your later plays. As for the other plays, a few minutes after I read your letter I read a manuscript preface by Gilbert Murray to one of his own plays in which he says: "I see that I am approaching the common pitfall of playwrights who venture upon prefaces, and am beginning to prove how good my play ought to be!" For "prefaces" read "letters". I think I have solved the mystery of your friend Shakespeare's premature end; he no doubt broke a blood-vessel in trying to prove to Ben Jonson that *Titus Andronicus* was a good play and *Hamlet* a bad one.

The amazing appearance of Mrs. Clifford on the theatre of war leads me to conjecture that you think she wrote *Alan's Wife*. She didn't, nor did Miss Robins, nor did I. *Und damit basta.*

Expect me at one tomorrow, Astrachan coat and all.

Yours,

W. A.

From GEORGE BERNARD SHAW

[Postcard]

21 *February*, 1900

The book herewith, ". . . and other Verses", by ——, has been sent to me with a request that I would put it in the way of being reviewed by the English press. I can produce an impression of having done so, if I report that I have placed it on your desk: hence the unwelcome offering. However, I always open such books, to sample the beginnings of poetry in the colonies. A small sample of this man will suffice for the present.

Some of your American book is very good—I mean supergood enough to leave a mark, especially the North and South article. I begin to have hopes that you will do me credit yet.

By the way, the Ibsen play[1] is powerful, and *frightfully* moral. The best review I have seen is in the last *Speaker*. It *must* be played.

G. B. S.

To G. G. A. Murray

12 *Nov.*, 1900

My dear Murray,

I am entirely confirmed in my original impression that this[2] is the best—most readable, comprehensible and delightful—rendering of a Greek play I ever came across. I also think that it could be made highly effective on the stage, though it would "ask" some money. Oh, why haven't we a decent theatre! (Come and meet Sachs[3] tomorrow at the N.L.C., if you are in town—lunch 1.15). As to the N.C.T. I can say nothing for the present—certainly I could not possibly stand in the way of anyone else doing it—but I am not without hopes that we might be able to tackle it.[4]

Many of the choruses I like particularly—but indeed the whole thing seems to me essentially good. You have an amazing facility without flabbiness of rhyme, and I think the diction excellent. I enclose a few notes—but I read it too hastily to consider

1 *When We Dead Awaken.*

2 Professor Murray's translation of the *Hippolytus*.

3 The distinguished architect and expert in theatrical construction.

4 The New Century Theatre did eventually "tackle it", though not till some three and a half years later.

minutiæ of style and metre very carefully—I did not want to interrupt the swing of the reading. I hope you will let me see it in proof, even if I should not see it again in MS.

Yours ever,

W. A.

[At the end of December 1900 the *New York World* addressed to "many notable persons on this side of the Atlantic" the question: "What, in your opinion, is the chief danger, social or political, that confronts the coming century?" Archer's answer was:]

"I think the need of the coming century is some sort of socialism; while the danger is that it should take the form of a military socialism mechanically enforced, instead of a democratic socialism organically developed."

From George Bernard Shaw

6th June, 1901

THANKS for the letter.[1] I return it, having copied the missing postscript. . . .

The warning—Vixere fortes etc.[2]—is interesting: he went back to the XVIII century to avoid the XIX, instead of going on to the XX. I believe that was why he did not impress me much at the time: I regarded him as a man I had not time to attend to, whereas now I delight in his romances (prefer The Black Arrow to Jekyll and Hyde) and boil with indig-

[1] Stevenson's letter of 1886 about *Cashel Byron's Profession*. Mr. Shaw had asked Archer for it in order to make use, in his preface to a reprint of *Cashel Byron*, of the postscript, which had been omitted from the letter as printed in the *Letters of R. L. S.*

[2] Stevenson had written: "*Vixere fortes*—O, let him remember that —let him beware of his damned century; his gifts of insane chivalry and animated narrative are just those that might be slain and thrown out like an untimely birth by the Dæmon of the Epoch."

nation at the Philistinism which complains of Macaire as a billiard marker complains of classical music. As I grow older I become professionalized, and expect presently to find myself outdoing Walkley, Wedmore, and Henry James in self-confident cabotinage.

Bashville[1] is certainly a masterpiece. Henry Arthur implores me to pursue this wonderful vein and recognize that my true genius lies in burlesque. Unfortunately, as I have to write the works I burlesque, I should have to spend the latter half of my life caricaturing the former half, which I am likely enough to do without any prompting and with the most serious intentions.

G. B. S.

To CHARLES ARCHER

[IN TRAIN FROM PUTNEY BRIDGE,
Sept. 6, 1901

As this happens to be mail day, I must jot down, while it is fresh in my mind, some impressions of a quaint experience I have just had—a luncheon with Swinburne and Theodore Watts-Dunton. Watts (bother the Dunton) got a man named Douglas who is an admirer of his to invite me to meet him (Watts) at his (Douglas's) house some days ago, and then asked me down to lunch at The Pines. . . . The luncheon was great sport. They are the oddest little couple—I really felt my height quite embarrassing when I was standing between them. Both are deaf, Swinburne extremely so. Watts has no chin, and a long moustache, just like a walrus's tusk. . . . As for Swinburne, he has a really fine, massive head, almost bald; but is the quaintest little cock-sparrow

[1] *The Admirable Bashville.* Archer had no doubt expressed his admiration of that *tour de force.*

in his motions—indescribably comic. At lunch, in a room largely hung round with Rossettis, Swinburne had his bottle of ale and Watts drank soda-water—I alone had wine. Then we went to the study, and Watts proposed that A.C.S. should read me a scene from the tragedy of *Cæsar Borgia* that he is writing. Swinburne was nothing loth, and proceeded to serve out all that he had written—about an act and a half. If only that reading could have been recorded by a phonograph and kinetoscope it would have been immortal. Anything like the little man's nervousness you never saw. . . . The hand that was not holding the MS. was never for an instant still, but always shaking and quivering and going on quite indescribably. Sometimes he would snap his fingers without rhyme or reason, but generally it was simply a violent wiggle-waggle that he kept up. It all arose merely from his delight in the poetry—not from diffidence or nervousness in the ordinary sense. He was perfectly at his ease, and rolled and chanted the lines with a sort of fixed smile of delight on his face, looking across to Watts whenever he came to a particularly sonorous line; as much as to say: "What do you think of *that*, my boy?" Some of the lines and phrases were very fine. There was a gorgeous description of Lucrezia Borgia, and this struck me as very good, placed in the mouth of Alexander Borgia:

Fiends and fools are men
Who play the fiend that is not.

I was interested to find on questioning him that he had not a ghost of a plan in his head, but was simply maundering on at large, without the slightest idea of a theme to be worked out or even a catastrophe to be arrived at.

Then we looked over Swinburne's Elizabethan quartos, and parted the best of friends. It was really an *impayable* experience. I wish you had been there, and yet if you had been I doubt if we should have escaped without catastrophe. By the by, I ought to tell you that at Watts' request I had sent him some days ago a copy of *Peer Gynt*; but apparently his feelings on the subject were unfit for publication, for he said never a word about it. . . .

Din,

W. A.

[Extract]

21 *May*, 1902

Do you see *The Times* in your fastnesses? When you do, you ought really to read Walkley's criticisms. I think he is better in *The Times* than he ever was before. I don't know that any one has ever done wittier criticism—and very sound too, for the most part. . . .

From G. G. A. MURRAY

April 29, 1902

MY DEAR ARCHER,

I have to attend a lecture by that man Murray at Oxford on Saturday evening—something about Euripides, of course, as usual! Would it suit you to lunch at the N.L.C. at 1 on Saturday? I should have to catch some moderately early afternoon train. If not, I will revisit the glimpses on Monday

and come to wait on you,

Even in London, where, in order due,
The books of Man are published one by one,
The teeth of Man extracted two by two.

You might send me a postcard at 1 Palace Green,—I suppose you could not come and lunch there? . . .

The Sthenobœa of Euripides was a mighty fine play, and no one, except me and those to whom I have told it, knows the plot! I will tell it to you. It is slightly under the influence of Sardou.

Yours ever,
G. M.

From G. G. A. MURRAY

Nov. 11, 1902

MY DEAR ARCHER,

I fear I cannot come to the Committee[1] tomorrow. We have got a visitor for the night, and apart from that I have been so interrupted in my work lately that I don't like to go away for a day just now. . . .

I have heard of a religious sect which really attracts me: "The grass-eating Atheists of Ham Common, who slept with their toes out of window. . . ." A weary soul might find peace there. I can find nothing more about them nor why they had their toes out of window. It must have been a sublime reason.

I have got too much to do, and can't write or improve my mind. Among other things an article for the Quarterly on the Homeric Question: masses of work for no earthly utility. I used to think that no one on earth read the Quarterly, but I now hear that John Murray does, and that in two or three large asylums it is read aloud to the lunatics in bed at night. But that is not the real public for the Homeric Question.

Yours ever,
G. M.

[1] National Theatre Committee.

From G. G. A. MURRAY

Jan. 10, 1903

MY DEAR ARCHER,

. . . . .

I am in a state of enthusiasm over Yeats. It is a little milder now, but a few days ago it was dangerous. I had read many poems of his before, and liked them, but the Countess Cathleen and the Land of Heart's Desire quite took my breath away. I did not know there was anybody living (not even Lord Rosebery) who could write such poetry. I will admit that you told me to read the Countess some years ago. Of course I am haunted by an uncomfortable dread that I may wake up and find the element of make-believe and fairydom too unsatisfying. . . .

I am in the throes of a tragedy. I have done the first line; got all the characters and some half-dozen scenes including the last. But I don't know whether the Lord will allow me to go further.

Yours ever,

G. M.

[Postcard]

Jan. 20, '03

WHICH I meantersay, the extreme edge of my enthusiasm for a certain W B Y is indeed wore off, which I hasten to mention the same, lest misunderstanding should occur, as there is no need, nor was, and far be it from me. It was the prose works as done it. Which of course I meantersay it don't make the plays any less beautiful than they was before, not nowise; but them prose books, and more specially the pictures as they have let get in 'em, which between me an you, some things is a pity.

JOE GARGERY

[The following letters are interesting as shadowing forth the project which was to take shape in 1904 as the Vedrenne-Barker management at the Court, and was to make theatrical history.]

From Harley Granville-Barker

April 21, [1903?]

Dear Mr. Archer,

I want to trouble you with rather a long letter. Do you think there is anything in this idea? To take the Court Theatre for six months or a year and to run there a stock season of the uncommercial Drama: Hauptmann—Sudermann—Ibsen—Maeterlinck—Schnitzler—Shaw—Brieux, etc.

Not necessarily plays untried in England.

A fresh production every fortnight.

The highest price five or six shillings.

To be worked *mainly* as a subscription theatre.

One would require a guarantee of £5000—if possible 50 people putting down £100 each.

I think the working expenses could be kept to £250 a week. I would stake everything upon plays and acting—not attempt "productions".

It seems to me that we may wait a very long time for our National Theatre, and that when it comes we may have no modern National Drama to put in it. We must get vital drama from somewhere, and if we can't create it we must import it first.

I think there is a class of intellectual would-be playgoers who are profoundly bored by the theatre as it is. Matinee productions don't touch these people (who are all workers) and Sunday evening is expensive and incapable of expansion.

Our actors—and worse still our actresses—are becoming demoralized by lack of intellectual work—

the continual demand for nothing but smartness and prettiness.

I think the Independent Theatre—the New Century —The Stage Society—have prepared the ground, and the time is ripe for starting a theatre upon these lines, upon a regular — however unpretending— basis. . . .

As far as I can judge there are a greater number of people interested in the pioneer drama than ever there were, and it seems to me that the regular managers are more timid and conservative than ever.

There'll be nothing new to you in all this—but this idea has been with me very strongly lately. If I am right and the time is ripe and passes unnoticed it will be a thousand pities.

Without doubt the National Theatre will come— but as Ibsen has leavened the whole English Theatre during the past fifteen years—so we ought to be getting some more leaven ready for the National Theatre when it does come.

I have the scheme in rather more detail than I have put it here. Of course the guarantee of £5000 is the practically insurmountable obstacle.

Please forgive this "epistle".

Very sincerely yours,

H. GRANVILLE-BARKER

April 28 [1903]

DEAR MR. ARCHER,

I have been meaning to write and thank you for coming and having that long talk with me. It is helpful to me in my impatience to get under the wing of your knowledge and experience sometimes.

I don't think my "Court Theatre" scheme will come to anything, and it is perhaps better that it should not.

But I do hope the National Theatre will hurry up and that it will fall into Liberal or even Radical hands, and deliver us to some extent from the manager with the wooden head and the stage-manager with the iron hand, before another generation of actors (mine in this case) has gone to the devil artistically. . . .

Very sincerely yours,
H. GRANVILLE-BARKER

From GEORGE BERNARD SHAW
[Extract]

2nd September, 1903

. . . Your Chronicle Review[1] roused the greatest indignation here. . . . You really are a very curious character. You admit the superiority of my talent and wit. You are quite wrong. Incredible as it sometimes seems, you have just as much talent and wit as I have. You have all the tools of the trade, but you have no conscience. There are a great many men who sin against the light because they can't do without wine and cigars and a thousand a year or ten thousand. They go to hell because the train has first class carriages, whereas the train for heaven has third class ones. There are other men so fond of money that they take the hell train because the ticket costs twopence less than the other. But you are perfectly content with plain living, and care so little for money that any publisher can get the better of you in a bargain; and yet you don't think the train to heaven worth taking. There is an absolute gratuitousness about your perversity that is inexplicable unless one sees you as a sort of child in

[1] *Mr. Shaw's Pom-Pom*—Notice of *Man and Superman*—August 24, 1903.

fairyland who has never learnt to live in the world, and who resents the intrusion of moral problems as angrily as it joyfully welcomes the advent of the poetic glamor. Blugginess you don't object to at all —quite the contrary. Fun is quite acceptable. But conscience avaunt! you turn pettish at the first taste of it. If Tom had not a mother as well as a father he would never to the end of his days walk out of Peona. . . .

From THOMAS HARDY

MAX GATE,
11.2.04

MY DEAR ARCHER,

Many thanks for the book,[1] which I have been looking into with interest. Mrs. C[raigie]s talk is, I think, the best, as would be natural, she being such an amusing companion. This bears testimony to the honesty of your report.

I must also thank you for a review in the Daily Paper of The Dynasts—that faulty performance, as nobody knows better than I. On one matter I disagree with you: that blank verse must only be used for what is essential poetry. I hold that it may be applied to narrative, annalistic, or ironical matter that comes between more poetical matter, to preserve harmony with the general form. So that the House of Commons debate, which could not possibly be poetical, was a right subject to bring under its rhythm, in the circumstances.

Believe me,
Yours very truly,
THOMAS HARDY

[1] *Real Conversations.*

To G. G. A. MURRAY

18 *Oct.*, 1904

MY DEAR MURRAY,

I have left the *Troades* along with Meilhac and Halévy at the Club. It seems to me one of the noblest and most moving things I know, and if, as I gather, it has hitherto been looked down upon by "color che sanno", I am sure you have done Euripides a great service in illuminating and rehabilitating it. Your part of it is quite admirable. I want to read it in proof—type-writing always obscures things a little—but my general impression is that it's at least as good as either of the others.

BUT

don't let Barker seduce you into putting it on the stage. As part of a Euripides cycle at the National Theatre—yes, by all means. Or even without the National Theatre, if you produced two or three other tragedies successfully and made Euripides a popular dramatist, then it might do. But it would be madness to make it the second production and do it at the Court. Everything is against it. It is not a complete and independent work like the *Hippolytus*, but an epilogue to an epos. Its effect lies in the associations it awakens, which are practically non-existent to even a fairly educated English audience. "What's Hecuba to them or they to Hecuba?" Then again it has no unity, or rather it gets its unity solely from the aforesaid associations. It is a fantasia on the theme "Fuit Ilium". It might have served Aristotle for the model of the episodic play—perhaps it did, for aught I know. It would strike the audience as three or four plays in one, the first (the Cassandra-play) wholly incomprehensible. Then there is the external difficulty that it wants *four* great tragediennes—and we know how hard it is to find one. And if you found them the experience of the *Hippolytus* seems to show that male parts get over the footlights better than female. Altogether, I am convinced it would be a great mistake to attempt the *Troades* at this stage.

I liked the text of the *Hippolytus* enormously to-day. You are really enriching English literature with these things.

. . . . .

Yours ever,

W. A.

From WILLIAM WATSON

[Referring to review—*Morning Leader*, December 24, 1904—of the two-volume edition of Sir William (then Mr.) Watson's poems.]

Dec. 26, 1904

. . . I was extremely glad that you liked "Semmerwater".[1] The legend itself is certainly picturesque, I should fancy of Celtic origin, though I don't know. I got it from no very recondite source—a local guidebook which I found in the Rose and Crown Inn at Bainbridge, Wensleydale—a place within an hour's walk of the lonely little lake itself, which lies in a collateral valley. At Bainbridge, by the way, was a Roman station, and they say the custom of blowing a horn at nine o'clock in the evening throughout the winter months to call in wandering legionaries has been kept up there from ancient times continuously to this day! I saw the horn at present in use—a very grand implement, kept in a cottage on the green. Perhaps the Romano-Celtic people similarly handed

[1] *The Ballad of Semmerwater*. "Deep asleep, Deep asleep, etc."

down the legend of Semmerwater to the aftercomers. About a mile from Bainbridge, in a little grey farm-house still standing, lived a great-grandfather of mine, who is buried with various others of his tribe in the neighbouring churchyard of Ascrigg, in which village my mother was born. So, in short, I have a certain native right to the use of the Semmerwater legend.

I haven't half expressed my sense of indebtedness for your splendid reception of my book. And what makes your praise most valuable is that I know you say exactly what you think and feel. I should like very much to come to see you in the summer as you so kindly ask me.

Meanwhile and ever,

Yours sincerely,

WILLIAM WATSON

XIII

1905–1908

LET YOUTH BUT KNOW—THE *TRIBUNE*—*THE WORKS OF IBSEN*—SIMPLIFIED SPELLING—THE NATIONAL THEATRE—*THRO' AFRO-AMERICA*

When the year 1904 opened, Tom Archer had completed his schooling, leaving Dulwich College as head of the sixth form and captain of the school; and at the spring term he went up to Oxford with a Christ Church scholarship. There was thus no longer any compulsory tie to Dulwich, and, the requirements of Mrs. Archer's nerve-training work having outgrown the space available in a single suburban house, a move to roomier quarters and more bracing air was decided on. "Did I tell you", wrote Archer in August, "about our King's Langley project? We have practically taken 2 (*two*) houses in that rural paradise, and I am, in leisure moments, composing an Ode on the Distant Prospect of Bankruptcy." Before the year was out the move had been made, and the then quiet Hertfordshire village, in its typically English setting —"a stretch of undulating country, arable, grass and woodland; a slow river winding down a broad, softly-moulded valley"—was the country home of the family for the twenty years of life together that remained to them. But rooms had still to be retained in London for the work of both husband and wife, and it was at these—from 1910 onwards in a tall old house of Fitzroy Square—that, when he was in England, most of Archer's days were spent and most of his work done.

Ever since Tom Archer had left his childhood and Peona behind him, his father's thoughts had been much, and in later years anxiously, occupied with the question of his future. A clever and bookish boy, with an apparent bent towards "the humanities", he had naturally been entered on the classical side at Dulwich College. His school record was distinguished, but even there, and still more clearly when he went up to Oxford, it was apparent that this was due to general ability rather than to any real bent towards scholarship.

Nor was it easy to say where his true vocation lay. He had shown at times an inclination towards a soldier's life; though his delicacy as a young lad had prevented him from distinguishing himself in active sports, he was a keen volunteer, and an excellent marksman; but, since he displayed no special interest in military history or military theory, his father took this to be a passing, boyish fancy, due to the study of Kipling and to the lure of the pomp and circumstance of war. It was a natural enough view to take in the case of a lad of delicate physique, with a strong taste for books, and, by the testimony of all his masters, an unusual aptitude for classical study. Yet, with the wisdom which comes after the event, we may think it probable that the boy's military fancies were more significant than they were judged to be; that it was the call of a true vocation, as well as the needs of his country, that nine years later plunged him into the Great War at the earliest possible moment, and carried him to Messines, to the Somme, and in the end to Mount Kemmel.

If this be so, it may be supposed that the non-satisfaction of the young man's real bent had set up what would now be called a "complex", which inhibited intellectual effort in other directions. At all events, it soon became clear that Oxford was not his spiritual home. His work, while conscientious, was lacking in keenness; and though no athlete and much above the average in intellect, he seemed to have adopted, almost wilfully, the average athletic Englishman's attitude of absorption in play and slightly bored indifference to the things of the mind and spirit.

As we have already seen, Archer had long had a keen sense of all that he himself had missed through the deficiencies of the Scottish educational discipline of his boyhood. Now, with profound, almost passionate, regret he witnessed what seemed the failure of the English system at its best to awaken his son, a youth of bright promise, to any sense of the true meaning of life. Under the spur of this feeling the ideas on education which he had long been revolving found utterance in what is perhaps the most deeply felt of all his works, the volume *Let Youth But Know*, by "Kappa".

The keynote of this "little volume of sermons", as the author himself called it, is struck in the passage already quoted,[1] on the true end and object of a liberal education. It sounds again and again throughout the book, in passage after passage driving home the thesis that "the essential task of education must be to beget and foster in the youthful mind the power of vivid and reverent realization of the external and internal universe", or, as it is called elsewhere, "the religion of the intellect".[2]

The existing public-school system, he urged, with its wholly disproportionate allotment of time and energy to "grinding" at the classics and to the cult

[1] P. 32.

[2] The ethical side of the thesis, dealt with in the book's last section, is further developed in the address on "Knowledge and Character", delivered before the Moral Education League, February 6, 1914.

of athletics, not only involved, from this point of view, enormous waste, but actually tended, in the case of the average boy, to dull and deaden his spiritual perceptions. "We are compassed about with glories and mysteries", he exclaims, "and we feed our children's souls on Greek accents and bowling averages!" "Time is short", he says elsewhere, "and the wonders of the universe inexhaustible. It follows (does it not?) that we must distribute our little allotment of time to the best possible advantage for the exploration, both extensive and intensive, of this wonderland in which we are placed. We cannot afford to waste a moment of work-time (reasonable recreation-time is not wasted) on anything which does not contribute, or contributes only in a negligible degree, to our appreciation of the marvellous dealings of the all-efficient Power in nature and in the soul of man.

"Now a great part of our current classical training is, from this point of view, perhaps the idlest of mental exercises. . . ."

The reasonable course, he maintains, would be to initiate the child step by step into the wonders of "Aladdin's Palace"—flower-lore, plant-lore, earth-lore, cloud-lore, rock-lore, star-lore—and into the romance of the "Adventures of Sindbad"—the history of man on the earth—and to let him approach and tackle languages, at a comparatively mature age, through, and as a part of, history.

Written by a layman, and a layman who, as he tells us, had deliberately refrained from studying beforehand the recent authorities on the subject, the book naturally offers an easy target for the objector, particularly as regards its constructive proposals. The author acknowledges this, and characteristically supplies, at the end of the Introduction, a fairly full criticism of his own work, the gist of which lies in its first sentence: "The lack of practical experience in teaching is evident throughout, and along with it the pure theorist's tendency to ignore or minimize the element of friction."[1]

Yet so inspiring is its general thesis, and so pregnant with suggestion its concrete proposals, even when least practical, that parents and guardians, masters, and even intelligent boys, may well find interest and profit in it. Its influence might have been wider if the circumstances of its origin had not dictated anonymity. But it did its part in shaping opinion, and one receives the impression that such progress as has been made in public-school education in the past twenty years has on the whole followed lines not remote from those advocated by Kappa.[2]

Though it was with no very great eagerness that Archer took up his post on the *Tribune*, he yet set to work with vigour to do all he could towards making the paper a power in the theatrical world. A carefully thought out "Private and Confidential" *Sketch of Policy for Theatrical Department* evidently dates from this time.

Whether success would have attended the policy

[1] This view of the matter was put, by a Scotch lady of his acquaintance, in a form which he relished greatly. The book, she said, reminded her of Cuddie Headrigg's account of his interview with his devout mother Mause on the eve of his trial: "Ou! she was juist bleezin' awa aboot a weddin' garment, when the job is, hoo to win by hangin'."

[2] "If I have made any addition at all to the stock of ideas upon education", writes Archer, "it is to be found, I think, in the co-ordination of History with Science, and the subordination of language to the very much widened concept of History." There seems some prospect that this idea may be realized now that Mr. H. G. Wells, in his *Outline of History*, has made a magnificent essay towards providing the necessary apparatus.

sketched, had the paper made good its footing amongst the great dailies, we can only conjecture. As things fell out, time to test its soundness was lacking, for the *Tribune* endured for two years only, coming to an end in February 1908, just when, in the opinion of some judges, it was within measurable distance of success. Archer's not very confident hope of acquiring, as critic of a daily paper, the influence which he had thought to be lacking to him on the *World*, thus remained unfulfilled.

For him, personally, the demise of the *Tribune* was doubtless a fortunate misfortune. The work that had fallen to him on the paper was heavy, including, besides a weekly column "About the Theatre", a large proportion of the overnight notices of current productions; and while his keenness for the betterment of the drama was, and remained to the end, unblunted, the physical strain of constant theatre-going must have been beginning to tell, and the other interests which his devotion to the drama had kept in the background were pushing more and more insistently to the front. "For myself", he wrote to Gilbert Murray in announcing the decease of the paper, "you can't think what a joy it is *not* to be going to the Sicilian Players tonight and to *The Woman from Kronstadt* tomorrow. But the holiday mustn't last too long. If only I could see something else than dramatic criticism at the end of it!"

None the less had these two years brought many theatrical events which interested him deeply. They covered the last eighteen months of the Vedrenne-Barker Court campaign, and the beginning of that management's less successful venture at the Savoy; and saw the production of much notable work, including Pinero's *His House in Order*, Shaw's *The Doctor's Dilemma*, and two striking plays by new dramatists, Galsworthy's *Silver Box* and Synge's *Playboy of the Western World*. And Archer's criticisms showed no signs of weariness, or of failing devotion to the causes he had at heart. His weekly column, too, gave him the means of dealing, more fully than had been possible in his *World* criticisms, with general questions of dramatic technique, and with the inter-relations of drama and life. Some of the technical matter he afterwards used in his volume *Playmaking*; but much interesting work remains as yet undisturbed in the files of the paper. Of these latter articles, one of the most notable is that entitled *Death and Mr. Bernard Shaw*,[1] in which he threw out the challenge that led to the production of *The Doctor's Dilemma*.

In the *Tribune*, too, appeared the first-fruits of an inquiry into the construction and conditions of the Elizabethan theatre, on which he had been engaged for some time past. He had long felt the importance of such an inquiry as a means of throwing light on the Elizabethan and Jacobean drama in general and on Shakespeare in particular, and in his friend Mr. W. J. Lawrence, who has since become so well known in this line of research, he found an enthusiastic helper. Their plan for a comprehensive treatise on the subject, to be written in collaboration, was never carried out, Archer's attention having been to some extent diverted by larger interests;[2] but, as the

[1] *Tribune*, July 14, 1906. See p. 296 below.

[2] "His temporary lukewarmness", writes Mr. Lawrence, "was a great grief to me, seeing that there were problems before which the unperceiving academic mind stood baffled, and which demanded the clear thinking which he almost alone could give, for their solution."

A selection from Archer's copious notes on the Elizabethan Playhouse (with an elucidatory preface kindly supplied by Mr. Lawrence) has found a fitting home in the admirably organized Dramatic Museum of Columbia University, New York, the creation of his friend, Professor Brander Matthews.

bibliographic appendix shows, much valuable work was done now and later towards clearing up the difficult problems involved.

Ever since, at the turn of the century, the sorrowful fact had become apparent that the Ibsen drama had indeed come to an end with the "epilogue", *When We Dead Awaken,* Archer had been engaged on a last thoroughgoing revision of his versions of the whole series of plays, with a view to a complete definitive edition. This began to appear in 1906, the year of the poet's death, and by 1908 was complete, in eleven volumes.[1] The text of this edition was the result of minute scrutiny and weighing of every speech, almost of every word, in the whole long series, often in consultation with friends and helpers; while the introductions which had been prefixed to the earlier versions, play by play, were also rewritten, and amplified by the inclusion of critical remarks.[2] Forty years had passed since *Pillars of Society* had reached the young journalist hot from the press, and he had "dashed off a translation in less than a week"; and thirty since, in his own words, "it slowly dawned upon me that the translation and editing of Ibsen's works was to be one of the chief labours, as it has certainly been one of the greatest privileges, of my life. Since 1887, or thereabouts", he goes on, "not many months have passed in which a considerable portion of my time has not been devoted to acting, in one form or another, as intermediary between Ibsen and the English-speaking public. . . . I can only trust that, by diligence in seeking for the best

[1] A twelfth volume, *From Ibsen's Workshop,* containing the poet's first drafts of many plays, was added in 1912.

[2] The introductions to *Love's Comedy* and *Brand* were furnished by the translator of those plays, Professor C. H. Herford.

interpretation of his thoughts, I have paid some part of my debt to that great spirit, and to the glorious country that gave him birth."

The results of this long labour of love have been variously appraised. The accuracy of the translations has been generally recognized, and their spirit has not wanted admirers; but in their earlier form, as we have seen,[1] they were attacked by some as being excessively colloquial in style; while it has more recently been the fashion, in some quarters, to depreciate the final text as being too literal, stiff, and stilted. Time must decide how far this complaint is justified, or how far it merely indicates that Archer's versions are, as he says, "translations, not paraphrases", and that actors, naturally inclined to follow the line of least resistance, prefer the results of paraphrase to those of translation. At all events it may safely be said that in the history of literature there have been few cases in which a task of translation of comparable magnitude has been carried out with a more loving care.

The movement for the reform of our chaotic spelling, which had languished since the 1860's, when the Spelling Reform Association had numbered among its members many of the most distinguished men of the time, had begun, with the new century, to show signs of fresh vitality both in America and England; and as early as 1901 Archer had[2] urged the case for moderate reform. In 1906, when the Simplified Spelling Board came into being in New York, and began to issue leaflets containing concrete proposals, and again when the question was forced into prominence by President Roosevelt's action in ordering the

[1] See letters, pp. 224–27.
[2] *Morning Leader*, August 10 and 24, 1901.

adoption in official documents of the changes proposed, Archer ranged himself on the side of the Board's propaganda (while criticizing the timidity and tentativeness of its proposals) in *Morning Leader* articles, and in a closely reasoned paper in the *Fortnightly Review*. Along with Professor Skeat, Dr. Furnivall, and other distinguished advocates of reform, he was invited to join the Board as an English member, and in March 1907 he writes to Gilbert Murray: "As a reward for spelling badly I am offered a free trip across the Atlantic to attend a meeting of the Simplified Spelling Board. It is on the cards (though scarcely probable) that I may go." The temptation proved too strong to be resisted. He spent something over three weeks in America, and during this visit, and again in 1908, when, as we shall see, he revisited the States on other business, a plan of campaign for England was doubtless discussed with the American Board and with Mr. Andrew Carnegie, the munificent supporter of the movement. In September 1908 the English Simplified Spelling Society was constituted, with Professor Skeat as its first President. Archer was offered and accepted the post of Secretary, and opened the office in Great Russell Street; and for several years to come much of his time was given to the organization of the Society, and to the furtherance of its objects by the usual methods of propaganda—pamphlets, newspaper articles and lectures. From 1909 onwards he was closely associated in this work with Professor Walter Ripman, who had meanwhile joined the Society. An important step was taken when, in 1910, the two in consultation prepared and submitted to the English and American Committees a comprehensive scheme[1] for simplification which

[1] Proposals for a Simplified Spelling of the English Language.

served as a basis for discussion at the various conferences held in the ensuing years. In 1909, again (with Professor Ripman) in 1911, and once more in the spring of 1914, we find Archer attending meetings of the New York Board, in the course of visits to America undertaken in part with that object; and, though he resigned the Secretaryship at the end of 1911, he continued for some years to take an active part in the proceedings of the Society, and to write and lecture on its behalf. Even after the war had thrust all minor interests into the background, he retained his belief in the cause, and in the last year of his life was a member of the deputation which presented to the President of the Board of Education a memorial urging the appointment of a Commission on Spelling Reform.

In his speech[1] in New York, at the inaugural dinner of 1907, Archer had laid stress on the difficulty of the task which confronted the reformers. The task was indeed even harder, the prejudice against change even fiercer, than he foresaw, and, if despondency had been in his line, he might well have desponded towards the end when he saw how little apparent progress had been made. But that things had so fallen out was certainly no fault of his. "His keenly critical spirit and clear and convincing pen", writes Professor Ripman, "were of very great service to the movement . . .; above all it was of inestimable value that a man of his wide reputation for sanity and sobriety of judgment should have led what so many were inclined to regard as a harebrained enterprise. His analysis of the current objections to spelling reform was unsurpassed."

Talking of the apparition of the spirits of the dead, Johnson remarked: "All argument is against it, but

[1] "A Speech on Spelling", *Morning Leader*, April 20, 1907.

all belief is for it." Of Spelling Reform we may almost say: "All argument is for it, but all feeling is against it." Yet reason, though a less powerful, is a more persistent force than feeling based on prejudice, and, even in England, often wins, in the long run, unlooked for victories. In this matter also the forts of prejudice may one day fall, and the work done by Archer and his fellow-pioneers in digging the first parallels may then receive its due recognition.

Being now no longer so strictly tied to the London theatres, and having, in the Simplified Spelling campaign, a second employment which rather encouraged wandering, since it took him from time to time across the Atlantic, Archer was free in these years to investigate the politico-social questions which had begun to interest him more and more, and at the same time to indulge his inherited love of travel, by undertaking a series of roving missions (made possible by the liberal policy of an excellent American magazine, *McClure's*) which led him over a great part of the United States and the West Indies, to Spain, Portugal, Mexico, and Russia, and eventually, for the second time, round the world. In March 1908 he crosses the Atlantic with Granville-Barker, in part to explore the possibilities opened out by a suggestion which had been put forward the year before, that one or both of them might join the directing staff of the "New Theatre", the repertory enterprise about to be set on foot in New York by a group of art-loving millionaires. The proposal came to nothing. But the episode was none the less a fortunate one, since it led to Archer's appointment from the close of the year as adviser to the management in respect of plays produced in Europe, a congenial post which he held, with advantage to the theatre and to his own finances, while the enterprise lasted; and this in turn was the beginning of a friendship with Mr. Winthrop Ames, the accomplished manager and producer who was ultimately appointed Director—a friendship which in itself and its consequences was to mean much in later years.

This business disposed of, he set out in pursuit of his main object—that of getting in touch with the facts of the colour problem, to his thinking one of the most urgent questions of the coming century, in the area where it was at that time acutest, the Southern States of the Union.

From Washington, where, under the conduct of the British Ambassador, Mr. Bryce, he renewed his acquaintance[1] with Theodore Roosevelt, now President of the United States, he followed a zigzag course through the Southern States east of the Mississippi, visiting all the most important centres, and everywhere using the introductions he had provided himself with, and the opportunities of travel, to get into touch with the representatives of the two (or the three) races. Then, crossing to Cuba, and thence to Jamaica ("where", he confesses, "I was too much occupied in sheer enjoyment of life to pursue with any ardour my researches into the colour question"), he paid a flying visit to the Panama Canal, now nearing completion, and returned to England in mid-June.

[1] At this time President Roosevelt was in the thick of one of his controversies with the Senate. The conversation happening to turn on a recent occurrence in the Senate of a Western State, where, during a sitting, someone had shot, or shot at, one of the Senators, Mr. Bryce made a playful suggestion that possibly, in the President's view, one or two of the members of the U.S. Senate might be "none the worse" for a similar experience. "Mr. Ambassador", said the President, slowly and gravely, "they might shoot—*at—random*."

The outcome of this journey was *Thro' Afro-America*,[1] a book which disappointed extreme advocates of the equality of the races, but gained the approval of some high authorities. A letter[2] from one of these, Mr. (afterwards Lord) Bryce, excellently summarizes its main conclusions.

On his return to England the traveller learned with delight that during his three months' absence the National Theatre movement had gained a notable reinforcement by the accession of the ardent Shakespeareans who had for some time past been agitating for the erection of an architectural memorial as a "world's tribute" to the poet at the approaching tercentenary of his death. "I found", he says, "that the idea of a National Shakespeare Memorial Theatre (whatever it may be called 'for short') was accepted in principle on all hands. I found an influential and widely representative body of men and women prepared to devote their best energies to its realization. . . . I found, in short, that the Utopian dream of yesterday had to-day taken a prominent position in the region of practical politics; and my heart was uplifted within me."

At the chequered history of this scheme—the high hopes and fair prospects of the early years, the forced suspension of the original plan following on the outbreak of the war, its revival on the return of peace in the face of difficulties doubled or quadrupled by the enormous increase of prices and the dislocation of men's minds and energies caused by the great convulsion, and its later struggle with manifold hindrances—at all this we can only glance in passing.

[1] Embodying a series of *Westminster* articles, and a review of the problem—"Black and White in the South"—in *McClure's Magazine*.

[2] P. 306 below.

It must suffice to say that during the sixteen years that remained to him the Shakespeare Memorial Theatre took much the same place in Archer's life that had theretofore been occupied by his work as an interpreter of Ibsen; few months passed in which a good part of his time and energy was not devoted to it. His numerous published articles and voluminous private correspondence dealing with the scheme represent only a part of his activities in the cause. Much time had to be given to service on committees, a type of activity little to his liking, for his patience was tried by the drawbacks inseparable from committee procedure in a matter involving many conflicting interests and many questions of individual taste—the delays, the fumbling, and the inevitable compromises—and his exaggerated sense of his deficiencies as a committee-man gave him sometimes an uneasy feeling that he was in part to blame for the slowness of the progress made. Yet he was never permanently discouraged, and we shall see the scheme towards the end taking an even more prominent place among his interests.

Meanwhile, to supplement the small salary derived from the Simplified Spelling Secretaryship, and the not very large income from the *Morning Leader* and his miscellaneous writings, he had fallen back once more on dramatic criticism, becoming, in November 1908, theatrical critic to the *Nation*, the weekly paper edited by H. W. Massingham. The paper had not a wide circulation among the theatre-going public, and, unlike the *World* and the *Tribune*, it did not lay itself out to record the general theatrical movement by noticing all productions at the chief London theatres. Its policy of taking cognizance only of specially significant productions suited Archer, from one point of view, since it left him comparatively foot-loose; but it gave him from the first a sense of being out of place, for to him, as he said, the interest of dramatic criticism lay "far less in the individual plays than in their relation to the general dramatic movement". And there were obvious risks of disagreement as to what were the "significant productions" that should be noticed.

The solitary public honour that fell to Archer's lot—the only one, probably, which he would have cared to accept—had come to him this year, when King Haakon VII of Norway conferred on him the Knighthood of the Order of St. Olav. No honour, we may be sure, could have more deeply gratified him than this recognition of the work he had done for his second fatherland and its literature.

XIIIa

LETTERS OF 1906–1911

From George Bernard Shaw

10th July, 1906

. . . Your remark[1] in the Tribune that a masterpiece is a play whose faults you learn to endure is a perfect breath-bereaver. You discover that my faults were only your blunders; and that is how you put it! And you still talk about "a farce". The thing is a poem and a document, a sermon and a festival, all in one. As to Valentine bamboozling the girl, was there ever such confusion of thought as your conclusion that he was unpoetic and insincere? He won her by perfectly legitimate strategy, she having defied him and pitted her heartlessness with contemptuous confidence against him. . . . Impervious Scotch rationalist that you are! Oh Jerusalem, thou that killest the prophets!!! . . .

You came up against it last night for the first time; and you only smile and scratch your nose as if I had poked it with an umbrella.

G. B. S.

10 Adelphi Terrace, W.C.

[1906]

Exclusive to the Tribune

Mr. Bernard Shaw has been taking advantage of his seaside holiday in Cornwall to write a new play. It will be of special interest to readers of the Tribune,

[1] "What is a Classic? It may be defined, perhaps, as a piece of work to whose faults we have grown blind." Notice of *You Never Can Tell*, *Tribune*, July 1906.

as it is the outcome of the article in which Mr. William Archer penned a remarkable dithyramb[1] to Death, and denied that Mr. Shaw could claim the highest rank as a dramatist until he had faced the King of Terrors on the stage. Stung by this reproach from his old friend, Mr. Shaw is writing a play all about Death, which he declares will be the most amusing play he has ever written. However, he has not evaded the challenge by a quip: the play is in five acts, with the fatal situation in the correct position—at the end of the fourth. The death scene will be unlike any ever before represented; and the consultations of the doctors will give full scope for the author's knowledge of modern therapeutics and for his views on the medical profession. The play, which is to be called *The Doctor's Dilemma*, will be one of the features of the forthcoming season under the Vedrenne-Barker management.

What price tragedy now?
Yah!

[1] In an article in the *Clarion*, June 1, 1906, Shaw had reproached the great writers of the past century, and Ibsen in particular, with making excessive and inartistic use of death as a motive in their novels and plays. In the course of his reply Archer said: "There may come a time, perhaps, when, to the vast majority of men, death will be scarcely more tragic than falling asleep. . . . But in the meantime, while death is still the touchstone of character, the supreme test of fortitude, the refuge of despair, the consecrator of greatness, the desecrator of loveliness, the crass intruder and the deliverer yearned for in vain, the matchless stimulant, the infallible anodyne, the signature to the stave of life, the mystery and the solution, the problem and the key—so long, in fine, as men and women envisage humanly the ultimate adventure of humanity—so long will the dramatic poet have recourse without shame to what is, in fact, the most penetrating search-light in the armoury of his craft. It is not the glory, but the limitation of Mr. Shaw's theatre that it is peopled by immortals." "Death and Mr. Bernard Shaw", *Tribune*, July 14, 1906.

From EDMUND GOSSE

31.10.07

MY DEAR ARCHER,

It is a very great satisfaction and pleasure to me to know that you are so well pleased with "F[ather] and S[on]". It tempers my acute disappointment that I am to miss the "golden largess" of a review from you. Was there ever such bad luck—to drop from quite the most indulgent and intelligent reader that I am ever likely to possess, to the least sympathetic possible, for I believe Mr. —— is particularly hostile to everything I write? Well, these are the things we have to bear.

I remember Browning saying to me that, old as he was, he never ceased to suffer from "puerperal fever" immediately after having published a book! If *he* did so, it is some comfort to a feverish minor mortal who has shamefacedly to confess that he suffers from a like infirmity. But this particular book causes me more nervous anxiety than anything I ever published before.

Well, thank you indeed for your kind, warm letter. Some day soon I hope you will let me talk to you about your own early experiences.

Yours very sincerely,

EDMUND GOSSE

To A. W. PINERO, ESQ.

NATIONAL LIBERAL CLUB,
14*th Novr.* 1907

MY DEAR PINERO,

Your handsome testimonial[1] fell as balm upon a wounded spirit. Only a few hours before, I had

[1] A burlesque testimonial, ending: "He is also strictly sober and clean in his habits and person."

received a letter[1] from an actor-manager—which his initials are *not* H. B. T.—saying that "he does not object to my unfairness, which is proverbial, but he does object to my impertinence". And what do you think was the impertinence? He sends me the cutting underlined. I had actually forgotten myself so far as to say that: "He is not a man of rich or deeply poetic imagination!" I have a considerable collection of such missives, but this, I think, is the masterpiece. I shall have it framed.

I hope C-B. is not going to funk the encounter with the infuriated dramatists.

Yours ever,

W. A.

DEAR MR. X.,

My first impulse was not to answer your letter; but silence might seem to indicate a resentment which I am far from feeling.

I am sorry we differ as to the quality of your imagination. Of course you may very likely be right and I wrong. In that case you will go down to posterity as a very great actor, instead of what I think you—an able and very valuable artist. Need I add that nothing would please me more than to be converted to your view? You actors perhaps do not realize what a delight it would be to a critic to hail a new Kean or Salvini—if only he could.

Of course you know the text of Shakespeare better than I do, since it is your business to study and repeat it. Whether you can feel its beauties better than I, and can perfectly convey what you feel, is a different question.

There never was a critic worth his salt, my dear Mr. X., who was not "proverbial for his unfairness".

[1] See W. A.'s reply below.

If I continue to write criticism, and you continue to do good work as an actor and manager, I am not without hope that you may one day view my imperfections with a more tolerant eye.

Yours truly,

W. A.

From WILLIAM WATSON

[Some speculations as to Coleridge's probable intentions with regard to the conclusion of *Christabel* had been formulated by Sir William Watson in a paper (never published) of which he had sent a copy to William Archer for remarks. In reply to Archer's letter of remarks and suggestions, he writes:]

Dec. 3, 1907

MY DEAR ARCHER,

I owe you many thanks for your very interesting letter just received, and for the careful attention you have given to the matter which I wrote about. I quite feel the force and pertinence of your query as to "the *method* by which Geraldine's blemish is to be transferred to Christabel". As you say, it cannot be physical contact—unless the process is to be supposed a gradual one, not taking effect immediately. Physical contact does work the spell which forbids Christabel to tell of the dreadful sight which she has seen:

"In the touch of this bosom there worketh a spell
Which is lord of thy utterance, Christabel", etc., etc.

I myself had thought of what you suggest when you say: "Was it by inducing some moral lapse on C.'s part?" As you say, Geraldine's identity does not really affect my theory, though the lines which you instance ("Sir Leoline, a moment's space," etc.) certainly go some way to establish her claim to be his old friend's daughter. But that again conflicts with the theory of her being a demon—a theory, which, as you emphasise, seems to receive such strong support from the incident of the lifting over the threshold "with might and main".

To your question whether I think that Coleridge really knew how he intended to finish the poem, I am inclined to answer affirmatively—there are so many incidents and little details which seem gratuitous unless we regard them as threads which are to be caught up later on. In some ways they remind me curiously of certain phenomena of dreams—of the kind of dreams which Frederick Greenwood calls "proleptic". You dream an incident which when it occurs seems perfectly inexplicable, but presently something else happens which makes the first incident intelligible and natural, seeming to suggest that there are two cerebral hemispheres at work, one originating problems or situations which the other states without an inkling of their solution, after which hemisphere No. I resumes its part and supplies the necessary illuminative sequel.

At any rate what you say fortifies me to make further study of *Christabel* and state my case more carefully and fully than in the paper which I sent you—as well as modifying it in some particulars in accordance with your own impressions.

I follow you with much interest in the *Tribune* with regard to dramatic matters, though I am not sure that I can range myself always on your side. I might find it difficult to state or define any æsthetic law or principle which "rules out" purely pathological, physiological, or surgical matter from the domain of art, but yet I have a feeling that such things as "illegal operations" have no proper place in drama or literature. . . . I felt, too, with respect to what you lately said about the avidity with which plays were *read* in the 18th century, that the explanation lay very largely in the "literary diction" which you deprecate on the stage. I fancy my own pleasure in reading a play would be almost in inverse ratio to the lifelikeness of the dialogue or colloquy. The blaze of wit in Sheridan, or the glow of poetry in Shakespeare, is quite unlifelike, and is delightful in proportion to its infidelity to nature. After all, as "somebody" says, art is art chiefly because it is not nature. . . .

But these are idle and irresponsible scribblings which have no value except as attesting the interest I feel—the very strong interest—in your dramatic criticism; and you must not waste your time—which can be vastly better employed—in answering me or in any way bothering about what I say. I have no doubt fifty other people have said the same thing—probably much better.

Ever, my dear Archer,

Yours sincerely,

WILLIAM WATSON

To CHARLES ARCHER

CHARLESTON, S.G.,
4 *May*, 1908

[Extract]

I received this morning your letter of April 5 . . . in which you take me to task for my onslaught on the Conservative spirit. I have the vaguest recollection of what I said, but of course it was (and was meant to be) something of an over-statement. I had neither the space nor the desire to state the necessary qualifications. But I was not attacking conservatism in individual political measures. . . . What I was trying to bring out was the contrast between the spirit that looks forward and the spirit that looks back: the spirit which cannot conceive the world other than it is (with a few trifling modifications of detail) and the spirit which realizes that the world must [some day?] inevitably be utterly different from that which we know—and immeasurably juster, humaner and more beautiful—and which seeks to minimize the mental friction involved in its passage to this inconceivable, and yet absolutely certain, future—certain, that is, unless the conservative, the static, spirit should get the upper hand, and mankind should become a regimented army of serfs driven to labour by a military oligarchy. (There is a sentence for you!) Of course you are quite right in saying that a recognition of facts as they are is the beginning of wisdom; but I think we ought also to recognize that psychological facts (which are the determinant elements of the future) are infinitely plastic, and that this is just what conservative psychology forgets or denies, thereby giving no end of unnecessary trouble. . . . Here, in this city, is buried a brother of A. H. Clough, who wrote an inscription on his grave; and that inscription has recalled to my mind the verses:—

Say not the struggle naught availeth,
  The labour and the wounds are vain;
The enemy faints not nor faileth,
  And as things have been, things remain.

. . . .

If hopes were dupes, fears may be liars;
  It may be, in yon smoke concealed,
Your comrades chase e'en now the fliers,
  And, but for you, possess the field.

The first phrase underlined sums up the conservative instinct which I attack, because I believe it to be flagrantly untrue—the exact opposite of the truth. The second [underlined] phrase seems to me magnificently and inspiringly true. It is not so much our own stupidity and self-seeking that retards the march of things, as the invincible cynicism with which we believe in the stupidity and self-seeking of everyone else—and are intimidated and paralysed by that belief. . . .

From GEORGE BERNARD SHAW

[Postcard]

[STOCKHOLM, postmark 17.7.08]

I achieved the impossible—a meeting with Strindberg—today. He said "Archer is not in sympathy with me".[1] I said "Archer wasn't in sympathy with Ibsen either; but he couldn't help translating him all the same, being accessible to poetry, though otherwise totally impenetrable." After some further conversation, consisting mainly of embarrassed silences and a pale smile or two by A. S. and floods of energetic eloquence in a fearful lingo, half French, half German, by G. B. S., A. S. took out his watch and said, in German: "At two o'clock I am going to be sick." The visitors accepted this delicate intimation, and withdrew.

G. B. S.

[Postcard]

[BAYREUTH, 1908]

This place, as far as the theatre is concerned, is incredibly unchanged: it is exactly as if you and I

[1] No doubt referring to a suggestion by G. B. S. that Archer should translate Strindberg's plays.

and Dibdin (Dibdin's dead, by the way, isn't he?) were there yesterday. The industrial end of the town has developed: there are more factories. The lunatic asylum has the same air of being deserted for the theatre. Richter looks older; so do I: otherwise it only needs you to be here (since you don't change) to make the illusion of yesterday complete. You will collapse some day like the one-horse-shay if you don't age naturally.

G. B. S.

[Archer having assured his friend that Dibdin was very much alive, and was Curator of the Walker Art Gallery at Liverpool, G. B. S. rejoins:]

MÜNCHEN, *6th August*, 1908

I am not at all satisfied about this Dibdin business. I saw the man's obituary notice; I said "Alas, poor Yorick" over him; I reflected on the shortness of the period during which I could hope to survive him; I thought of the many worse men I could have better spared; and at last I became resigned to the loss and invested his memory with a certain poetry. And now he upsets me and falsifies history by not being dead at all. I am not disposed to accept your rather off-hand and unfeeling statement without some investigation. I am going to Liverpool to lecture in October; and I shall make a point of visiting the Walker gallery (the name is suspicious) and satisfying myself that the alleged curator is really Dibdin. If not, I shall tell the impostor what I think of him. If so, I shall do my best to resume our old relations with as little sense of anti-climax as possible.

Somehow, strange things are happening. You will not attempt to deny that Davenport Adams has been dead many a long day; yet I saw him to-night at the Residenz Theatre, listening to Mozart's *Figaro's Hochzeit*—in which, by the way, the part of Figaro was taken by T. P. O'Connor. Perhaps he is dead too: I haven't seen an English paper for a month past. There was a time that when the brains were out the man was dead; and if there was a man in the world at whom Macbeth might have pointed this remark, it was Davenport Adams; and yet there he was pushing the Residenz opera-goers from their stalls, as large as life. I have not seen Joe Knight yet, but shall probably do so in the course of the week.

The hand of Providence was shown plainly on my arrival here yesterday by the sudden revival at the Residenz, for one night only, of *Candida* and *How He Lied*. I asked the hotel porter to get me tickets. He told me that I was mistaken about the play—that it was in German and that I would not understand it. I said I would go all the same. He then told me to pay at the doors, as the house would be empty. I thanked him and took his advice, which I found to be based on fact. Eugene was a thick-necked young motor agent out for a bank holiday, in a striped suit and collar of the flashest fancy. Morell was an Archimandrite who would have put Moses out of countenance on Mount Pisgah. His hair came down to his shoulders; and his coat came down to his ankles. Candida was not at all bad for a Gertrude Kingston sort of woman. Burgess made me laugh, and even gave me some tips in the way of stage business. They played it straight through in 90 minutes, dropping the curtain for a moment only, and hurrying on as if the police were at their heels. In *How He Lied* (same cast) Morell lifted Eugene on to the keyboard of the piano and bumped the bass with him. The woman was again good; but the thick-necked Bursch made the piece simply disgusting. On the whole, it was a devastating experience, and confirms my opinion that Germany has everything to learn from Vedrenne and Barker.

G. B. S.

From JAMES BRYCE

21 Aug., 1911

DEAR MR. ARCHER,

Thank you very much for the copy of your book "Through Afro-America," which I have read with great interest and with general agreement in your observations and conclusions. Three points especially seem to me to be stated by you with much force and truth, viz.:

That there is no use trying to pooh pooh the Southern repugnance to the negro. It is an ultimate fact; and whoever lives among black people gets to understand it.

There is a dangerous side to negro progress. The richer and more educated he becomes, the less will he bear insult and injury; and the more may the worse sort of Southern white fear him.

A general mixture of blood would be a misfortune for the human race. It may be, as you say, increasingly difficult to prevent it. But the Americans are right to try. If they could prevent illicit intercourse as well as marriage, they perhaps would try that.

Segregation is desirable—is on the whole the most practicable remedy. But the difficulties are immense. There is really now no vacant space for the negro in the U.S.A. No existing State would consent to be given over to negroes. When one sees how statesmen fumble over simpler problems, one expects nothing in our time towards a real grappling with this one.

Meantime, there seems to me to be nothing for it but to try to make the negro more useful to the white as well as himself, and hope that the Southern white may slowly mend his temper and his manners. They have slightly mended in the last twenty years.

. . . . .

Believe me

Very truly yours,

JAMES BRYCE

XIV

1908–1911

THE CENSORSHIP AGAIN—*FRANCISCO FERRER*—MEXICO—SHIPWRECK

THE two years 1908 and 1909, not barren in important productions (Galsworthy's *Strife* and *Justice*, Pinero's *Mid-Channel*, and Granville-Barker's *Madras House* belong to this time), were also notable in theatrical annals as marking the climax of the anti-Censorship movement, which had been steadily though slowly spreading and gaining strength ever since the institution had received the blessing of the Select Committee of 1892. The Examiners of Plays who had held office during these years (or the Lord Chamberlains who nominally controlled their actions) had not shown much tact in exercising their unpopular functions, nor much agility in avoiding the pitfalls of inconsistency and absurdity with which the paths of all Censors, and particularly Censors of the acted drama, are thickly beset. Their proceedings had given much warrant for the contention of the opposition, that the Censorship operated, in the main, on the one hand to protect frivolous licence from the control of public opinion, and on the other hand to suppress serious thought. At each instance of the licensing of what is described in Blue-Book language as "frivolity trenching on indecency", or of the vetoing of classic masterpieces or of modern dramas of ideas, the assault on the institution had been renewed with ever-increasing vigour, and Archer had been in the forefront of the attack. And in these twenty-five years a body of dramatists had arisen who were no longer disposed to suffer without protest the arbitrary suppression or mutilation of their work, and whose numbers and literary standing made it inexpedient altogether to ignore their protests.

Before the new century was far advanced the Censorship was put on its trial once more. In 1907, shortly after it had committed one of the most harmful of its harmful deeds in vetoing Granville-Barker's tragedy, *Waste*, the dramatists decided on concerted action. The Prime Minister's consent was sought and obtained to receive a deputation on the subject, and in the meantime a strong protest against the Censorship, signed by seventy-one authors, appeared in the Press, the list of signatories including, besides practically all the working dramatists of the day, a number of leaders in the world of letters, potential rather than actual dramatists, such as Conrad, Hardy, Frederic Harrison, Henry James, Meredith, and Swinburne. The deputation, after some delay due to Sir Henry Campbell-Bannerman's illness, was at last received on February 25, 1908, by the Home Secretary on behalf of the Prime Minister, being introduced by Mr. J. M. Barrie and Sir W. S. Gilbert. The Home Secretary, Mr. Gladstone, "could only promise to represent the deputation's views to the Prime Minister"; and the matter stood over for more than a year, when the deliberations of the official mind issued in the appointment of a "Joint Select Committee on the Stage Plays (Censorship)".

The proceedings of the Committee, which met on July 28, 1909, examined forty-nine witnesses, and continued its deliberations till November 2nd, may be studied at large in a portly and very interesting Blue Book of xl+375 pages. This time the odds in favour of the established order were not so overwhelming as in 1892. The thirteen representative dramatists examined were practically unanimous in demanding that the Censorship be ended or substantially amended. On the other side were arrayed the managers, anxious to retain an institution which, as the Committee noted, relieved them from "the responsibility of judging what is proper for representation and what is not", and gave them practical security against any risk of interference, after production, by public opinion or by local authorities; and the actors, who, for similar reasons, regarded the Censorship as a safeguard for their interests. Dramatic criticism spoke with a divided voice. Archer, called as the first witness for the prosecution (perhaps in honour of his record as the sole challenger of 1892), reiterated his arguments against the Censorship, and was able this time to enforce them by examples not only of the licensing of noxious frivolity, but also of the suppression of serious plays of genuine merit and wholesome tendency; while Walkley, viewing the matter with Olympian detachment, found the advantages and disadvantages of the institution so evenly balanced, and the question at issue of so little importance to the art of drama or to the public welfare, that, he said, had it been for him to decide it, he would have been tempted to do so by tossing up a coin.

The Examiner of Plays, Mr. G. A. Redford, less fortunate than his friend and predecessor, Mr. Pigott, was exposed to a good deal of heckling by the left wing of the Committee; and his evidence, like Mr. Pigott's before him, was distinctly damaging to the Censorship cause, not only as demonstrating that he himself possessed few of the many and rare qualifications required by the perfect Censor, but also as showing that the practice of the Examiner and of the Department in general rested on no clear and consistent principles, but was largely governed by the taste and fancy of the officials concerned.

The Committee, steering a middle course,[1] recommended a compromise, following the lines of a scheme of "optional censorship" suggested by Professor Gilbert Murray. The details of the scheme need not detain us, since no legislative action has ever been taken on the Committee's recommendations. It might seem, then, as though the time, money, and labour expended in threshing the question out had been altogether wasted. Indeed, when, a year or two later, the adapter-author of a "frivolous" farce, the licensing of which had been one of the counts in the indictment of the Department, was nominated as Assistant to the Examiner of Plays, it looked as though the sole effect of the proceedings had been to harden the heart of Pharaoh, and make him seek, rather than avoid, grounds of offence. It would seem, however, that this may have been an accidental indiscretion, and that the Report of the Committee may at least have served to bring home to the Lord Chamberlain's Department the necessity for setting its house in order and taking its responsibilities, or irresponsibilities, more seriously. On Mr. Redford's retirement in the end of 1911, the place of the well-meaning ex-banker was filled by a man of letters of some distinction; and, while the futility of the Censorship as a bulwark against lubricity has never been more glaringly evident than in recent years, and while it still shows itself, on occasion, ready to smother any stirring of unconventional thought, it would seem on the whole to have been

[1] It may be worth mentioning that the one legal member, Lord Gorell, had, on second thoughts, moved the abolition, his motion being defeated by a narrow majority.

conducted latterly with more circumspection and common sense than in the Pigott-Redford days.

It should perhaps be recorded here that the post-war "revolt against decency", and the consequent lowering of the tone of literature and the drama in both America and England, led Archer to modify the view so often expressed by him, that the censorship of the stage may safely be left entirely to public opinion, supplemented only by the provisions of the ordinary law against gross breaches of decency, libel, etc. "I now think", he wrote in 1924, "that there ought to be some authority to be appealed to; but that authority should have no power to kill an unborn play, and a dramatist should have the right to plead openly the cause of his intellectual offspring and publicly to defend his means of livelihood against capricious annihilation."

Not once or twice in the story of Archer's life, an effort, in itself not fully successful, towards some public end had happy results for him as an individual. This was eminently the case with the Censorship struggle, for it drew closer his intimacy with John Galsworthy—an intimacy which ripened into one of his closest friendships. It was not strange that he should be drawn to the man of whom, speaking long after in America, he said: "It is, after all, his love of humanity that is the first and last word of his genius."

Archer's wanderings in 1909 had taken him over familiar ground—to Copenhagen, to deliver two lectures on "The Revival of Modern Drama"[1]—and twice to the United States, in the spring on Simplified Spelling business, in the autumn for the opening of the magnificent "New Theatre". But the

[1] Repeated at the Royal Institution, February 4th and 11th.

next year's travel broke new ground, and filled up the only gap remaining in his first-hand knowledge of the countries of Western Europe. The occasion, in the first instance, was a commission from *McClure's Magazine* to investigate the case of Francisco Ferrer, the secularist educator, whose execution, on October 13, 1909, after trial by a military court on the charge of having been the "author and chief" of the Barcelona riots in the previous July, had aroused violent controversy throughout Europe and in America. An article in the magazine by Mr. Perceval Gibbon, denouncing the action of the Spanish authorities, had been vehemently assailed by American Catholic apologists, and the editor, while printing a rejoinder by one of the Catholic champions "to keep the balance true", determined to ascertain the facts, if possible, by independent inquiry, and turned to the author of *Black and White in the South* as the person best qualified for the task.

Having already some knowledge of Spanish, which he improved, in the course of the summer, by taking lessons in the colloquial tongue, Archer was able to study in the original all the available literature and documents in the case; and a flying visit to Paris and a longer stay in Barcelona and its neighbourhood in the late summer brought him into touch with many of those best qualified to speak from first-hand knowledge of the events of the so-called "bloody week" at Barcelona, and of Ferrer's life, character, and fate. The results of his inquiry appeared in two articles[1] in *McClure's Magazine*, republished in book form in the spring of 1911 as *The Life, Trial, and Death of Francisco Ferrer*.

In a controversy so embittered it was not to be

[1] November and December, 1910.

expected that the party against which the finding went should accept the result of the inquiry as conclusive. Yet it is difficult to see how anyone accustomed to weighing evidence who reads this volume with a mind reasonably free from prejudice can fail to agree with its conclusion—that Ferrer's trial was a gross travesty of justice, and his conviction on the charge brought against him wholly unwarranted. The book is written frankly from the point of view of advanced Liberalism, and those of an opposite way of thinking may consider the treatment of Ferrer's educational propaganda unduly tender, though the writer shows little sympathy with its naïve, half-informed rationalism, and still less with its "acratism".[1] But throughout, in the story of Ferrer's life, his daily walk and conversation, while much that had been set down against him in malice is swept away, none of his limitations and weaknesses are extenuated; and, in regard to the matter mainly in issue, the alleged instigation of the riots, the writer's consciousness of his own anti-clerical leanings has clearly operated to make him doubly scrupulous in giving due weight to every grain of evidence that might possibly tell in favour of the prosecution. As a whole the book is a solidly documented "footnote to history", and its picture of the narrow, but single-minded and indomitable idealist, whose death, in the words of the daughter who loved him but did not share his views, "was imposed on the Spanish Government by reasons of State", is all the more impressive and moving because of the sobriety and restraint of its treatment and its freedom from all passion, save, here and there, a touch of the passion of pity.

[1] "Acracia"—the term applied in Spain to theoretical, non-terroristic anarchism.

Returning, in the late autumn, from a second visit to Spain (the richer by a strong affection for that fascinating country and a lasting enthusiasm for the architecture[1] of its magnificent cathedrals), Archer passed through Portugal, then busily celebrating with tumultuous joy the revolution which, less than a month before, had given birth to the young Republic, and by November was back again in theatre-land. Not, however, for long, for within a few weeks he had cut loose entirely for a season from dramatic criticism. The space assignable to the drama in the *Nation* was insufficient to give him elbow-room and a free hand, conditions indispensable, in his view, to satisfactory work. When, therefore, he found himself at variance with Massingham (a man who, like himself, held strong views on most subjects and held them stoutly) as to the disposal of the space available—the choice of plays to be noticed—he was not sorry to bring his regular connection with the paper to a close with the end of the year. He and his editor parted excellent friends, and in the coming years many of his occasional articles on theatrical subjects appeared in the *Nation*.

Released for the time from the drudgery of professional playgoing, he promptly set to work to arrange and set forth the thoughts on the technique of drama stored up during his thirty years' experience of theatrical criticism. It must have been early in 1911 that he conceived and began to write the book which, appearing the year following under the name of *Playmaking*, was to prove the most widely read, or at least the most widely bought, of his critical works. He wrote, in this instance, from such a full mind that the work did not tie him to the neighbour-

[1] Celebrated in *Things in General*, November 19, 1910.

hood of theatres and libraries—a great part of it, indeed, was written on shipboard—and 1911 was a year of wide and adventurous travel.

After Old Spain came Hispania Nueva. At this time a multitude of eyes in the United States and many in England were turned on Mexico, where Porfirio Diaz, after a long and dazzlingly successful reign, was visibly tottering to his fall. Revolts were on foot in most States of the Federation; the chaos which Diaz's admirers deemed that he had conjured away, for his lifetime at least if not for all time, was evidently come again; the investments of American and English capitalists were in great peril, and the lives of the English-speaking foreigners in Mexico far from secure. A study of these conditions and of the causes which had led up to them was wanted for *McClure's Magazine*, and a journalist with a judicial mind, a good knowledge of Spanish, and no objection to a mission flavoured with a spice of risk, was clearly indicated for the work.

The beginning of April, then, found Archer in New York once more, busily preparing for a Mexican adventure, while attending, with Professor Ripman, the meetings of the American Simplified Spelling Board. This time he had with him Tom Archer, who, since leaving the University, had shown no decided bent towards any of the callings open to him in England, and who, it was thought, might be helped in his final choice by making something in the nature of a Grand Tour and seeing a little of the world outside Europe. And indeed this visit, which included a prolonged stay with the kindest of friends in New England, was successful in rousing in the youth a strong taste for America and things American, and, had the Fates not intervened, would probably have led to his making his career in the New World.

Leaving his son behind him in the north, somewhat to the youth's disappointment, Archer set forth before the middle of April by way of St. Louis, and arrived in due course in Mexico City, where he found a climate that realized his ideal, "warmth without stickiness", a population endlessly, fantastically picturesque, and a highly interesting political situation. His account[1] of his stay in

> the land where the cactus and yucca
> Are emblems of deeds that are done in their clime,

shows how greatly he enjoyed the experience; and he was able, in a very short time, to collect the materials for his McClure article[2] of the following August, with its penetrating analysis of the facts which underlay the "specious fabric of statistical prosperity and lawless law-and-order" erected by the great President. Of the new régime under Francisco Madero he speaks with sympathy, but with a lack of confidence in its stability only too fully justified by the events of eighteen months later, when a counter-revolution swept that well-meaning idealist from the Presidential chair and out of the world. By the beginning of May the traveller had made his way to Vera Cruz without misadventure, and on the 4th he sailed by the good ship *Merida* for Havana and New York.

But his adventures were not over. Thirty-six hours out from Havana, at twelve o'clock of a dark and foggy night, the *Merida* was rammed by the *Admiral Farragut*, a fruit steamer bound for Jamaica, and in due course, though fortunately not for some hours, went to the bottom, taking with her practically all

[1] "A Glimpse of Mexico", *Morning Leader*, May 27 and June 3, 1911.
[2] "The Collapse of the Diaz Legend."

the possessions of everyone on board. There was no loss of life, the 350 castaways being successfully transferred, in the course of the night, to the *Admiral Farragut* (herself in an almost sinking condition), and from her next day to the s.s. *Hamilton* and the battleship *Iowa*, which, summoned by the *Farragut's* wireless, had groped their way to the rescue through the fog. The *Hamilton* passengers, Archer among them, were landed on May 12th at Norfolk, Virginia, after what seemed, in the circumstances, the superfluous ordeal of a prolonged examination by the Health, Immigration, and Customs offices. And the fact that all his personal belongings, except the scanty garments he stood up in, all his money (placed in the purser's charge for safe keeping) except a 20-dollar bill, and all his Mexican books and papers (with the fortunate exception of his note-books) were at the bottom of the Atlantic, seemed of comparatively small moment as he sat that night at dinner in the Monticello Hotel at Norfolk. His cabin companion, who had been at his side through most of the adventure, was an accomplished American artist, who had the misfortune to be deaf and dumb. "As we sat at dinner", Archer says, "I wrote on my friend's tablet: 'This is better than Davy Jones's locker.' He nodded emphatically."

His published account[1] of the disaster is a human document impressive in its simplicity and candour, even to-day, when we have so many descriptions of like, or far worse, experiences. Throughout he is watching his acts and sensations, like a spectator at a play, and none of them, whether more or less creditable, is dissembled.

Some of the episodes have a picturesque grimness. There is the moment, not, he confesses, a cheerful

[1] "A Shipwreck", *Morning Leader*, June 10 and 17, 1911.

one, when the lights of the *Merida* "all of a sudden fainted and went out"; and the moment, a little later, when, having seen two ladies,[1] his table-companions, into the first boat (wrapped in his great coat and warm jacket, and carrying his electric torch, the only light in the boat), he watches, "with a curious feeling of combined relief and apprehension, the little circle of light drift heaving away into the fog". Thereafter, all the women and children being gone, "I began to think it was time to take my own passage. Nothing, I hope, would have induced me to leave earlier; but as soon as it came to the turn of the men, I was distinctly conscious of a resolve that I would not, if I could help it, be the hindmost." Least agreeable of all, perhaps, was the hour or so spent in transit to the *Farragut,* during which he tries to help with an oar, but is overwhelmed with sea-sickness—his infallible remedy having been left behind in his trunk. "Behold me, then", he writes, "in a frightfully overcrowded boat, with nobody (or rather with everybody) in command; in a dense fog, on a sea which . . . on closer acquaintance proved to be rolling pretty heavily. . . . There was no room to work the oars; there was no light; everyone was shouting contradictory orders; the man at the steering-oar apparently could not steer, and certainly did not know where to steer to. . . . Suddenly, however, a steamer loomed out of the fog a few yards ahead of us. She had a notable list to starboard; but, as her lights were all burning, she was evidently in no immediate danger. She was the most comfortable sight I had seen since the lights went out on the *Merida.*"

[1] Mrs. and Miss Seeger, the mother and sister of Alan Seeger, the young American poet who fell, five years later, fighting for France, and whose volume of Poems, with an Introduction by Archer, was published in 1927.

Received with open arms by friends in Washington, he spends some time there, filling up, so far as possible, at the Library of Congress, the blank left by the loss of his Mexican documents. Then, having returned to New England, completed the results of his mission and rejoined Tom Archer, he sets out homewards; but cannot resist giving himself and his son a glimpse by the way of Jamaica, the island that had enchanted him three years before. On June 21st he is writing from St. Ann, Jamaica, to Sir Arthur Pinero:

"My ignorance of what has been passing in England is colossal; but I see in today's paper the knighthood of G. A. [George Alexander]. Except yourself, no man of the theatre has better deserved the honour, and I am sending him a line of sincere congratulation. I also read of Gilbert's death. Poor old fellow! He gave an immense deal of pleasure in his day.

"I have been in a great rush of travel and business. I went to Mexico with the sensation of doing something rather risky, and had absolutely no unusual experience. When I got on board the U.S. Steamer *Merida*, I thought all danger was over; and behold! the *Merida* went to the bottom with all my belongings, and if it hadn't been an exceptionally calm night, I should doubtless have gone too.

"I am now taking Tom for a fortnight's round of Jamaica, as a consolation for *not* taking him to Mexico. We shall be home (D.V.) about the middle of July. There is nothing like shipwreck for making one pious."

XIVA

LETTERS OF 1907–1911

To THE LADY MARY MURRAY

1 November, 1907

DEAR LADY MARY,

It was very kind of you to write to me, and you may be sure that if anything should occur to bring me to Oxford—and perhaps "whether or no"—I will not hesitate to descend on you. But for the present there is no chance of my being able to leave London. This Censorship fight is taking up all my time, and even the Elizabethan Theatre has had to go to the wall.

You will be glad to hear that all arrangements are now completed for the deputation to C. B. The Dramatic Authors of England are to assemble in Trafalgar Square. Barrie will address them from the base of the Nelson column, and the Savoy orchestra will play "Britons never will be slaves". The procession will then form, and will be headed by Pinero and Shaw walking arm in arm. Immediately behind them will come Garnett and Galsworthy, each bearing the pole of a red banner with the inscription "Down with the Censor!" An effigy of Redford, which is being prepared by the Savoy property-man, will be carried by Frederick Harrison and W. B. Yeats; and over its head will wave a banner, carried by Gilbert Murray, with the inscription "Ecrasez l'Infâme!" Arrived in Downing Street, Swinburne will declaim an "Ode to C. B.", and the speakers will be Ford Madox Hueffer, Desmond MacCarthy, Maarten Maartens and Ernest Rhys—dramatists who cannot be suspected of interested motives, as they have never written any plays.

The managers are believed to be organizing a counter-demonstration; but it is thought that anything like a massacre may be avoided by a mutual agreement to leave the question to the arbitrament of a single combat between Vedrenne and Barker, to take place in Whitehall, C. B. being umpire. So we have lively times before us.

Yours ever,
W. A.

From THOMAS HARDY

MAX GATE,
9.1.1909

MY DEAR ARCHER,

I have just read your amusing article[1] in "The Nation"—and not only amusing but strong and intellectual, like all your articles—which, as I cannot enter into the discussion (not having seen the play) has set me thinking on another branch of the subject, and leads me to ask you why you never write an article on the unfair and disproportionate difference of standard applied to works of the theatre and those of us poor scribblers—I mean imaginative writers—who depend upon the press for making our ideas known. A situation, for instance, which is a stale thing in a novel or dramatic poem, is hailed as one of dazzling originality when, after some years, it . . . appears behind the footlights. Surely a readjustment of terms is wanted here, so that the two arts might be reduced to a common measure. As you stand so independent of all necessity to flatter the theatre, you might do the thing well.

[1] "De Juventute", the *Nation*, January 9, 1909. A reply to some attacks on W. A.'s recent criticisms. The question raised in this letter was considered by W. A. in a *Morning Leader* article, "Novelist and Dramatist", January 23, 1909.

This is an impromptu note (or I should never have written it at all) and I wind up with wishing you a happy new year.

Sincerely yours,

THOMAS HARDY

From A. W. PINERO

29th April, 1911

MY DEAR ARCHER,

I have just finished reading your *Life, etc., of Francisco Ferrer*. I must tell you, to satisfy my own feelings, how much I have been moved and impressed by it. You have told the terrible story finely and moderately, with a clearness of style which, I honestly think, is all your own today in literature. Most heartily I congratulate you on your valuable work.

If there is ever to be a Day of Judgment your book will lie on the Judge's table!

Begging that I may be kindly remembered to Mrs. Archer, I am, my dear Archer,

Yours sincerely,

ARTHUR PINERO.

From G. G. A. MURRAY

May 29, 1911

MY DEAR W. A.,

What a marvel of youth and adventurousness you are! "A green tree with birds singing in the branches" is the description to which Galsworthy was moved when I told him of your adventures. Spain and Ferrer, then Mexico and Revolution, and then a shipwreck: and apparently no check to your wish for further and wilder experiences. We all admire you.

Ferrer seems to me exceedingly good: so absolutely convincing and judicial. Of course you have not tried to make it exciting, rather the reverse; but I found it did excite me. . . .

It greatly decreases the amenity of this island having you so long resident in America. If you stay there I shall have to come out and teach at Amherst, which has been inviting me. . . . By the way, you will be pleased to hear that we have let the science and mathematics students take a course without Greek, this Dust-like One speaking for the proposal. Of course other steps will follow, but Greek and Latin are put on a par by the present scheme: they can take either one or the other, which is the point I lay most stress upon.

Farewell, and my respects to Tom. . . .

Yours ever,

G. M.

To MRS. ARCHER

HOTEL BELMONT,
NEW YORK,
2 *June*, 1911

MY DEAR FRANCES,

I have today received from McClure's office your letter written after hearing of the shipwreck. It is rather a good thing that when you heard of the wreck of the *Merida* you didn't associate it with me . . . if you had tumbled to it, you would no doubt have been on tenterhooks till my letter arrived, so it is best as it was. . . .

I enclose a nice letter I had from Mr. Seeger. Mrs. Seeger has evidently made the most of what I did for them, which was little enough; but, after all, in such cases to *seem* helpful is almost as important as to *be* helpful. As for my trying to find their cabin [to look for warm clothing for the two ladies] I very soon gave that up as a bad job. And you must remember that at no time was there any imminence of danger. Of course one didn't absolutely know "which moment gwine ter be de nex' "; but there was every appearance that the ship would float a long time, as in fact she did. It would have been a very different matter if the weather had been bad, or if the ship had been filling so rapidly that we had only had 10 minutes or 20 minutes or half an hour to clear out of her. . . .

Poor old Diaz! one can't help being sorry for such a come-down. He was an old ruffian, but he thoroughly believed in himself as the benefactor of his country —he was the first dupe of his own legend. If only he had died two years ago, he would have passed into history as one of the greatest of rulers, instead of supplying an almost unique example of a reversal of fortune. I feel my article a good deal like kicking a man when he is down; but I can't forgive him his absolute neglect of the common people of Mexico.

I must close this hurriedly to catch the mail.

Sempre tuo,

W. A.

XV

1912–1914

PLAYMAKING—THE GREAT ANALYSIS—ROUND THE WORLD—*INDIA AND THE FUTURE*

IN September 1911, two months after Archer's return to England, a chapter in his life was closed by the death of his mother, in her eightieth year. The great divergences of outlook and opinion between these two had never impaired their deep mutual admiration and affection; and in these later years, particularly when, after the death of Thomas Archer in 1905, the mother's health began to decline, the sense of her strong eldest son's nearness had become an important element in her comfort and happiness. That sense was hardly diminished by the son's travels during those years. The rest of her children were for the most part away in remote parts of the globe; and in this family in which the Antipodes set the standard of distance, a son who had his domicile in England, and wandered no farther afield than the Continent and America, was felt, by comparison, to be easily within reach. Thus, while his mother yet lived, a plan which Archer had long had in mind for a second *Wanderjahr* round the world had to remain in the region of vague possibilities.

Now that this tie was broken, there was nothing to prevent the dream being realized, and it was natural that Japan and India should be the chief objects, both as the most interesting countries of the East and as the temporary homes of members of his widely scattered clan, who would be able to put him in the way of seeing those fascinating lands and their civilizations to good advantage. The winter was devoted to clearing the decks for the adventure and paying a farewell visit to Norway. *Playmaking* and *The Great Analysis* (a smaller treatise on a greater subject, flung off in the previous autumn) had been completed by January 1912; in February he had made time to prepare and deliver the Conway Memorial Lecture, choosing for his subject "Art and the Commonweal"; by March the further arrangements for a year's absence were complete, and on the 23rd of that month he sails on the *Mauretania* for New York. While he is crossing we may glance at the works left behind.

Playmaking, though styled in the sub-title "A Manual of Craftsmanship", seems better described as a study of the distinguishing conditions, the possibilities and limitations, of the dramatic form. It disclaims at the outset all attempt to lay down hard and fast rules. "There are no rules for writing a play", the first sentence runs, and the purpose of the three hundred pages which follow is thus indicated in a later passage: "Rules there are none; but it does not follow that some of the thousands who are fascinated by the art of the playwright may not profit by having their attention called, in a plain and practical way, to its problems and possibilities." The book treats avowedly of what Archer used to call the "vertebrate" as distinguished from the "jelly-fish" play; for to the end he held strongly the view, of late years so unfashionable, that story or plot, while not the noblest or most important, is the fundamental element in drama.[1] It follows, of course, that, with regard to what some hold to be the highest form of drama, that which has no plot at all, or a negligible plot, a good deal of the discussion in *Playmaking* goes wide of the mark. But it may safely be predicted

[1] See in particular pp. 18 and 19.

that for many years to come plays which tell a story will continue to be produced in large numbers, and that their success will continue to depend in no small degree on the skill with which the story is told. And, while this state of things lasts, *Playmaking* will doubtless continue to be helpful to the budding dramatist. Nor is it without more general interest. It assembles from a wide range of drama a great variety of apt and entertaining illustrations, while its analysis of the mind of the average audience (notably in such chapters as those on "'Curiosity' and 'Interest'", "Tension and its Suspension", etc.) is no less illuminating than the study of the psychology of acting in *Masks or Faces?*

Of *The Great Analysis: A Plea for a Rational World-Order*, published anonymously,[1] with a preface by Gilbert Murray, Archer wrote in 1913: "Nobody paid the slightest attention to it, and possibly it deserved none; but it contained the outline of a scheme for an International Institute of Sociological Research, whose business it should be to take stock of the whole earth, systematize the data of the world-problem, and try to shape a reasonable course for the future of humanity, not from a national but from a planetary point of view. It pointed out that only of recent years had discovery and intercommunication rendered it possible for the world to 'know itself', and argued that, this being now possible, it was time for man to show himself a reasonable being."

"Nobody" is a modest exaggeration, for the little treatise found appreciation here and there. But it came both too soon and too late—too soon, because

[1] "I tried anonymity", Archer wrote later, "because I felt that anything serious I chose to say was discounted as proceeding from a practitioner of the despicable trade of dramatic criticism."

it was too far in advance of its time to bite on the general mind—it has taken a world-convulsion to convert that mind to something like Archer's point of view; too late, because the evils it foresaw and would have guarded against were even then in the gate, and there was no time left to set up barriers against them. Yet the suggestion it threw out is one towards the fulfilment of which in one form or another, if no second cataclysm should come to confound all orderly development, it seems certain that the world must move.

Looking back on the little book in the last year of his life, its author, while feeling to the full its deficiencies due to lack of expert knowledge (deficiencies admitted in its mottoes from Lord Balfour and the Psalms: "I am a child in these matters" and "Out of the mouth of babes and sucklings"), could yet say: "I verily believe I went straight to a point which, as yet, all you League of Nations people are only fumbling after. What you want—I mean one of the things you most urgently want—is an organized World-Brain, in the shape of an International University."[1]

The stages of Archer's pilgrimage in the footsteps of the sun are traceable in his *Things in General* articles. Crossing the United States from east to west in a luxury of travel that contrasted strongly with the bare boards and picnic commissariat of his eastward journey thirty-five years before; giving a day or two in San Francisco, newly risen from its ashes, to memories of Bret Harte, of Stevenson, and of his

[1] *The Great Analysis* has now been re-issued (Williams & Norgate, 1931) at the instance of the International Industrial Relations Association; and there are not wanting other signs, such as the formation of the "Committee for International Co-operation" of the League of Nations, that the idea set forth in it is gaining ground.

own youth; spending "A Day in Paradise" at Honolulu; he entered Tokio Bay in a cold grey morning of May, and saw at sunrise Fujiyama "floating lightly above the interloping hill-crests like a giant bird with wings outspread".

Several of his Japanese articles appear under the modest heading: "The Surface of Japan", but he went farther below the surface than most travellers, for, in the course of his two months' stay, besides visiting the recognized sights, he spent many days in tramping through the mountains, under expert guidance, by paths untrodden of the ordinary tourist, and many hours in study of the Japanese stage—both the venerable *No* performances ("by far the oldest form of drama surviving in the modern world"), and the *Kabuki-Shibai,* or popular theatre, a comparative parvenu, the origins of which go no farther back than the early seventeenth century. These, as well as the Chinese stage (known to him of old in America, and now to be studied afresh in its native land), had a vivid interest by reason of their close analogies with the Elizabethan theatre. "In both countries", he wrote, "I have found myself much nearer to the theatre of Shakespeare than I ever did at Elizabethan performances in England." Less interesting were the puppet-plays of Osaka, which, however, were duly visited; while at Tokyo he came in touch with the most recent developments, lecturing to the students at the Waseda University on "The Future of the Drama", and witnessing at a charming little private theatre Japanese performances of *A Doll's House* and Shaw's *Man of Destiny.*

Passing on to Dairen, he visits Port Arthur, and there, fresh from the appalling object-lesson of "203-metre Hill" and the Forts, he is moved to take up again the parable of *The Great Analysis.*

"To-day", he wrote[1]—little thinking how soon such descriptions were to become mere commonplace—"they [the forts] are, in very truth, the abomination of desolation. They look as though some tremendous earthquake had splintered their rock, riven their concrete, and made of it all a sort of petrified stirabout. And while it was being stirred about by every infernal agency known to science, it was full of living, sentient, writhing, agonizing human beings. There is a covered way in one of these forts, for the possession of which the Japanese and Russians fought at close quarters for three weeks on end, mowing each other down with machine-guns, blowing each other to fragments with dynamite hand-grenades. One of the historians of the siege, describing this episode, heads his chapter with the single word 'Hell'. When you see the spot, the word seems scarcely adequate. And, in pauses in the carnage, the kindly human creatures, returning for a moment to sanity, are said to have exchanged cigarettes! Then the bugle sounded, and they were back in hell again. . . .

"I am not a Tolstoyan. I do not believe that nations in which the spirit of militarism is both theoretically and practically dominant will listen to reason without a substantial display of force behind it. But surely it is time that reasonable men of all the nations should get together and challenge the militarists to think out their position. What is it that they want? Is there anything that a whole nation—as distinct from a military caste—can in justice or even in policy desire, that they may not more certainly and cheaply attain by peaceful than by sanguinary methods? . . .

1 "Militarism, the 'Prestige' of War", *Daily News and Leader*, July 27, 1912.

"... It is on plain lack of imagination that theoretical militarism is founded.... The last thing that the man of sluggish imagination can realize is the omnipotence of the human will, and its power to remake the world in its own image. History, as he reads it, has been one long record of wrangling tribalism; and he cannot conceive that the days of tribalism are numbered. But to the intelligence that is capable of a larger view it is manifest that, whether we like it or not, terrestrial conditions are changing, and civilization must soon choose between suicide in tribalism and self-preservation in solidarity."

The articles sent home by the traveller from China give forcible—perhaps over-forcible—expression to the lively disgust which the surface aspects of that huge and ungainly country are apt to inspire in the foreigner visiting it for the first time—particularly if the visitor comes straight from the daintiness of Japan. In the highly insanitary theatres, into which he ventured six or eight times "from a stern sense of duty", and feeling like a hero imperilling his life in the cause of Science, there was little to detain him, when once the resemblances to the early English theatre in construction and arrangements had been noted. Having seen, with heartfelt dissatisfaction, Peking, Tientsin, Shanghai, and Canton, he went on his way rejoicing, landing at Colombo in the beginning of August, and thence crossing the straits to Tuticorin.

In an address[1] to Indian students, delivered four years later, Archer summarized his travels and doings in India and their effects upon him.

"I landed in India", he says, "in a state of ignorance upon which I now look back with shame—

[1] "The Future of India", 1916.

indeed I had even then the grace to feel ashamed of it. But I had not been twenty-four hours on the soil of your motherland, before she had cast her spell on me. I plunged right into the heart of Indian India, not by way of Europeanized Bombay or Calcutta, but crossing from Ceylon to Tuticorin, and proceeding straight to Madura, with its gigantic, marvellous, terrible temple. My very ignorance intensified the impression it made on me. I had never heard of Madura. But for a chance remark of a fellow-traveller, it is quite likely that I should never have thought of stopping there. But stop I did, and that day at Madura marks an epoch in my life. It awoke in me a new, and eager, and, I trust, sympathetic interest, which has coloured my thoughts, and in some measure shaped my actions, ever since. I did not remain long in Southern India, for the month was August and the heat intense. I returned to it afterwards; but for the moment I went on, with only a few pauses, to the hills of Baluchistan, and there settled down for two months, to try, by assiduous reading, in some measure to correct my ignorance. Then I came down again into India proper, and wandered far and wide, from Peshawar to Trichinopoly, seeing many strange and fascinating things, talking with many men, both Indian and European, steeping myself in both the romance and the reality of Aryavarta. After I left India, a great part of my reading and thought for more than a year was still devoted to Indian subjects. The war has partially broken the spell—but nothing less could have done so."

The pauses referred to brought him, at Poona, into touch with officials, English and Indian, of the Bombay Government, and with some of the ablest non-official Indians, and at Ahmedabad gave him a foretaste of what he called the "rational magnificence" of Indian Muhammadan architecture. Thence, through the burning fiery furnace of the Sind desert, he made his way to the uplands of Baluchistan, and there, first in a tent pitched amid the aromatic junipers and artemisia of Ziarat, 8,000 feet above sea-level, and later at Quetta, he remained immersed in a sea of Census Reports, Blue Books, histories, Sanskrit classics and exegetics, and modern Indian fiction, until the approach of the cold weather made leisurely wanderings in the plains possible.

From Quetta to Peshawar and the Khyber, thence to Lahore, Amritsar, Simla, Hardwar, Delhi, Agra, Rajputana, and Bombay these wanderings took him; once again to the toe of the peninsula, for another taste of the "wonder and horror" of the giant southern temples—Madura, Trichinopoly, Tanjore—thence by Ootacamund and Bangalore to Hyderabad for the great Langar festival; to Bankipur for the Indian National Congress; to Benares, Allahabad, and Lucknow. When he embarked for England at Bombay on January 7, 1913, he had seen in his five months' sojourn more of India than most English residents see in half a lifetime, and had seen it with fresh and eager eyes, unclouded by the cataract of habit and daily routine.

He came away obsessed by the problems of Indian society and government, and from what he had seen and learned on the spot, and from the results of further study, there emerged very definite views on those problems, to which he felt constrained to give utterance. This he did in the volume *India and the Future*, completed in the summer of 1914, on the eve of the outbreak of the war.

India and the Future is the work of a man believing whole-heartedly in the ideals of Western civilization (though alive to its shortcomings in practice), and with small reverence for the wisdom of "the brooding East" in so far as concerns the conduct of life and of politics. "The relations between West and East . . ." he says, "were determined from the moment when the East adopted the static ideal of civilization, which happens to be in the long run false and impossible, and left the West to discover the dynamic ideal, which happens to be alone consonant to the inward nature of things." Again, in his address to Indian students, he urges them not to take too seriously the claim made by worshippers of Hinduism that India has a profound genius for religion, and is in this respect superior to the rest of the world. "It is quite true", he says, "that from prehistoric ages onward there have always been men in India who had great gifts of metaphysical penetration. Many of the philosophic doctrines of Greece and of modern Europe had been anticipated in the India of the Upanishads. But, for the purposes of practical life, metaphysical insight is not so much a gift as a disease. I am not laughing at the metaphysicians. I am quite alive to the fascination of going at night into a cellar without a candle to search for a black cat that isn't there. But this sport does not make for efficient citizenship. I know quite well that the universe is an illusion; but it is an illusion sufficiently constant for all practical purposes, and the first point of sanity and morality is to behave as if it were real."

Those who, setting a high value on "metaphysical aid" in sublunary matters, deny and contemn these premises, can hardly be expected to look with favour on the conclusions drawn from them. The present writer, on the other hand, feels himself disabled from judging the book with strict impartiality, because it arrives, by a process of admirably clear and incisive reasoning, at results substantially the same as those to which, quite independently, he had gropingly felt his way during a period of thirty years' Indian service. The passages of the book dealing with modern Hinduism might at points be over-severe, but their plain speaking seemed to this reader to be justified in the main, and to be greatly needed.[1] Even the strictures on Hindu art in general, and on Hindu sculpture and architecture in particular, however out of tune with modern theory, were welcome to one who had long felt, with Goethe, that

> Nichts schrecklicher kann den Menschen geschehn
> Als das Absurde verkörpert zu sehn.

The manuscript of *India and the Future*, handed to the author's agent on the day the war broke out, was held over, with a view to publication when peace should come again. But when three years of war had dragged by without bringing the end perceptibly nearer, it was decided to wait no longer, and the book appeared in the summer of 1917. Fate had dealt unkindly with it in two respects. Stealing into existence in the thick of tremendous events and emotions, it necessarily attracted less attention than it deserved. And the delay had thrown its thesis, as it were, out of focus, and given it, in the eyes of those who might have benefited most by its doctrine, a deceptive appearance of one-sidedness; for in three years of storm and stress Archer's conception of the British mission in India, as the welding of a conglomeration of races into a people capable of independent nationhood, had ceased to be a heresy of advanced thought, and was in a fair way to be adopted as official doctrine, so that his championship

[1] The indictment has since been repeated, in *Mother India*, in much severer and more sensational form.

of Indian aspirations seemed like beating at a half-opened door; while, on the other hand, the changed conditions must have rendered the wholesome, bitter tonic of his strictures on Indian shortcomings more than ever distasteful to the Indian intelligentsia and their Western partisans.

Back in London, after a year of expensive travel and small incomings, Archer had to give part of his attention to bread-winning, and he turned again to dramatic criticism as the readiest resource. Apparently he had some little difficulty in discovering an opening, but by the end of February 1913 we find him established as dramatic critic of the *Star*. He was to hold this post for more than seven years, and to relinquish it only when he finally retired from regular journalism; his career as dramatic critic thus ending in the service of the paper on which, thirty years earlier, Walkley's had begun. The post suited him well, for the work, while not so exacting as the dramatic criticism of a morning paper, served to keep him in touch with the theatre—without that contact he would not long have remained happy—and the salary[1] was to prove a valuable stand-by during the hard times that lay ahead.

But the dramatic harvest of the eighteen months that followed his return was not a rich one. Apart from Shaw's *Androcles and the Lion*, there is scarcely a single new play of importance on the list of productions; the most interesting events are one or two revivals, as of Shaw's *Cæsar and Cleopatra* and Galsworthy's *Strife*; Granville-Barker's spirited struggle to set on foot a Repertory Theatre fails of success;

[1] Though in the years of stress, when things theatrical were thrown into the background and small space could be given to them, it was considerably cut down, at his own suggestion.

and, in looking through the files, we find that, as in all seasons poor in new productions, the most interesting criticisms are those of acting—Forbes Robertson's Hamlet and Shylock, for example. Perhaps this merely meant that the theatre was in the trough of the wave that had risen so high in the first decade of the century. But one is tempted to think that in those days political and social conditions were unfavourable to healthy art of every kind, that already the stormy state of men's uncertain minds may have begun to throw a blight on the dramatic growth that had seemed so vigorous. At all events, the most noteworthy of Archer's by-works, during this time when the Indian book was on the stocks, are not those which deal with the drama, but such things as the address[1] on education, delivered at the meeting of the Moral Education League in February 1914, developing the ethical side of the argument of *Let Youth But Know*; and some of the *Things in General* papers, in which coming events cast their shadows before—notably the article of March 27, 1914, with the ominous title, "If the World Went Mad", setting forth how terribly contagious is the *folie lucide* of the reputedly sane; how delicate, in these latter days, when "the world has become, as never before, one great organism, linked up by a thousand nerve-filaments," is the balance of the world-brain; and how easily it might come to pass that "an epidemic of disequilibrium" should "run like wildfire round the earth, and leave civilization in ruins".

In April 1914 Archer is in New York once more, attending the annual meeting of the Simplified Spelling Board, and sees, with dismay, the beginnings of the invasion of African barbarism in music and

[1] *Knowledge and Character: The Straight Road in Education*. Published 1916.

dancing.[1] Here, too, no doubt, the plan was matured which should have launched Tom Archer on a business career, for, soon after Archer's return to England, his son set forth to take up a post in the New York office of an American friend. And then the summer came, and a shock, no greater seemingly than other earlier shocks which had been safely absorbed, chanced to upset that delicate balance of the world-brain, and the best-laid plans went fatally astray, and all things were changed.

1 "Tangomania", *Daily News and Leader*, April 24, 1914.

XVa

LETTERS, ETC., OF 1912–1917

To G. Bernard Shaw

The Galle Face Hotel,
Colombo, Ceylon,
August 7, 1912

My dear G. B. S.,

I think you owe me a salary as Travelling Inspector of your Theatre. After *The Man of Destiny* in Tokyo, I come in for *Candida* here. The theatre was about half full; which was not bad, considering the counter-attraction of Mr. R. G. Knowles and his wife (described as "the Kubelik of the banjo"). The performance, of which I saw two acts, was quite respectable, considering they played *Othello* the night before and were to do *The Sign of the Cross* next night. Both Morell and Eugene were quite decent; the people loved Burgess ("Don't be vulgar, Candy" was the success of the evening); and the Candida had the good fault of being too young for the part—she looked quite as young as Eugene. In this way she was the most inadequate of the lot—but she was agreeable. You will see from the enclosures what an excellent dodge it is to write your own criticism and print it on the program.

Such is your popularity in Ceylon that the name of Candy has been given to the capital. I spent the day there, and only returned to Colombo in time for the performance.

My first impression on the threshold of India is that we are a hopelessly insignificant and vulgar lot in comparison with the extremely handsome and distinguished people we rule over. You see sinister and even ugly faces here, but scarcely any that are common, half-baked, shapeless. And the number of noble and impressive figures is extraordinary. I daresay they are awful scoundrels, but æsthetically they are magnificent.

Love to Mrs. Shaw from

Yours ever,
W. A.

THE TAJ MAHAL

[Fragment]

Yes, it is filmy-fair—It seems
Built of the stuff of poets' dreams;
A fabric of enchantment, hewn
From lucent quarries of the moon;
Or curdled by some thaumaturge
From lace-like foam of southern surge;
From earliest drift of blossom-spray,
And starlit snows of Himalay.
Whence then the vague disquietude,
The doubt that flaws my halcyon mood?

. . . . .

From J. M. BARRIE

June 4, 1913

MY DEAR ARCHER,

Certainly I have not had any letter about this business that has pleased me more than yours.[1] As certainly, if my plays have given you any pleasure, I can tell you that, however poor they may be, they would have been poorer things if there had not been you, for there was a time when the feeling that you were looking on and wishing people would do things

[1] Letter of congratulation on Baronetcy.

a bit better made me do a bit better. It was no outside influence, but yourself, that made me struggle at plays as I have struggled at books.

Quite apart from my own work, I consider you have done more for the English stage than any man living.

Yours very sincerely,

J. M. BARRIE

From G. G. A. MURRAY

[On reading the sheets of *India and the Future*]

OVERSTRAND, NORFOLK,
April 10, 1914

MY DEAR ARCHER,

You really are a dam good writer. You seem to me to have a power of candid and wise and disinterested appreciation of things which I have rarely seen in literature, and also a power of putting your results in a wonderfully clear and persuasive way. And all this about Indian art needed saying. It is curious how people long to go mad about something or other; they only want a handle or a word of encouragement, and off they go, raving. And then it needs great patience and firmness to stop them . . . just a few of them. . . .

Am getting very lazy here and enjoying myself.

Yours ever,

G. M.

OXFORD,
April 28 [1917?]

MY DEAR ARCHER,

Sunday has been a tornado, as usual, or I should have written sooner to say that I found the Indian chapters most interesting—surprisingly interesting, considering how many books there are on the subject. I think you have a great power of seeing the important and interesting points in a mass of detail, and an extraordinary fairness of judgment. You carry me with you on every single question, and I think your frank discussion of Hinduism and the Castes may be very useful. We have allowed ourselves to be hypnotized into a senseless admiration of the supposed wisdom of the east. I found the whole book fresh and striking, and, as a matter of fact, did not put it down till I had finished. . . .

Yours ever,

G. M.

XVI

1914–1919

WAR WORK—*WAR IS WAR*—THE LEAGUE OF NATIONS

To tell in full the story of the five years 1914–1919 would be needlessly to renew unspeakable pain; but some account of them, however brief, must be given. Archer, like so many of his countrymen, was spared the worst pain of all, that of doubt and misgiving, by the capital blunder with which Germany opened the war, the invasion of Belgium. Had England been drawn in merely on the strength of her commitments to the Dual Alliance, he would doubtless in the end have recognized the inevitability of the decision to fight, but only as the lesser of two evils almost equally appalling. But the German action, by making it clear from the outset that neutrality could not be maintained without the sacrifice of national security and national honour, saved him much searching of heart; the two evils ceased to be commensurable; the worst that might come of war was preferable to the almost certain consequences of standing out. Already, on August 28th, he is writing:[1] "I have too much faith in the ultimate decency of things to conceive the possibility of final defeat. But even if sheer ruin should ensue, and I am still alive, I trust I shall have the grace never to repent that we stood by democracy, we stood by France, and we stood by the small nations."

Neither during the war or after it did his view of the rights of the matter waver at any time; for "the pseudo-impartiality which delights in weighting the scales against its own country",[2] and the sophistry

[1] *Daily News and Leader.* [2] H. A. L. Fisher: *Life of Lord Bryce.*

which, not content with the easy demonstration that pure white and unmitigated black do not exist, goes on to argue that all shades of grey are indistinguishably alike, were equally alien to his habit of mind.

He set himself, then, to do what he could to help, with no divided mind, and with more and more fervour as the German methods of warfare developed. But for a man long past military age, without scientific training or manual dexterity, whose bread-winning occupation seemed for the time to have become infinitely unimportant, it was not easy to find work that satisfied the craving to feel that he was pulling his weight in the boat. On the outbreak of war his son had recrossed the Atlantic by the first steamer, had rejoined his volunteer corps (the London Scottish), and before long was serving as lance-corporal in the Flanders trenches.[1] To the father no such simple and obvious course of duty presented itself. He was able to do something for the cause in his *Daily News* articles, which were devoted in these months mainly to three topics: a closely reasoned pro-ally polemic, encouragement for the "home front", and the driving home of the moral of the war, the calamitous insanity of militarism. And he made during 1915 other not unimportant contributions, including a clear and convincing account[2] of the events of the fatal thirteen days following the Austrian ultimatum.

But such occasional tasks were not sufficient. What was needed was regular employment of some value to the country, which should fill up the space

[1] His account of "The Soft Side of Messines" in the *London Scottish Magazine* reads, in its graphic simplicity, like a chapter from *The Red Badge of Courage*.

[2] *The Thirteen Days: A Chronicle and Interpretation.*

left by the shrinkage, both in quantity and in importance, of his theatrical and literary work, and should help to deaden, by busyness, the continual gnawing of public and private anxiety. A somewhat ironic turn of fate solved the problem, by providing him, the inveterate foe of censors, with a desk in the postal censorship. In October 1915 Gilbert Murray, whom he has evidently asked to be one of his sponsors, writes to him:

"Who can deny after this the workings of Providence? . . . Now you will know how Pigott and Redford felt, and you will learn how easily and simply they slid into their worst follies. I never knew Providence express its disapproval in such a gentlemanly way before. It clearly cannot be on the side of the Germans. Well, I have thrown a veil over your past and testified to your humble and chastened spirit in the present."

His command of the languages of Western Europe and his robust common sense must have made him a valuable worker in the censorship hive at Portugal Street. But his spirit was not so far chastened as to find itself at home in the censor's trade, and it must have been obvious, even to himself, that he was wasted on such work. "As for me", he writes in March 1916, "I am still toiling on most unwillingly in that abode of imbecility, the Censorship. There were rumours that something else was to be offered to me, but nothing has materialized. I shall rebel and get the sack before long." Fortunately the "something else" materialized shortly after in the shape of an appointment in the recently formed bureau of War Intelligence at Wellington House, and he seized the chance with alacrity. Here, in the intervals of routine work, he found time to produce a series of pamphlets, in the form of open letters to prominent neutrals, and in one case to an eminent scholar[1] in the enemy's ranks, setting forth, with lucidity and strength, the case of the Allies, and in particular that of Britain. It is hard to say what the effect of a single voice, and one which strove to speak the language of reason, may have been in the hurly-burly of passionate polemic which at that time filled two hemispheres; but it is probable that the pamphlets were not without effect, at all events in the Northern Kingdoms and America, where their author was known. Particularly effective, perhaps, was *Colour-Blind Neutrality* (1916), a letter to Georg Brandes (whose utterances in the character of Mr. Facing-Both-Ways were doing harm), which was translated into Danish and Spanish, and drew a long reply from the great Danish critic.

A by-product of Archer's employment at Wellington House, important not only in itself but for its indirect influence on his later years, was the short three-act drama, *War is War*, published in 1919. His close and prolonged study of the documents relating to the German invasion of Belgium, and first and foremost of the German official apologia,[2] had led him to a firm conviction that the excuses alleged for the atrocities of the invasion were baseless, and to a vivid realization of the full horror of the tragedy. It would seem that, as he studied the grim story, indignant sympathy broke down the inhibition which had so long held him back from any serious attempt at creative work, and the events of the twenty-four hours of August 5–6, 1914, in a

[1] Professor von Wilamowitz-Möllendorf.

[2] The White Book entitled *Die völkerrechtswidrige Führung des belgischen Volkskrieges.*

typical Belgian frontier village, shaped themselves in his mind into dramatic form, and were recorded with stark simplicity in this poignant little piece.

Finished in 1918, the play never reached the stage, for, before there was time to overcome the difficulties due to the size of the cast and the large number of supernumeraries, peace came, and checked or killed the interest of the theatrical public for serious war plays. But on its publication (with a Postscript giving some of the evidence in the case) the reception given it must have gone some way towards shaking its author's fixed idea that he was incapable of producing effective dramatic work.

Meanwhile the wasting months had been dragging by, and as they passed, and all effort was increasingly focussed on the war, the normal activities of civil life had shrunk and dwindled more and more. Already in April 1915 Archer's articles in the *Daily News* from weekly had become fortnightly; in March 1917, when the paper was reduced to a single sheet, they ceased altogether. Before many months were out the theatrical notices in the *Star* had dwindled to mere snippets; and throughout the war Archer's most important dramatic criticism was to be found in a series of letters on the English Stage contributed to the New York *Nation*, which, if they only here and there deal with matter of intrinsic interest, are historically curious as a picture of the London theatre in war-time.

In 1917 Archer found time to produce, in his booklet *God and Mr. Wells*, a searching criticism of H. G. Wells's *God the Invisible King*; and this led on to a series of essays in rationalistic theology, contributed in later years to the *Literary Guide* and the

Rationalist Press Association Annual, and collected in book[1] form after his death.

The burden of private anxiety, which had been lightened for a time, again lay heavy on Tom Archer's parents as the war entered on its fourth year. A severe attack of illness had sent the young lance-corporal home as an invalid at the end of 1914, and, since it was clear that he was not robust enough for service in the ranks at the front, he had, on recovery, obtained a commission in the Ordnance Department, and for a year worked at the base in comparative safety. But as time went by, and the war seemed to drag on endlessly, "it irked him to be there". Quoting from the family favourite, *Huckleberry Finn,* in a letter to a friend, he says: " 'This ain't no thirty-seven year job; this is a thirty-eight year job', and I must get back to the line." He exchanged into an infantry regiment, the King's Own Scottish Borderers, and at first all was well with him—better than well, indeed, for he was happy with his Corps, and more than happy in his marriage, which took place in February 1918, while he was with a battalion on home service. Then, at the end of March he went with his battalion to the front; was in the Mount Kemmel section when, a month later, the defence was overwhelmed by the second German "push", and appeared in the returns as "wounded and missing". No further authentic trace of him could be discovered at that time, and many months of suspense and slowly ebbing hope had to be endured before it became known that he had died in a German hospital and lay buried at Courtrai.

One fine day of July in that summer of black depres-

[1] *William Archer as Rationalist,* 1925.

sion a friend walked into the room at Wellington House where Archer and a colleague were working, and said: "Do you see that Foch is beginning to hit back?" The two men looked up with a startled question in their eyes. The friend, Archer knew, was no irresponsible peddler of rumours, yet how could any one tell that this might not merely be one more false dawn? It would be tempting Fate to rejoice in it for the true one; and Archer turned to his work again with a "Well, at all events the Germans don't seem to have made much headway this time". But henceforth the hour was marked with a white stone in the recollection of all three, for the enemy had indeed been flung back across the Marne, and the vast peripety, so often heralded before, so often almost despaired of, was begun at last in earnest.

Now that the end of the long struggle was in sight, many schemes were being set afoot for the constitution of that "organization for ensuring future peace", proclaimed by President Wilson to be one of the chief ends for which the war was being waged. None of these, we may be pretty certain, included in its scope the International University of Archer's ideal; but, to his opportunist spirit, half a loaf was always better than no bread—it was clear to him that the foundation of almost any League of Nations, provided that its constitution was reasonable and workable, would be a step, and, if the scheme were sufficiently bold and comprehensive, might be a long step, in the right direction. From August onwards we find him busy as a member of one of the two associations formed to spread the gospel of the League in England, and to do preliminary spadework towards the framing of a sound scheme; and when, somewhat later, the Wellington House organization came to an end, he was able to give much of his time to the cause. With Gilbert Murray and others he worked for the amalgamation of the two societies, which finally came about at the end of the year, when the League of Nations Union was founded, under the Presidency of Lord Grey.

Meanwhile there were signs that the ideals for which the Allies were professedly fighting, and the hope of realizing which had been to him the soul of goodness in the gigantic evil of the war, were in danger of being trodden under foot in the drunkenness of victory. The best hopes of saving them seemed to rest with President Wilson, whose utterances showed him to have the will, and whose commanding position as the head of a mighty and seemingly united country appeared to give him the power, to bring about a peace that should heal and not exasperate. The popular enthusiasm for the President, however, was exceedingly ill-informed, and it was in the hope of supplying a little solid fuel for what, without some knowledge, was likely to prove a fire of straw, that Archer wrote the short sketch[1] of Wilson's career and achievements which was published shortly after the Armistice.

Throughout the early part of 1919 Archer's energies were largely devoted to work for the League of Nations Union, on whose staff he was for some time employed. In January he is in Paris, attending the Conference of League of Nations Societies, and for the next few months he is engaged, as Secretary to the Research Committee of the Union, in contributing to the framing of a draft Covenant for the League, and to the working out of a permanent organization for the Union. The draft completed, the

[1] *The Peace President: A Brief Appreciation.*

Research Committee seems to have been absorbed, and, proposals for his taking up a more permanent position on the staff having fallen through, his official connection with the Union ended in May, though he continued to the end of his life to give it his hearty support. Thus the summer of 1919 found him once more thrown back on dramatic criticism pure and simple, and, since his *Daily News* articles on "Things in General" had come to an end, with even less outlet for his energies in other directions than five years before.

XVIa

LETTERS OF 1914–1918

To Sir William Barrett

8 *June*, 1914

Dear Sir William Barrett,

I have read your *Creative Thought* with great interest, and am much struck with the idea (which I own had not occurred to me) that the form of sensitiveness which we encounter in telepathy has no doubt played its part in the processes of evolution. . . .

Your chapter on the Problem of Evil, and especially paragraph (ii), recalled to my mind some verses I wrote a couple of years ago to serve as the motto to an essay that was never written. As they are very short, I will venture to copy them. You will understand, I hope, that I would not for a moment class you with the "glib apologists" of the second line:

"If things were ordered otherwise",
The glib apologists aver,
"The soul would lack the needful spur
To earn its mansion in the skies.

"The hero must have foes to quell;
Evil is but the foil of good;
Anguish accents beatitude,
And heaven were vapid but for hell."

So runs the circular excuse:
God is constrained by God's decree,
Or by a mightier God than he;
Anangké dominating Zeus.

The argument, it seems to me, is perfectly sound if we postulate two antagonistic principles in the universe: an intelligent but extremely limited power making for ever higher consciousness, but condemned to work in a clumsy way through an extremely recalcitrant pre-existent medium, which we may roughly call matter. That seems to me an arguable hypothesis, though it is, of course, "une griefve hérezie, dont maint concile ha faict iustice". But if it be presented in the guise of a justification for all the groaning and travail of conscious existence, I can only say that (as at present advised) I am sorry the postulated power did not recognize its fatal limitations and let the task alone. But of course I admit the whole thing to be so densely mysterious that there may quite well be some good explanation of it, though wholly inconceivable to our present faculties.

Yours very truly,

W. A.

To CHARLES ARCHER, QUETTA, INDIA

6 *August*, 1914

MY DEAR C.,

The enclosed copy of a letter I wrote to Murray today will show you pretty much where I stand in this black business. Now that the die is cast, I am beginning to pluck up heart a little, and to wonder whether, in one way or another, it may not be the final flare-up of militarist madness in Western Europe, and may not result in a federation of West European states, with vastly reduced armaments maintained for the purpose of keeping Russia in check until she is civilized enough to stand in. It is no use remarking on the events of the moment, for two reasons—firstly that no one knows anything for certain, and secondly that it will all be ancient history before it reaches you. . . .

Murray has been passing most of his time in the House and was enormously impressed by Grey's statement on Monday. It certainly seems to have been a statesmanlike utterance in so far that it made nothing like the appeal to passion that might have been made. The case for war is much stronger in the diplomatic correspondence now published than it was in Grey's speech. Murray says the reception of Asquith's statement on Wednesday was very curious. He began, "I have to announce to the House that from 7 o'clock last night a state of war has existed between England and Germany." This was received with absolute silence. Then when he went on, "We propose to ask the House for a credit of a hundred million pounds", there was a great roar of applause, as if he had been announcing a windfall of a hundred millions.

People I think are behaving very well. There is no panic and no mafficking, or very little that I can hear of. . . .

Din,

W. A.

To G. G. A. MURRAY

27 October, 1914

MY DEAR MURRAY,

Many thanks for the pamphlet. It seems to me excellent and very helpful. I should have been inclined to emphasize the point that not to have fought would have been a betrayal of the cause of peace—unless we were prepared to accept the peace conferred by an all-embracing military despotism. And even that would be illusory: our grandsons would be doing the goose-step preparatory to a war against the Americans or the Chinese. If we want peace, we must crush the philosophy that idealizes war. Also we must study and realize the social conditions that can alone make peace possible—See *The Great Analysis, passim.*

Among my sister's refugees at Wadhurst is a gigantic Belgian whom no clothes could be found to fit. So I wrote to Chesterton for a cast-off suit, and he has sent one which he had offered in vain to his local refugees, as no one could be found to fill it. Thus is the eternal fitness of things once more vindicated.

You don't happen to possess any of the works of Treitschke, do you?

Yours ever,

W. A.

To ANDREW CARNEGIE

21 *January*, 1915

DEAR MR. CARNEGIE,

Many thanks for your New Year's greeting, with the sentiments of which I most heartily agree. At the same time it sets buzzing what I am afraid you think the bee in my bonnet—namely, the idea that what is most urgently required in the cause of peace is an organization of thoroughly qualified students of history, politics, geography, sociology, etc., who should devote themselves to paving the way for world-peace by studying the causes of war and pointing out how they can be eliminated and counteracted by the exercise of reason. The defect of the Hague Tribunal is that it can only take cognizance of quarrels which have actually arisen; and the really serious quarrels spring to a head so quickly (as did this Austro-Servian affair) that there is no time for reason to make itself heard. That watchword of black magic "mobilization" sets the avalanches rolling, and no power on earth can arrest them. The Hague Tribunal, in short, is like a searchlight which can only cast its ray backward. To make the peace-apparatus complete, we want a searchlight aiming forward, showing what pitfalls lie in the path and how they can be filled up or avoided. We want an International World-Brain thinking ahead for Peace, or, if you prefer it, an Organized Will for Peace with the best available intelligences working in its service. This would not be a costly institution to create—not costly, at any rate, in comparison with many of your beneficences—and I feel sure that it would one day be recognized as putting the crown to your work in the great cause.

This is no new idea of mine. Indeed I fear that it must in one form or another have reached you before and been rejected by you. In that case forgive my troubling you afresh—you must be accustomed to monomaniacs. If, however, this brief statement of it interests you at all, I shall be glad to develop it at greater length.

Yours very truly,

W. A.

From HARLEY GRANVILLE-BARKER

H.Q., BRITISH RED CROSS,
A.P.O.3. B.E.F.,
Feb. 4 [1915?]

MY DEAR W. A.,

Some day we'll meet! and I'll tell you whys and wherefores.

Meanwhile £25—the first subscription to that

scheme.[1]—Well, that has gone by the board with many other things—and someone else will now do the job.

Do you know, W. A.—if the millionaires had taken up that Blue Book of ours when it was written—I'm not sure we shouldn't have found it a little easier (we the B.P.) to win this war.

Was so glad to get your message the other day.

Yours,

H. G-B.

To BRANDER MATTHEWS

16 *November*, 1918

MY DEAR MATTHEWS,

. . . .

You will understand that there is for my wife and myself, as for so many thousands of others, a shadow over what would otherwise be a time of wonderful relief and joy. My wife and Tom's wife have not yet given up hope—I wish I could share it.

But what a victory! What days to have lived through! It is almost to belittle it to say that there is nothing like it in history; for the fall of Napoleon was, after all, the fall of a mushroom adventurer; whereas the Hapsburgs and Hohenzollerns had all the prestige of age-old legitimacy behind them. They had everything in their favour except honesty, humanity—and intelligence. For it seems to me that this is the moral of the whole affair—the Germans are an immensely able people, but they are not *intelligent*. They were content to leave their honour and their fortune in the hands of a man who believed

[1] Granville-Barker's Repertory Theatre Scheme, to which W. A. had been the first subscriber. When it became clear that the war was going to last, all subscriptions were returned.

fanatically in such a mouldy old superstition as the divine right of kings, and thereby wrote himself down an ass.

. . . .

And the best part of the victory is the American share in it. There are almost as many Stars and Stripes as Union Jacks in the streets of London to-day—far more than there are of any other flag.

. . . . .

Ever yours,

W. A.

Read *The Great Hunger* by Johan Bojer. It is a remarkable book.

December 28, 1918

MY DEAR MATTHEWS,

Forgive pencil. My typewriter is in London and my penmanship is painful and infamous.

I am much interested in your letter about Wilson, and am moved to give you my views. When I first heard he was coming over, I was very doubtful of the wisdom of the move. Of course I couldn't estimate its domestic bearings; but it seems to me that the head man, the big boss, ought never to descend into the arena of debate, even as arbitrator or moderator. But it now appears that Wilson has no intention of personally sitting at the conference table, and if that is so my objection vanishes; and I cannot tell you how much reassurance his presence on this side brings me. For things are going ill here. Both in England, France, and I gather in Italy, the intoxication of victory is playing havoc with the sanity of politics. Here the Coalition is this very day being returned to power, by a huge majority, on a platform which, if it were literally carried into effect, would be nothing short of infamous. Wilson is our only security against an act of perfidy to Germany as vile as her perfidy to Belgium and far more stupid. Of course this "Parliament of all the Ruffians" will not work the havoc it threatens, for the worst of the follies to which it is nominally committed are mere dishonest election talk, impossible of realization. Still, irreparable harm may, and perhaps will, be done, and sane men look to Wilson to minimize it.

I think, if you had seen his reception two days ago, you would have felt that his trip across the Atlantic had not been all a mistake. The crowd was immense, and the enthusiasm absolutely spontaneous and genuine. I have never seen so moving a public spectacle, or one of such encouraging symbolism. How crazy would anyone have seemed who should have told me, four or even two years ago, that I should live to see the President of the United States driving to Buckingham Palace cheek by jowl with the King of England—the successor of Washington, after less than a century and a half, the honoured guest of the successor of George III, and enthusiastically acclaimed by the hugest London crowd on record. The crowd was much denser than at the Diamond Jubilee—but it is true that then the route of the procession was much longer.

There will be difficulties yet between Britain and the U.S. There are hot heads and narrow views on both sides. But nothing can cancel the significance of that day. We have downed the Big Bully together, and we're not going to forget it.

. . . .

With all good wishes for 1919,
I am, my dear Matthews,
Ever yours sincerely,
W. A.

WILLIAM ARCHER
(*about* 1920)

XVII

1920–1923

THE GREEN GODDESS—LECTURING IN NORWAY—*THE OLD DRAMA AND THE NEW*—THE NATIONAL THEATRE

THE long strain of the tragic five years had told heavily on Archer's highly-strung temperament. Already in 1916, even while declaring that he would not on any account have wished to be a neutral, he had written:[1] "To myself . . . this war has been a pain unspeakable. Though I have hitherto had less of direct personal anxiety than hundreds of thousands of my country-men and country-women, I seem to have been living for two years in a nightmare. . . . I often wonder whether there was ever a time when I could waken in the morning without a sense of black oppression, and open a newspaper without a tremor." The oppression had gone on deepening for two years more, and personal anxiety, and in the end private grief, had been added in full measure. Then, after the feverish exhilaration and high hope of the armistice winter, had come heavy disappointment in the peace settlement, which seemed to do so little towards realizing the great good, the hope of which had helped him to endure the war years. Small wonder if he came out of the ordeal with head unbowed indeed, but a little dizzy.

His health, too, hitherto notably robust, was visibly shaken. From early manhood onwards he had scarcely had a day's serious illness. But now, as a consequence of attacks of influenza caught during visits to France, he had begun to suffer from an

[1] *Colour-Blind Neutrality*, p. 52.

obstinate catarrh and cough, which defied all the doctors' remedies and troubled him henceforth not a little.

Nor did he regard his immediate worldly prospects with much satisfaction. Though his devotion to the drama was undiminished, he felt that he could best serve it now by special work—such as lecturing, furthering the National Theatre Movement, and helping on the work of the New Shakespeare Company at Stratford—which brought little or no grist to the mill; and that it was time to leave the strenuous paths of journalistic criticism to younger men. But, having throughout life saved only so much money as was strictly necessary to ensure for him and his "the glorious privilege of being independent", he could not afford, in those hard times, to discard the only remunerative trade in which he was an acknowledged expert. It seemed then as though he must remain indefinitely tied to the field of dramatic criticism.

Escape came in a quite unexpected, and to him very astonishing, fashion. Six years earlier he had begun to take a keen interest in dreams, his attention having been attracted to the subject by Freud's well-known book, and further stimulated by his experiencing at that time one of those deeply impressive dreams of unspeakable and seemingly unmotived well-being that probably visit most men twice or thrice in a life-time. He had begun, from that day forward, to register all his remembered dreams, training himself to write down their substance immediately on waking, at whatever hour of the night or day; for his habit of constant reading—in his study, in trains, on shipboard, wherever he might be—brought with it the habit of frequently dropping off into a doze over his book. Practice no doubt made him expert in the art of remembering and noting, for many of the dreams recorded in his voluminous notes[1] are long and complicated. But the dream of September 1–2, 1919, which changed the course of his life, was a comparatively simple one.

"What do you think I was doing all yesterday?" he writes on September 8th. "Sketching a play which came to me in a dream! How much of it I really dreamt it is hard to say, but certainly the root idea—the idea that constitutes the originality (if any) of the theme." The idea, as recorded in his notes, was that of "cultured barbarians applying a sort of torture by courtesy to Europeans. I have a vague idea", he adds, "that the leading spirit on the barbarian side was a woman, whom I conceived as a singularly able personality." The construction and even the writing went, up to a certain point, with unwonted ease. His incorrigible diffidence caused some delay by inducing him to suggest collaboration to Bernard Shaw (a suggestion met by an exhortation, in the usual affectionately abusive terms, to overcome his laziness for once, and do the work himself), and to Sir Arthur Pinero, who remarked that the scenario shown him was already so complete, that there was nothing of much interest left to do. But before the end of the year Archer was writing: "I have finished my great melodrama, provisionally entitled *The Raja of Rukh* . . . There are many things in it that I'm far from satisfied with; but on the whole it's much liker a real play than anything of the kind I've done before. The inspiration is simply the desire for filthy lucre—I want an Old-Age

[1] These formed the basis of two lectures delivered at the Royal Institution in May–June, 1920, and he had made some progress with a book on the subject in the year of his death.

Pension. The worse of it is, it'll want a tremendously big production; and if it is ever produced it may fall between the two stools of the Highbrows and the Lowbrows. It's too good for the Lyceum and not good enough for—what shall I say?—the Comédie Française. And alas! no sooner did I begin writing it than the one man who could have played the Raja went away and died—H. B. Irving. . . ."

Apart from this misfortune, all things seemed to conspire in the play's favour. Confided to the good offices of Granville-Barker, then on his way to America, it was read by him to Winthrop Ames, and accepted with enthusiasm by that prince of producers. In his expert and friendly hands the arrangements for the production of the play at the end of 1920 went forward smoothly (helped by a flying visit paid by Archer to the States in July-August), and by the autumn a Raja had been found whose performance was to prove as masterly in its way as that of the distinguished actor for whom the part was intended could possibly have been.

Satisfied that the fate of the first heir of his dramatic invention was in the best of hands, the budding dramatist could take up in good heart the current work of the year, which was fairly strenuous. Since the "old-age pension" was as yet in the lap of the gods, prudence required that the resources in hand should be made the most of, and from May onwards Archer took up an engagement to contribute a weekly review of the theatres to the *Illustrated Sporting and Dramatic News*. No extra theatre-going was entailed, and he was more at ease in this class of work than in the day-by-day criticisms for the *Star*. His *Sporting and Dramatic* articles were as forcible as any of his work, and rather more uncompromising than had been his wont. The season produced several interesting home-grown dramas, but it was his criticism of a much-admired foreign play, Tchekhov's *Cherry Orchard,* that attracted most attention. Influenced, perhaps to excess, by his dislike of formlessness in drama, and his distrust of what he called "æsthetic attitudinizing" in the theatre, he boldly avowed his inability to appreciate this extremely exotic dramatic work, as interpreted by actors who, in his view, obviously did not understand the characters and the life they were trying to represent. His very last article, too (November 20, 1920), was an onslaught on a much less defensible fashion of the hour—the attempt to reverse the verdict of two centuries and gain indiscriminating acceptance for the fruit of the Restoration medlar-tree as a wholesome and agreeable article of dessert in the theatrical banquet.

When Archer reached America in December, followed by many good wishes, preparations for the production of his play were already well advanced. It had been decided to give it a trial trip before the production in New York, and the enlarged and renovated Walnut Street Theatre, Philadelphia (occupying the site of the earliest American theatre, and of the more modern playhouse in which, forty-three years before, Archer had witnessed the "elegant, chaste, and complete" performance of Offenbach's *L'Archiduc*), was chosen for the experiment. On December 27th the new theatre opened its doors with *The Green Goddess*—so *The Raja of Rukh* had been finally renamed.

The success of the play was immediate and striking—so striking as to amaze the author, who, as his letters show, was at first inclined to fear that it must be a flash in the pan, that his play "had gone up like a rocket in Philadelphia only to come down like the stick in New York". The fixed idea, which had obsessed him for thirty-five years and had become almost an article of faith, that he was incapable of producing theatrically effective dramatic work, could not be uprooted in a moment. But it had to yield to the experience of the next few weeks, which made it evident that, with the advantages given it by Winthrop Ames's admirable production and by George Arliss's "subtle, serpentine, terrible, and fascinating" performance of the chief part, the play was to be one of the great popular successes of the time, amply fulfilling its author's double purpose of adding to the stock of harmless pleasure and earning for himself such an "old-age pension" as should set him free from drudgery. Transferred to the Booth Theatre, New York, the piece repeated its Philadelphia success, and "ran" for fifty-five consecutive weeks (weathering one of the hottest and most unfavourable summer seasons on record); and thereafter continued its prosperous career at Boston, at Chicago, and "on the road" throughout the North-Eastern States. When, on May 5, 1923, the American run came to an end, it had lasted, with a brief recess in the summer of 1922, for nearly two and a half years.

We have spoken of the "comparative leisure" of William Archer's last years, but when one examines the records of the work done by him in those years—dramas, lectures, a large book on dramatic history, essays in rationalistic theology, voluminous correspondence and committee work connected with the theatrical movements in which he was interested, and especially with the work of the Shakespeare Memorial Theatre Committee—one is disposed to think the phrase an inappropriate one. He was engaged as unrestingly as ever in forwarding the causes he had at heart; and any spare moments were now devoted to play-writing, for, convinced at last of his ability to produce "something like a real play", he had taken up that fascinating pursuit with eagerness and found it an excellent pastime and anodyne for care.

He was free also to take up such public tasks as came his way, and one of these took him once more to Norway in the late autumn of 1921. Lord Robert Cecil's engagements having prevented him from delivering, as had been intended, the inaugural address at the opening in Christiania of the newly founded Norsk-Britisk Forening,[1] Archer was invited by the Committee to take his place. His reputation as a British patriot who was also a world-patriot, and as one who from a boy had loved Norway, and who had done as much as any man living to interpret Norway to England, made it fitting enough that he should now be chosen to interpret England to Norway. His address on "The British Empire", delivered to an audience which included many of the leaders of Norwegian thought, was warmly received, and the banquet and reunion which followed had a tone of informal friendliness rarely to be found at such functions. Having spent the next few days in the enjoyment of the cordial hospitality of the Norwegian capital, in diligent theatre-going, and in a flying visit to the old home at Larvik, Archer returned to England by way of Stockholm and Copenhagen, not failing to see by the way the most noteworthy plays of the moment in both cities. The visit to Norway had been entirely successful, and made delightful by the kindness of

[1] Norwegian-British Society.

old and new friends; but too few of the former were now left, and his enjoyment, like the austere beauty of the late autumn landscape, was deeply tinged with sadness. For Norway, and especially that angle of the country which he knew and loved best, was now for him a land thickly peopled by ghosts.

After a journey in search of health in the early spring of 1922 to Spain, the Balearic Islands, and the Italian Riviera, Archer settled down to the work of revising, for publication in book form, two courses of lectures delivered at King's College in the foregoing years on the invitation of the Education Authority of the London County Council.

The argument of this, his last large critical work,[1] had been foreshadowed, some thirty years before, in a *New Review* paper on "Webster, Lamb, and Swinburne", and at times during the intervening years he had returned to the theme; writing, for example, in 1908: "It is high time for a revaluation of the whole domain" (of Elizabethan drama), "and I hope I may live to see it. Where is the critic who has sufficient youth, energy, and grasp of the fundamental principles of drama to undertake it with success?"

Though the first of these qualifications was now left far behind him, he took up the task in *The Old Drama and the New*, and, not content to deal with the Elizabethan-Jacobean drama as an isolated period, attempted to relate his revaluation to a general theory of the evolution of drama. The course of that evolution, as conceived by him, had been from an originally mixed or impure art form (in which interpretation through imitation held a com-

[1] *The Old Drama and the New.*

THE RAJA OF RUKH
MAKES OBEISANCE TO THE GREEN GODDESS

paratively small place, the preponderating element being lyrical or exaggerative passion) to a relatively pure art of imitation, the lyrical element being relegated to opera and music drama. And his contention was that the criticism of the past century, blinded by the glamour of the lyrical, exaggerative element in the drama of the past, had tended to overestimate its purely dramatic merits, and to undervalue as greatly the achievements and possibilities of the modern art of sober imitation—the most flagrant instance of this tendency being the glorification of the minor Elizabethans and their imitators and the failure to recognize the merits of the modern prose drama as newly developed in England in the preceding thirty years.

"Whatever comes of it", the author wrote to his friend, Dr. Kellner, "I can say 'liberavi animam meam'. It is, I think, the first systematic attempt to apply dramatic (as opposed to literary) criticism to the English drama as a whole. I regard it as a sketch for the history of English drama that must some day be written." Had Archer developed his "sketch" into a finished picture (the work, he says, would have demanded from five to ten years of unremitting labour, and "I have arrived at a time of life when one does not lightly undertake such long engagements"), he would probably have adopted a less polemical tone, and softened a few trenchancies of expression. These perhaps hindered the acceptance of the book's thesis, and at least gave a shadow of excuse for misconceiving its purpose and the author's tastes and ideals, as some devotees of the fashionable cults to which it ran counter did not fail to do. But the "sketch", taken from a point of view which has been too much neglected, is comprehensive and firmly drawn; its protest against the attempt to galvanize into life the unhandsome corpse of Restoration drama was as timely as it was vigorous, and it will doubtless be of service till, and when, the final History is written—at a time, one may hope, when some at least of those cults will have had their day and ceased to be.

The presentation of a portrait of Ludvig Holberg, on behalf of the Bergen Holberg Club, to Magdalen College, Oxford, in memory of the "many dinners" which the great dramatist tells us he enjoyed in that hospitable Hall—in the days when he was a poor outlandish student, boring into books at the Bodleian and keeping soul and body together by teaching French and music—was an occurrence of this summer that warmed the heart of the Holberg-lover, and we find him speaking at the unveiling ceremony. And another joyous event was the great success of the New Shakespeare Company's performances in Christiania, in the arrangements for which he had taken part; he is hard at work at the end of June translating the enthusiastic yet discriminating notices which had appeared in the Norwegian papers.

But most of his time during this summer and autumn was given to a vigorous effort to speed up the National Theatre movement—an effort evidently prompted by the feeling that there was no time to lose if he himself was to witness any real advance. The voluminous correspondence shows him engaged in an uphill struggle to obtain acceptance for his views on policy and methods of action. The struggle was in the main unsuccessful, and for once he was somewhat discouraged. By enlisting the help of the British Drama League, however, he was able to arrange for the distribution to "as nearly as possible all the leaders of the national life and thought" of a

Declaration ("Towards a National Theatre: a Statement of Principle") for signature[1] in token of general approval of the movement. "I consider this", he writes, "a sound initial step to take, which will be of value whenever anything is done and whoever does it." And with the Declaration was issued a pamphlet[2] ("a romance not quite as long as *The Forsyte Saga*; I wrote it in four days") entitled *The Foundation of the National Theatre: being a Chapter from the History of England after the Great War*, setting forth a possible method for the realization of his ideal. Feeling that, for the moment, he had done all he could, he thereafter withdrew to some extent from the fray, awaiting a more propitious time—which, unhappily, he was not to see.

Falling back on play-writing, he puts in three weeks' concentrated work in a Devonshire retreat, finishing an historical play of the American Revolution,[3] begun a year before. It is, as he writes, "the most historical play that ever was: every episode . . . is dated by year, month and day; a great deal of the dialogue is absolutely historical; and nothing (to the best of my belief) occurs that can be proved *not* to have occurred". He might have added that there is a successful suggestion of the atmosphere of the period which would, one fancies, have pleased the author of *The Virginians*, though with a generation which likes its drama, in sentiment and setting, "up to date", it doubtless counted as a defect. This, perhaps, of his more ambitious efforts in drama, comes nearest to complete success; though there is strength in *Beatriz Juana*,[4] a blank-verse play suggested by

[1] A substantial number of signatures was eventually obtained.
[2] Afterwards published through the British Drama League.
[3] *Martha Washington*, published in *Three Plays*.
[4] Published in *Three Plays*.

Middleton and Rowley's *Changeling*, and tenderness and charm in *Lidia*,[1] his other experiment in blank-verse, founded on Massinger's *Grand Duke of Florence*. Here, too, his work was to be cut short—he had taken up playwriting so late that time was not given him to develop his full powers.

[1] Published in *Three Plays*.

XVIIa

LETTERS OF 1920–1922

To CHARLES ARCHER

THE PHILADELPHIA CLUB,
31 *Decr.*, 1920

I AM giving myself a holiday from "The Green Goddess" tonight, partly because it is doubtful whether I could get a seat. It appears this is the great theatre-going night of the year, and they expect a full house even at increased prices. The theatre is a very large one, seating, I believe, 1700 people; and hitherto it has never been quite full, except, I believe, at the Wednesday matinee. Nevertheless they have taken close upon £2000 at the 5 performances up to last night, and expect to bring it up to £3000 or thereabouts for the week. So far, then, the thing is astonishingly successful; but this is a holiday week, and all the theatres are doing good business. A considerable drop next week is more than probable; but on the whole Ames thinks the prospects quite good. . . . The whole experience is weird and incredible. If anyone had told me two years ago that on this New Year's Eve a play by me would be drawing something like £400[1] in Philadelphia, of all places, I should have thought him bindegal [raving mad].

Thanks to having for manager and producer an extremely "white man" like Winthrop Ames, the experience is on the whole a pleasant one. But I am yearning for the time when the play shall have hardened into its final form and there shall be no

[1] [Pencil note] The actual figure (at increased prices) was £760 = $3800.

more patching or paring or sandpapering to be done to it. Rehearsal is to me an unspeakably tedious business, and the performance bores and annoys me extremely. It is full of little things that affect me like misprints in an article—all the more annoying for the fact that few people except myself detect them. No essential changes have been made in the action, but the dialogue has in some places been cut more than I theoretically approve, in order to adapt it to Arliss's slow and subtle manner. He is an excellent actor, and a quite intelligent man; the greater part of this week's success is certainly due to him; but whereas I imagined the Raja a voluble, mercurial man, loving to hear himself talk, Arliss relies enormously on pauses and facial expression, so that several of my scenes would certainly have appeared tedious had he delivered the whole of the Raja's speeches. He has the great vice of the star—always wanting to follow the line of least resistance and cut or alter anything that he finds at all difficult. On the other hand many of his suggestions have been excellent, and he always "dit juste" as Sarcey used to say. I never have to ask him to correct an emphasis, as I am constantly having to do with the others. . . . I except a man named Simpson who plays Watkins —an excellent, most intelligent actor. . . .

I always thought it foolish of Pinero never to see his plays in the theatre; and I still think it foolish, but now I entirely understand and sympathize. If I did my duty, I should be sitting it out at this moment and noting things to be put right before it approaches the ordeal of New York. But after the first night I have never succeeded in sitting it out. . . .

K. came over here and supported me on the first night of the play, which was pleasant, but . . . I never felt less nervous in my life. . . .

Jan. 2

The total receipt of the week has been $19,164—nearly £4000 at pre-war rates, and I suppose a good deal more at the present exchange. Rather surprising, isn't it? I hope it hasn't gone up like a rocket in Philadelphia to come down like the stick in New York. . . .

To GEORGE BERNARD SHAW

22 *June*, 1921

MY DEAR G. B. S.,

All the time I have been reading "Back to Methuselah", I have been mentally writing you a series of letters that would fill a small volume. Now that I have come to the end, I have providentially forgotten most of them; but Providence (or Satan) having arranged that I should have a little time on my hands, I can't resist the temptation to give you a few extracts from the fragments that remain.

And first of all I want to protest against your affectation (p. lxxxvii) of being a He-Ancient. It won't do. Your mind was never more infernally agile, your intellectual muscle was never better. To put it in another way, you never were further from years of discretion. Throughout the play (I'm not speaking of the preface) you are almost indecently young and irresponsible. When a man can walk on a tight-rope over the Falls of Niagara, turning three summersaults to a minute, it's no use his appealing to the census-paper to prove himself decrepit.

There is, then, no just cause or impediment in your age to prevent you from accepting the following challenge: Why not prove once for all the reality of Creative Evolution by creatively evolving from the privileged lunatic all the world knows (I remember when Tom used to call it "pivileged loonatit") a Leader of Men and a Saviour of Society? If this last Bible of yours is ever going to have any effect, it will be 100 or 1000 years hence; and it's tomorrow that needs salvation. If there are today a few intellectual smelters who can separate the gold from the slag, they are about as many as can understand Einstein. The mass of people will simply laugh, shrug their shoulders and pass on. What's the use of a wisdom concealed in indecipherable hieroglyphics, however amusing?

There are two really tragic passages in the preface: "I have spent forty years in writing in this fashion without, as far as I can see, producing any visible effect on public opinion" and, with regard to MAN AND SUPERMAN, "The effect was so vertiginous, apparently, that nobody noticed the new religion in the centre of the intellectual whirlpool."

I doubt if there is any case of a man so widely read, heard, seen and known as yourself, who has produced so little practical effect on his generation. I am strongly under the impression (I may be wrong) that you have less of a following to-day than you had twenty years ago. Don't tell me that that's merely the natural effect of the lapse of time, a new generation having supplanted the generation that hailed you as a delightful novelty. Neither Carlyle nor Ruskin (great writers, but men of very limited intelligence) had, at your age, lost any part of his influence. It isn't as if any newer prophet had arisen to oust you. You have no serious competitor; but your public (small blame to them) declines to take you seriously. Can't you fix your will upon the high-growing frondage of Practical Influence and elongate your neck so as to reach it?

You will say it's no use badgering you to "hatch

yourself over again and hatch yourself different". But that's just what, on your own showing, Creative Evolution should be able to do. Besides, it wouldn't really be a matter of Creation, but rather of Suppression. The wisdom is *in* you, right enough; it has only to be liberated from the tyrannous, irrepressible idiosyncrasy. Do your own smelting: let us for once, or twice, or thrice, have the gold without slag, working it into whatever artistic form you please. . . .

To put the same idea in another way, why not set the dramatist in you to work, and project a new avatar of your godhead, persuasive and convincing, instead of merely startling and titillating. The G. B. S. we know is partly a deliberate creation; and it has done its work. Why not shift the mask, and adapt the voice and manner (not the essential matter) to a new and more ingratiating prosopopœia?

You may think it rather unfair of me (not to say d——d cheek) to seize upon two casual sentences and make them the text of a sermon. But it isn't a sermon—it's an appeal. I believe firmly in the wisdom of the essence of your thought: there are hundreds of pages in your prefaces that I read with a passion of assent and admiration. I believe there is no one living who has more light and leading in him, if you would only purify your light and condescend to give a little study to the psychology of leadership, or rather of followership.

What we really want is a great orator—a "spellbinder"—who should be at the same time a thinker and a right thinker. I don't suppose even Creative Evolution could make you a Bright or a Bradlaugh, effective debater though you be. But all that the pen can do you could an if you would. I think you have quoted with approval Ibsen's "To be yourself you must slay yourself"; I think that a grossly overstated doctrine; but anyway no one was ever further from acting up to it than you—I mean, of course, in a literary sense.

. . . .

Yours ever,

W. A.

To Harley Granville-Barker

7th Jany. 1922

. . . My general criticism of your dialogue[1] with Fisher would be that it encourages the erroneous habit of talking and thinking of "the theatre" as one and indivisible. Until the general elevation of the British brow has reached a pitch at present inconceivable, the mass of theatrical productions will always be poor and trivial, with a bias towards baseness. A system of good theatres at the top will no doubt tend to raise the general level, but nothing will ever place the theatre, as a whole, on a uniformly high level. I find no sufficient admission (in that dialogue) of this basic fact. Also I think your Man of the Theatre is too resolutely high-browed. He does not sufficiently admit and stand up for the function of even the best theatre as a place—occasionally, and even frequently—of mere harmless, unpretending recreation. We can't always be listening to Bach—there is also a time for Offenbach—and if anyone is so devoted to Bach as to have no ear for Offenbach, that is his misfortune, not his merit, and he oughtn't to make it a law, or an ideal, for others. Remember, I have not yet read beyond Chapter I—the subsequent chapters may allow for all that I am

[1] Dialogue between Man of the Theatre and Minister of Education in Granville-Barker's *Exemplary Theatre*.

saying—I merely note my general impression of the attitude of your Man of the Theatre.

Don't say that my plea for the Average Human Being is suggested by the fact that I myself can only write trivial plays. I have stood up for the theatre as a place which ought sometimes (and frequently) to be devoted to pure recreation ever since I began to stand up for anything—forty years before I dreamt of writing plays. Such is the inferiority of my taste that, much as I should like to have written WASTE, I'm not sure that I wouldn't rather have written THE WHITE-HEADED BOY—and I'm quite sure that I'd rather have written AS YOU LIKE IT than CORIOLANUS. Vive la bagatelle!

XVIII

1923-1924

THE GREEN GODDESS IN ENGLAND—THE LAST YEAR

ARCHER'S health had benefited little by the many and varied remedies prescribed from time to time, and he was now advised to try what wintering in a warm climate would do for him. He accordingly spent the next winter and spring in the West Indies and the Southern States; finding Jamaica still entrancing; falling for the first time under the charm of the "still-vexed Bermoothes", though finding the Shakespearean epithet curiously apt; and, as recorded in a characteristic letter, experiencing at a Carolinian health-resort all the discomforts of modern luxury. There were sojourns besides in New York, highly successful socially, but less so from the business point of view. *Martha Washington,* in whose possibilities he had a strong belief, shared by other good judges, was, it appeared, too domestic and unsensational in tone to inspire either managers or actresses with confidence; and the Elizabethan experiments were doubtless too experimental to commend themselves as theatrical wares. In May he was home again, ready to take up the arrangements for the English production of *The Green Goddess.*

Good fortune followed the play across the Atlantic, for Winthrop Ames joined forces with an English manager in the venture, and personally supervised the staging and rehearsals;[1] and George Arliss returned for a time to the English boards to play the

[1] The relation between manager and author, perhaps unique in theatrical annals, is illustrated in the charming note (p. 399), in which, after the production, Mr. Ames said farewell. The two men never met again.

part of the Raja, which he had made so thoroughly his own. The production at the St. James's Theatre (September 6, 1923) was brilliantly successful; congratulations showered in on the author; and there ran through the theatrical world of London a little ripple of genuine pleasure, tinged with amusement at the paradoxical nature of the achievement. That a man who for forty years had been proclaiming, in season and out of season, his inability to write an actable play, should, at his first essay, produce one of the greatest successes on the stage of the time, was in itself a piquant enough event. But that the successful dramatist was also a critic who was generally (though quite wrongly) believed to have been all his life exclusively devoted to the "high-brow" theatre, and the successful play in effect a glorified melodrama, gave the situation, in the popular view, an added touch of paradox. "I was amused", the author wrote, "by a remark of Desmond MacCarthy's in *The New Statesman*. He said he was glad I was no longer a critic, for this was not the sort of play I would have approved. But I don't know—I always had a weak spot for melodrama."

In the event, the play "ran" the year round in London, and, in an abbreviated form, toured the provinces successfully for some years more. It is still a standby with "stock" companies in America.

The calamity with which 1924 ended stains backwards, in retrospect, through the records of the year, tinging them, to our sense, with a feeling of sadness and frustration; but this was certainly not present to Archer's own consciousness, except during occasional fits of depression evidently due to disordered health. True, we find him from time to time a good deal troubled and annoyed, now that he has an income worth attention, by questions of Income Tax assessment. To a conscientious man incapable of figures, Income Tax complications in these latter days must always be sufficiently mysterious and troublesome; and in his case the controversies[1] as to principles of assessment, due to his sudden tapping of new and rich sources of income in America and England, were particularly complicated and irritating. But these were passing clouds. His access of fortune brought him, on the whole, keen enjoyment; he had always valued money mainly for the pleasure of giving it away, and this taste he was now able to indulge more freely. His diary, too, shows many good days of work on magazine articles and lectures, on the book on dreams, on contributions to the Rationalist Press, above all on projected plays; and much enjoyment in the entertainment of friends—English, American, Scandinavian, Austrian, German—at King's Langley, or at the Reform Club, where he was now a member and much at home—and in visits to the numerous houses where he was a welcome guest. Of the dramas, only one, a light and amusing "crook-play" entitled *The Joy Ride*, reached completion; but in the autumn a more ambitious piece, intended for George Arliss, was on the stocks, a hopeful first act had been completed, and work was proceeding on the remaining acts, when Archer was called away by an invitation to visit Denmark and Sweden on a lecturing tour.

He set out, accordingly, in the latter part of November, on what proved to be his last visit to the Northern capitals, and, appropriately enough, his last important piece of work. He lectures at Copenhagen before the Anglo-Danish Society, on "Ludvig Holberg, with special reference to *Jeppe paa Bjerget*",

[1] They were not finally settled till two years after his death.

and before the Students' Association on "The British Empire"; and, passing on to Sweden, repeats "The British Empire" lecture at Lund, at Gothenburg, and at Stockholm. At Stockholm some of his audience noticed that the lecturer was obviously out of health, and that the delivery of the lecture cost him a considerable effort. He himself says nothing of this, merely remarking in his diary: "Crown Princess present—also Branting", and adding without resentment (being himself a notorious offender in that kind[1]) that the eminent statesman "slept solidly". Only one day could be given on the return journey to friends in Christiania, and on November 29th Archer bade farewell to Norway for the last time.

For before December was far gone the enigma of his recurrent ill-health had at last been cleared up, and he had been served with what was in effect his death-warrant. It was found that, while he had been undergoing all kinds of treatment for a superficial ailment, a more deep-seated and deadly evil had for some time been in progress undetected, and that a dangerous operation was now urgently necessary. Though, for the time being, he felt unusually well—the excitement of the impending adventure, perhaps, buoying him up—and though he fully realized the risk involved, he did not hesitate to accept the verdict of the experts. After fulfilling, with great enjoyment, an engagement to lunch at the Norwegian Ministry, to meet the King and Crown Prince of Norway, he set to work to clear the decks for his possible departure, and was able, in the next twenty-four hours, to dispatch a surprising amount of business, including the writing of a very comprehensive

[1] He himself once remarked that he had, in his time, slept through the greater part of the world's drama, from Æschylus and Sophocles to Ibsen and Shaw, inclusive.

letter of instructions for the settlement of his complicated literary and financial affairs, and of letters[1] of conditional farewell to one or two friends. The following day's entry in the diary—the last—gives a succinct account of his occupations and state of mind during his day of waiting in the nursing home: "Decr. 19th—Went to Mr. ——'s at 11, where F. met me. Final examination satisfactory. Returned to [the Nursing Home in] —— Street. Received Johan Bojer's *Vor Egen Stamme.*[2] . . . Wrote long letter[3] to Middleton Murry. Feel so well, I cannot persuade myself that there is anything wrong with me. If the worst comes to the worst, have had my innings."

The operation the next morning proved even severer and more extensive than had been anticipated. It was only the unusual strength of the patient's constitution that carried him through and enabled him to rally temporarily, so that on the fourth day there even seemed some hope of recovery. But the shock had been too great. From Christmas Eve onwards his state grew rapidly worse, and he died in the early morning of December 27th. He lies in the pretty little churchyard at King's Langley, close by the Memorial to men of the village Fallen in the War, which bears among the rest his son's name.

[1] Of these the most notable is the letter below to Bernard Shaw, already printed in Mr. Shaw's Foreword to the *Three Plays* volume.

[2] The fine work known in English as *The Emigrants*.

[3] On Spiritualism, published in the *Adelphi* for March 1925.

WILLIAM ARCHER
WITH HIS WIFE AND DAUGHTER-IN-LAW, 1924

XVIIIa

LETTERS, ETC., OF 1923–1924

To Harley Granville-Barker

[Extracts]

R.M.S.P. *Orca*,
In Havana Harbour,
30 *Jan.*, 1923

. . . If climate is going to cure my ailments (which it isn't) I have certainly come to the right shop. I sit all day on deck under an awning and watch the brilliant sunshine on the pink walls of Morro Castle, and over this gay, amusing, busy harbour. There is a breeze all day long, and the shade temperature is ideal, though the sun is hotter than in an English July. . . .

I have been very little ashore. The place has sad memories for me, and is, moreover, Americanized out of all knowledge. . . .

As I was coming off in the launch last night, I heard a lady say a nice thing. "They tell me", she said, "that this is just about where Hobson sank the 'Maine'." N.B. She was an American lady. Lord —— and I are the only British Anglo-Saxons on board.

My dramatic affairs in New York do not greatly prosper. Ames's failure to rise to *Martha Washington* is a disaster. I can't conceive that it will altogether fail to find a manager, but there aren't two Ameses. He certainly shows a disinterested love of art in spending thousands on *Will Shakespeare* and turning down *M.W.* As for *Beatrice Joanna*, Miss Marbury says Sam Harris would produce it if I would have Miss —— for Beatrice, but I flatly decline; just as my eminent colleague Shakespeare would decline . . .

if she had been proposed for Lady Macbeth. . . . Providence doesn't seem to have provided in the matter of actresses for my appearance in the character of "the William de Morgan of the drama". . . .

ASHEVILLE, N.C.,
12 *April*, 1923

. . . . .

I suppose you and Helen are back in England long ago—as I shall be myself about a month from now. . . . It seems to me I wrote you from somewhere in the Gulf of Mexico, though what I said I have no idea. Probably I broke to you the sad news that America regards *Martha Washington* with chilling aloofness. The only chance for her, it appears, is to get her translated into Czecho-Slovak and retranslated into American, when the Theatre Guild will produce her expressionistically, or Arthur Hopkins will commission Robert Edmond Jones to design one scene (principally consisting of stairs) to serve for all the seven tableaux. Well, well—I daresay poor Martha's turn will come some day—if only my exit doesn't precede her entrance. . . .

Well, a rivederci fra poco.

Yours,
W. A.

To MRS. JOHN CORBIN

—— HOTEL,
FINEST RESORT HOTEL IN THE WORLD.
ABSOLUTELY FIREPROOF.
OPEN ALL THE YEAR.

3rd April, 1923

DEAR MRS. CORBIN,

I have hitherto—perhaps rashly and presumptuously—reckoned you among the best of my

American friends; but if you ever had a spark of friendship for me, how could you find it in your heart to send me to this ridiculous, incredible, exasperating place? In a sense, I am glad to have come, for no one knows America who has not been here; but oh, I am paying dearly (in every sense of the word) for this crown and pinnacle added to my education. It only remains that I should spend a few weeks in Sing-Sing.

Mentioning your name, as you suggested, I wrote to the Grand Lama at the head of the establishment, and requested him to reserve me a room. After requiring me to make an affidavit that I had neither tuberculosis nor leprosy, he indicated that I might have a second-rate chamber with board for the modest consideration of £23 a week. Without tremor or hesitation I accepted, thinking within myself: "It will be fun, for a week or two, to play at being a millionaire." Well, I arrived from Florida on Sunday afternoon (April 1st—Providence is witty!) expecting that the magic of your name, and my disguise as a millionaire, would secure me an enthusiastic and obsequious reception. What did I find? On entering the palæo-megalithic hall, I was received by a casual gentleman who informed me that the room-clerk was not there, and suggested that I should play about until he came. I took his advice for a quarter of an hour, for half an hour, and then mildly remonstrated: he looked at me as much as to say: "What is this the cat has brought in?", and replied that the room-clerk was still absent. It did not occur to him that a man who has been travelling for two days and a night may perhaps be rather impatient for a wash, or even for a glass of water ("the purest in the world"). No—he suggested no mitigation of my penance; and being a poor-spirited creature, I went back to my rocking-chair and consoled myself for *another whole hour* with the "Detective Story Magazine". Then again I ventured to approach the desk, only to learn that the missing room-clerk *had appeared and disappeared again.* At this even the worm turned, and I rushed to a time-table to find out whether it was possible to escape that very day from the palæolithic age and return to the twentieth century and the Pennsylvania Hotel. Half an hour's research assured me that there was no escape until the morrow; and at the end of that time the room-clerk did actually condescend to notice me (two mortal hours after my arrival) and to assign me a temporary room—my *pukka* room I could not have till next day. No one uttered a word of apology, or seemed to think that I had the slightest ground to complain of this reception. Remember, I was not a casual arrival, but had been assured, by telegraph and letter, and fondly believed, that my room had been reserved for me.

My further experience has confirmed me in my suspicion that the millionaire's lot is far from being a happy one—at least in North Carolina. I shall be glad when my fortnight's sentence is over and I go forth into the world a free man again. There is more pretentiousness and less real comfort in this hotel than in any other I ever struck. They can't even give you a cake of soap or a glass of water without a long printed rigmarole vaunting its superexcellence and the enormous pains that have been devoted to inventing and procuring it for you. Every dish in the menu is introduced with a flowery eulogium or a hygienic dissertation. At every corner of your bedroom you are adjured to behave like a good little boy, and threatened with pains and penalties if you don't—if, for instance, you slam your door or drop your boots. There is only one consolation—if the place becomes quite unbearable, I have only to slam my door and decline to pay for damaging the slam-preventer, in which case I shall be forcibly ejected, and can, like Mr. Babbitt in Maine, "loaf and cuss" at my own sweet will.

Really, there is an insolent pharisaism about the place that is beyond belief. I don't know if the Grand Lama is a personal friend of yours, but he is evidently a platitudinous ass of the worst description. The mottoes on the megaliths are a haunting insult to one's intelligence, and the megaliths themselves (or I'm much mistaken) are titanic shams—the real structure of the place is steel and concrete, and the "labor of an age in pilèd stones" is nothing but veneer and window-dressing.

The horrors of the place culminate in the organ, which converts music into silly stunts—meaningless pianissimos and fortissimos, whispers from the cellarage and echoes from the third floor back—the very essence of musical vulgarity.

The only friendly human being I have encountered in this Ogre's Castle is the darkey who runs the elevator. He receives me with an affectionate *empressement* which touches my heart. But he seems to have no influence on the establishment at large.

I hope you realize that I am in fact profoundly grateful to you for sending me here. It is an experience I wouldn't have missed for a great deal. I am doing some work that interests me, and rather enjoy being at enmity with my kind. If I were idle, I should certainly go mad; but as it is, I look forward to the expiration of my sentence on the 14th without undue eagerness.

I hope John has quite got over his accident, and I

trust you have taken a passage for Southampton by the *Homeric* on May 5th.

Yours ever,

WILLIAM ARCHER

P.S.

7th April, 1923

The latest: a framed announcement on the office desk:

> All the money we give you in change has been boiled in Ivory Soap and thoroughly cleaned.

"Mark Twain, thou should'st be living at this hour."

An article by Mark on the —— Hotel would be one of the gems of American literature.

N.B.—Whether boiled or raw, they give you as little change as possible.

W. A.

[The following extracts are from a discursive correspondence with Bernard Shaw arising out of Mr. Shaw's remarks on *The Old Drama and the New*. They present, of course, only a portion of one side of the discussion, and are included here, in the impossibility of setting forth both sides, "without prejudice" as to the merits, for the sake of the light they throw on the writer.]

To G. BERNARD SHAW

12 *June*, 1923

MY DEAR G. B. S.,

[After discussing at length various questions relating to drama, W. A. goes on:]

I have only a few minutes to deal with your old superstition about my hard-shell rationalism. Why, even Dean Inge sees that I am not a rationalist in any offensive sense of the word; and only last night I had a letter from Galsworthy accusing me of having abandoned the whole rationalist position in the enclosed pamphlet. The trouble with me is that I am too old a metaphysician to be taken in by metaphysics. I know too well that each new philosophy is only a new terminology—in fact, a new dialect—and, fundamentally, a new failure to express the inexpressible. I don't despise the inexpressible—in a sense, there is nothing else that matters. But in expressible things I think reason, however imperfect, is the best and only guide we have. The trouble with you, on the other hand, is that you are incurably credulous. Someone comes along and tells you that wool is the only wear; and instantly you go in for woollen boots, which lead, in due time, to a course of crutches. Then Wagner comes along, and you are a Wagnerite; Ibsen, and you are an Ibsenite (I never was); Nietzsche, and you are a Nietzschean; Bergson, and you are a Bergsonian. And all the time you are no whit nearer the real secret of things. All these men, I admit, had something to say, though Nietzsche to my mind was only a crack-brained poseur who was vastly overrated in his little day. But the best of them has only advanced the border of light a little way, and has shot no penetrating beam into the surrounding darkness. . . .

20th June, 1923

MY DEAR G. B. S.,

It won't do. In your determination to defend your later manner of play-writing against all the rest of the world, your earlier self included, you have undertaken to remake the English language. I say a cat is a quadruped, with a brain, a backbone, and (unless of the Manx variety) a tail. You say, "Oh no—a cat is a round, mushy, iridescent object with long streamers, usually observed on the shingle at low tide." "Why", I reply, "that is not a cat, but a jelly-fish." "Nonsense", you say, "your natural history is mid-Victorian. It may have been called a jelly-fish about 1870; but Tchekhov has changed all that, and we now call it a cat—and furthermore the only admissible form of cat. It is true that Shakespeare, Ibsen, Sophocles and the other pre-Tchekhovians had not *quite* mastered the art of dispensing with vertebræ. But by carefully neglecting the articulations of their works, we can reduce them to very plausible imitations of the Tchekho-Shavian cat."

The substantial points on which we differ are really few, though not quite unimportant. Your wild and whirling methods of dialectic make them seem greater than they really are. We differ as to *Heartbreak House*; we don't really differ as to *The Wild Duck*, *Rosmersholm*, *Hedda Gabler*, and the *Master Builder*, though it suits you to call them unconstructed plays, whereas in fact they are the most complex jigsaw puzzles ever invented in this world. Ibsen was as convinced a constructor as Sardou; but he was also a poet, and he had elaborated the art (in which he had been anticipated by Sophocles) of constructing his plays backwards instead of forwards, whereby he gave them a new depth and richness of texture. . . .

To Harley Granville-Barker

11 *June*, 1923

My dear H. G-B.,

I spent a whole Sabbath day over The Secret Life; a very exciting day; and at the end I felt like Napoleon after the Sabbath of Waterloo—defeated in spite of numerous close calls upon victory. I read with constant admiration for the abounding originality, wit and even profundity of the thing, but with despair at the pervading sense that I am at least three generations removed from it. It is written for next generation, if not for the next again; while I belong to the last generation, and cannot hope to overtake it. I thought again and again in the brilliant second act that I was really getting the hang of the thing and saw the drama crystallizing; but in the third act the crystals seemed to dissolve again, leaving behind them a sort of shimmering opalescence from which I could extract nothing solid. This means that I was looking for something that you didn't want to give, and could not find the thing you did want to give. In very great measure my fault, but also, I think, partly yours—for it *is* possible to be "though deep, yet clear". The greatest people have done it. In fact, I'm not sure that any of the really great—except perhaps Æschylus, whose obscurity is in part mere remoteness—have failed to do it.

I think I realize (though even in this I may be mistaken) that I am in part quarrelling with the very task you set yourself. Putting the title and the play together, I take it your theme is the importance of the undercurrents of life that never come to the surface. Therefore, if I am right, the absence of outward and visible drama is the very thing you set out to portray. But will you get even an audience of élite to see and accept this? Yes, one audience, two, three—but scarcely more. Perhaps thirty years hence audiences may be purged of all lust for the event, and may have their faculties sharpened and speeded-up to the sort of salmon-spearing by torch-light which the apprehension of your dialogue demands. But the theatre of thirty years hence leaves, and will leave, me strangely cold. I want another VOYSEY INHERITANCE and WASTE; and in this play you seem to be drifting away from, not towards, the theatre that is understanded by the people—even the fairly intelligent people. . . .

Believe me, I'm not trying to make my own dramatic diversions a law for you. In *my* theatre the bones show through everywhere, because I have mighty little flesh and blood to put on them. But if you *could* strike an average between my obviousness and your elusiveness, posterity might think less of you, but the contemporary theatre would profit more.

I am perfectly certain, in all sincerity, that I shall see much deeper and more clearly into the play when I have time to read it again. But I read it yesterday with all deliberation, and a play ought to get home the first time, however much further it may get home the second and subsequent times. It is true I thought comparatively little of Ibsen's greatest play —THE WILD DUCK—the first time I read it. That ought to make one humble.

Let us talk these things out when I come down. I don't offer you your revenge upon my improvisations, for no one realizes more clearly than I that there is no common measure between such plays as yours and my little melodramas.

Yours in affection and admiration,

W. A.

From HARLEY GRANVILLE-BARKER

COLYTON,
19.9.23

MY DEAR W. A.,

Well, of course the double theatre makes for actual economy in running a repertory—say 1½ times the receipts at one and a quarter to one and a third times the costs. This is the only important discovery I've made since we wrote the book.[1] My idea is that this competition[2] may "document" designs as the book has to a large extent "documented" the rest of the scheme. Hence the importance of this. . . . I fancy the more unusual task might make it *more* interesting to the architect. . . . Blessings on you.

About the Secret Goddess—I mean the Green Life:—I met a politician here the other day—or a "statesman" may be, as he has been in the Government; and he had got the hang of it all at one go—never asked whether it would "act" or anything: which pleased me.

H. G-B.

To HARLEY GRANVILLE-BARKER

20 *Septr.*, 1923

MY DEAR H. G-B.,

There's a lot in your views on the duplex theatre question. They shall be duly submitted to the Committee.[3] I fancy it is really a matter for architectural opinion—will the architects come forward? As you say, they might be tempted by the larger problem.

1 *Scheme and Estimates for a National Theatre.*
2 A proposed competition for a design for the National Theatre.
3 Of the Shakespeare Memorial National Theatre.

But what is this about the alleged "statesman"—a d--d diehard I hope—who showed his intelligence by never asking whether *The Secret Life* would act? If you are going to ignore that question, why do you write plays at all? Why subject yourself to the manifest and manifold drawbacks and trammels of the dramatic form, if you are writing for "the study"? That slip-shod, go-as-you-please thing, the novel, is the thing for the study, and all Downing Street shall not persuade me that it is a matter of indifference whether a play "would act". I daresay *The Secret Life* would act very well. I daresay that is just what it wants to clear up what I find cloudy in it. Of course your statesman might feel a delicacy in putting the question to *you*; but if he did not ask *himself* whether it would act, he was one of those drama-blind numskulls who are the curse of the British nation, and the real obstruction to the National Theatre. So there!

I attended last night a Green Room Club supper to Arliss—du Maurier in the chair—quite good fun.

Love to Helen from

Yours,

W. A.

From HARLEY GRANVILLE-BARKER

COLYTON,

22.9.23

No, no, no, no, no, no, no, no! What I meant to imply was that the statesman (none of your diehards; vice-chairman of the L. of N. Union) had found the S[ecret] L[ife] simple enough, possibly because his understanding of it was not balked by the recurrent question, "Will this act?" When I told him he need not expect to see it on the stage he said, indeed, "Why not? Couldn't you get it acted?" I answered, too optimistically: "Yes. I could get the actors, but not the audience that would listen."

I protest I never have—I cannot—write an unactable play; it would be against nature, against second nature anyhow: I act it as I write it. But there is no English company of actors so trained to interpret thought and the less crude emotions, nor, as a consequence—any selected audience interested in watching and listening to such things. But that, believe me, human fallibility apart—mine, to begin with—is the extent of the difficulty.

So blessings on thy still unfrosted pow
John Anderson, my Jo.

H. G-B.

[On January 12, 1924, the following document, apparently intended for the Press, found its way into the hands of the author of *The Green Goddess* :

"NOTICE

The Murray Family have given notice to the Heralds' Office of their intention to change their family motto: 'Uni æquus virtuti', and, in consequence of their experiences during an evening spent en masse last week at the St. James's Theatre, to adopt in future the motto

WHAUR'S YOUR WULLY SHAKESPEARE NOO?"

His reply, of even date, reads:]

My dear Murray,

Commendation from (the descendants and representatives of) Sir Hubert Stanley is praise indeed.

It *is* a better play than *Love's Labor's Lost*, isn't it? And my black man is at all events more chaste in his language than Othello.

When are you coming to lunch at the Reform?

Yours ever,

W. A.

To THE RIGHT HON. J. M. ROBERTSON

6 July, 1923

MY DEAR ROBERTSON,

I am not "oppugning" your position.[1] I quite agree with you as against Clutton-Brock. But I do think and have always thought, that the difficulties of the play have been enormously exaggerated. I don't in the least "puzzle over the fact that everybody else" has dwelt upon the difficulties. It arises simply from the no less manifest fact that three or four generations of critics have approached the play with microscopes, whereas Shakespeare did not even write for opera-glasses. The delay, you say, is "self-charged"—it is evident you have no personal experience of the procrastinator's psychology, else you would know that we unhappy mortals who put off from day to day our disagreeable duties (even when there is no particular danger about them) are constantly abusing ourselves in soliloquies, saying "O, what a rogue and peasant slave am I!" "How all occasions do inform against me!" and so forth and so on. Who is it that says, very pertinently, something to the effect that Hamlet's dilatoriness is denounced in no measured terms by college dons and country clerics, as though they themselves made nothing of murdering a stepfather or two?

You have got the argument of my lectures[2] wrong.

[1] As to *Hamlet*.

[2] *The Old Drama and the New.*

I am no champion of "realism" as an æsthetic doctrine. I am the last man to argue that all plays should be "realistic". What I do say, and what is a plain matter of fact, is that *realistic technical methods* —the use of prose, the avoidance of soliloquies and asides, the use of stable instead of constantly changing scenes, and so forth—have proved themselves to be applicable to the highest imaginative, and the most graceful fantastic, uses. You may have heard that I am an admirer of a playwright called Ibsen, whom only fools take for a "realist" in the narrow sense of the word, and whose ROSMERSHOLM, MASTER BUILDER, LITTLE EYOLF, etc. are in my judgment among the highest imaginative achievements of our time. Do I not praise warmly a great deal of Barrie's work, which is purely fantastic? Am I not an ardent admirer of J. M. Synge? The LOST LEADER, which you attack, is certainly not "realistic"—it is a romance, a denizen of that no-man's-land between the possible and the impossible which has always been beloved of poets and other feeble folk. I scarcely dare whisper in your ear the disgraceful secret that I have myself written two blank-verse plays! And my GREEN GODDESS, which I hope you will one day view without too much disgust, is not in the least realistic, but a mere picturesque melodrama.

Yours ever,

W. A.

From WINTHROP AMES

SOUTHAMPTON,
8 *Sept.* '23

Good-bye for a little while, dear W.A.

I can't sail without telling you that I quite know what torture it must be to sit at rehearsals and see point after point go by unrectified. Thank you for your sweet patience.

Now that is all over, I realize that I've had a very good time!

Good-bye.

WINTHROP AMES

To A. GOWANS WHYTE, ESQ.

27 Septr., 1924

DEAR MR. WHYTE,

I see that, in the last LITERARY GUIDE, you find "mysticism" in an old remark of mine about music. I wish very much that you and some other of our friends would reconsider your use of this word, which seems to me neither correct by the test of good usage, nor convenient from the point of view of common sense.

[A paragraph follows on the subject of music.]

But all this I say in parenthesis. What I really wish to ask you is: what meaning do you attach to the word "Mysticism"? In good literary usage, I take it, a mystic is a man who believes himself to have some special insight into the mystery of things, and to stand in some peculiarly intimate relation to it. He believes in intuitions in which the intellect has no part, and often in visions vouchsafed to him by God. Mysticism, as I understand it, is properly the state of mind characteristic of such a person; and nothing can be more foreign, more repellent or more ridiculous to me than such a state of mind. You, on the other hand, and some other contributors to the GUIDE, seem to regard as mysticism any admission that there *is* a mystery in existence; and this seems to me a most inconvenient and unilluminating use of the term. I cannot believe that any intelligent man can really hold that the blessed word "evolution" has solved the riddle of the universe and banished all mystery from life; yet that I think might be justly inferred from the general use of the term mysticism in the GUIDE. To me it seems that with every advance in our knowledge the mystery of existence deepens; if, indeed, there can be degrees in a mystery which is, from the outset, infinite. All the discoveries of science bring us no nearer to the whence, why and whither of life. They reveal the amazing and inconceivable complexity of the mechanism on which life is based and by which it is carried on; but they do not bring us one jot or tittle nearer an understanding of how matter ever came into existence or was endowed with what we call its "properties". Why we should hesitate to admit this perfectly obvious fact I totally fail to conceive. If the admission be mysticism, then assuredly I am a mystic; but so, I am quite sure, are all thinking men.

Yours sincerely,

W. A.

To CHARLES ARCHER

17 *Decr.*, 1924

MY DEAR C.,

It is my turn now[1]—it appears to-day that I shall have to undergo an operation for the removal of a tumour, they think connected with the kidney. . . . I have known, since Friday, that there was some suspicion of something of the sort, but could not take it very seriously, I felt so well. . . . However, I have had so long exemption from this sort of thing that I mustn't complain. . . . How serious the business

[1] His sister-in-law had just come safely through a severe operation.

is I don't know, but of course it can't be quite slight. The doctors agree that I am in good condition.

This means, of course, that you may enter upon your executorship sooner than we anticipated. I will do what I can to leave things in order: if I have time tonight, I shall put together all sorts of notes for you as to where things are to be found and so on: but with all the help I can give you, I don't envy you your job, especially when it comes to dealing with the income-tax fiends. . . .

Who do you think I have been lunching with today? None other than Kong Haakon den Syvende! . . . The King produced a very pleasant impression—no side at all, talked in quite a lively way with everybody in general, and indeed stayed so long that several people, I among the number, in defiance of etiquette, went away before him. The lunch was at 2.15 and, though I took a taxi home, I did not get here until nearly 5.

Din,

W. A.

To George Bernard Shaw

17 Decr., 1924

My dear G. B. S.,

Since I wrote you, I have learnt that I shall have to undergo an operation one of these days—I go into a nursing home tomorrow. I don't know that the operation is a very serious one, and as a matter of fact I feel as fit as a fiddle, so I suppose my chances are pretty good. Still, accidents will happen, and this episode gives me an excuse for saying, what I hope you don't doubt—namely, that though I may sometimes have played the part of the all-too candid mentor, I have never wavered in my admiration and affection for you, or ceased to feel that the Fates had treated me kindly in making me your contemporary and friend. I thank you from my heart for forty years of good comradeship.

Whatever happens, let it never be said that I did not move in good society—I lunched today with the King of Norway and Prince Olaf.

Very kind regards to Mrs. Shaw, and all good wishes for 1925.

Yours ever,
W. A.

Last Verses

(19*th Decr.*, 1924)

[This fragment of verse, scribbled in pencil on the night before the operation, to while away the tedium of waiting, takes on, in the light of the event, an almost ironical poignancy—for his week's struggle for life was not without suffering. But even had he known that Nature's "balsams anodyne" were in some measure to fail him, the knowledge would not have affected the spirit the verses breathe.]

Dread not, my soul, the ether's drowsy breath;
Quail not, my flesh, before the surgeon's knife;
Rather exult—"Where is thy sting, oh Death?
How blunted are thy ruthless fangs, oh Life!"

My brother-men I praise, those men divine
Who fought with Pain and hurled it back to Hell;
From Nature wrung her balsams anodyne,
And told the secrets God forgot to tell.

The Fates I thank, too, who delayed my birth
Till Pain was bridled for all time to come—
But oh! what anguish has the groaning earth
Endured for æons because God was dumb.

And oh! what spiritual bugbears—worse
Than torments of the flesh—haunted of yore
The men who, cowering 'neath a fancied curse,
Approached, as I do now, Death's mystic door.

If I with brow serene can face to-night
The Great Perhaps, whose praise shall be my theme?
The men's, God wot, who said: "Let there be light!"
Where God left Ignorance and Fear supreme. . . .

XIX

ONE WORD MORE

WILLIAM ARCHER's sudden death came with a shock of surprise to almost all who knew him (especially to those who had not had occasion to notice his sometimes sadly changed appearance), for in physique, as in character, there had always been about him a suggestion of

> the tower of strength
> Which stood foursquare to all the winds that blew.

The appreciative obituary notices naturally dwelt chiefly on his services to the drama as critic and translator. In so far as they dealt with his mental equipment in general, they found his strength to lie in the capacity for clear, logical thinking, and his weakness in a somewhat narrowly rationalistic habit of mind. Yet, if the reading of his mind which emerges from the foregoing pages is the true one, it seems clear that the chief of his cradle gifts was not logic, but keen, intuitive perception, not untouched with imagination.

The master qualities of his criticism were spontaneity and independence. From the beginning, we find him taking nothing in drama or in literature on trust. He cannot be infected with or awed into admiration or enjoyment by other men's judgments —not even when the judgment is that of all the world. "The one critical faculty on which I pride myself", he wrote, "is that of knowing when I am bored"; and he would have maintained that this faculty is a much rarer one than is commonly supposed, particularly in the theatre, where mass contagion acts most strongly and the "æsthetic attitudinizing" which he disliked is consequently most rife. Conversely, where he admired or enjoyed, his admiration or enjoyment was so keen that he could not, if he would, have refrained from giving it utterance, though by doing so he might incur the disesteem of the superfine on the one hand, or contumely from the Philistines on the other. He was, perhaps, sometimes a little impatient of the epithet "incorruptible" currently attached to his name—for he was apt to consider honesty in a critic, like chastity in a woman, a virtue which it is more seemly to take for granted—but he would have valued highly the praise of intellectual integrity, immunity to the subtler influences of tradition, fashion, and the popular breath; and this praise cannot be denied to him.

Will his critical writings, or the cream of them, live in literature, as some of Hazlitt's may be said to live? The question is one which would have given him little concern; for, provided that his criticism did its work in the present, he would have been well content that it should live in the future only in its effects. "Be helpful if you can, 'and let who will be clever,'" was the principle he followed, and, in pursuing it, he discarded, of set purpose, some of the ingredients which tend to make criticism permanently entertaining. Except when carried away by indignation, he eschewed invective, and, once he had outgrown the cruelty of youth, he was very sparing in the use of ridicule; for he knew that, in all but extreme cases, the bludgeon, as a critical weapon, does more harm than good, and that the barbs of raillery are apt to fester and rankle.

His criticism of contemporary dramatic work, moreover, was frankly opportunist; the standards he applied were not rigid and unalterable, but relative, varying with the general level of the drama, the class of play in question, and, to some extent, the capabilities of the author. More than once, in later years, he confesses to a feeling of amusement and surprise[1] on re-reading one or another of his notices of plays which had marked an advance in their day, but which the progress of the drama had now left far behind. But he is quite impenitent. "The worst sort of criticism", he said,[2] "is sterilizing criticism. I would rather see columns of fatuous gush about a foolish play, than a brilliant but discouraging and sterilizing criticism of a play with any germs of good in it." Certainly none of his critical work can be described as "fatuous gush", but it is clear that the opportunist criticism at which he aimed, being professedly of and for its age, must survive, if at all, rather in spite than in virtue of the critic's chosen method.

The opportunist method, moreover, which led him to assess the merits of dramatic work in some degree in relation to the powers of the author, sometimes tends to mislead as to his essential estimate of the value of a play. "His aim", as Sir Arthur Pinero says, "was to get the best out of a writer that was in him, and not to be satisfied till he got it." Therefore, the higher his estimate of a dramatist's powers, the more exigent was his critical attitude towards him, and the less likely was he to praise his work unreservedly. His "candid criticism", for instance, of Bernard Shaw's dramatic work (which at times, even to himself, must have seemed like an attempt to lay down a course for the wind that blows whither it listeth) was in reality one of the highest tributes ever paid to Mr. Shaw's genius. It was his unbounded belief in his

[1] See, for example, remarks on "The Lights o' London", p. 281 of *The Old Drama and the New*.

[2] Speech at O.P. Club dinner, 1902.

friend's intellectual power and potential capacity as a dramatist that prevented him from ever being wholly content with his achievement, remarkable as that was.

In the literature of the past, nobility and large humanity of feeling, clearness and harmony of form, melody of utterance, were the qualities that touched him most nearly. No sort of literature, save the "lubrique and adulterate", the pretentiously dull and the wilfully obscure, was alien to him; but of mere virtuosity, uninformed by humanity of outlook, his appreciation was comparatively cool. For Shakespeare his admiration, while remaining on the hither side of idolatry, deepened in intensity with every year of his later life.[1] And, after Shakespeare, it was the great humanists—Chaucer, Holberg, Scott, Mark Twain (the Mark Twain of *Huckleberry Finn*), above all Dickens—that commanded his warmest devotion. Hear him on Chaucer: "But if he seldom awes and never appals us, he has in the richest abundance every quality that can charm and refresh us, every gift that makes for health, sanity and 'gentilesse'. Matthew Arnold chose as his specimen line from Chaucer, 'O martyr souded in virginitee', and placed in the balance against it his favourite, 'In la sua voluntade e nostra pace'. It may be true that 'the accent of such verse is altogether beyond Chaucer's reach'; but there is another verse in the *Divina Commedia* at least equally impossible to his benign

[1] In 1923, feeling the inadequacy of the substitutes for the Burial Service used at the funerals of agnostics, he drafted a "Form of Farewell to the Dead". He probably failed to satisfy himself, as the draft remained unused among his papers. But it is noteworthy that Shakespearean passages bulk as largely in it as Biblical passages do in the Prayer Book ritual.

On the other hand, in the contents list of his handy-volume Shakespeare he has marked twenty plays as "clearly alive", fourteen as "clearly dead", and three as "doubtful".

and gracious spirit: 'E cortesia fu lui esser villano'."[1] His love for Dickens grew to be almost a cult; in his last years he was prone to think there must be something seriously amiss with any man who had not Dickens in his soul; and at the time of his death he was at work on an address, to be delivered to the Liverpool Dickens Society, under the title: "The Greatest Since Shakespeare."

In poetry his tastes were largely conditioned by the inherited passion for rhythm and melody which, as we have seen, so strongly influenced his criticism of acting. He had no technical understanding of music, and little sense for virtuosity of execution; but his emotional response to the soul of music (so to speak) was deeper than that of many adepts. His writings are full of expressions of the wonder and awe inspired in him by "that ultimate miracle of the human spirit—the creation of great music". "Music, in all its higher forms", he says, "may not unfitly be called the language of the gods—rather brainless and helpless gods, perhaps, but infinitely sympathetic and well-meaning." Again: "As I sit in my chair and silently think the notes ot 'Voi che sapete', I feel that if it were given to me to decide whether I would rather invent such another melody or carve another Venus of Milo, I should unhesitatingly choose the melody, and consider that I thereby conferred the greater benefaction on the world."[2]

Accordingly, in poetry, beauty of rhythm and melody of diction were for him more than half the battle, and harsh or crabbed work, however richly freighted with thought and imagination, was heavily handicapped by its form. He delighted in the com-

[1] "That atrocious line of Dante's" (*India and the Future*, p. 111).

[2] In 1923–24, he went to hear the piece *Lilac Time* seven or eight times—taking anyone he could lay hands on with him—purely for the sake of Schubert's melodies.

plicated organ-harmonies of Milton, but the occasional dissonances which that master permitted himself were to him not beauties but blemishes. Of the attempts made by Stephen Phillips and other poets to lend variety to their blank verse by imitating and exaggerating these disharmonies, he writes: "It is a question of physical sensation. When a line hurts me—yes, physically hurts me, like a fly in my eye or a nail in my shoe—I cannot help crying out, though Milton himself should rise from the grave to swear it is beautiful."

Yet rhythm and melody alone, uninformed by clear thought or potent imagination, would not serve. Swinburne's magnificent command of metre could not bribe the critic to give him a place among the great poets; and, of the unquestionably great, Shelley appealed to him less than many others, by reason of the cloudiness and insubstantiality of his thought.

In his work as publicist we find the same quality of penetration, and the same independence of judgment. "We see what we want to see", he himself has said, "and he who sees rightly is he whose will impels him to select the essential, the perdurable, the efficient element in things." That will was strong in him. Whether he is dealing with a specific inquiry, such as that into the case of Ferrer, or with large questions of education, economics, sociology, or politics, he invariably goes straight to the root of the matter in hand.[1] His insight may be that of an outsider—of the looker-on who proverbially sometimes

[1] Even in politics, of which, till late in life, he made no special study, he had a notable gift of prevision. "I am not afraid of Russia", he said in 1879, when "the Russian menace" was in most men's thoughts, "but I *am* afraid of Germany." The letter of 1887 to Mrs. Stevenson,

sees most of the game; he is doubtless often astray in detail; often, perhaps, he is "right too soon";[1] but always his concentration on essentials, his freshness of judgment, and the intensity of his will for the betterment of things, enable him to throw out fruitful suggestions, seed-corn for the harvests of the future.

On the other hand, these very qualities were closely bound up with his chief defect—a certain impatience with speculative opinion which seemed to him to hinder the march of progress. For the frailties of men and women he had almost infinite tolerance; for, by a failure in logic that made for happiness, he was apt, while giving them full credit for their virtues, to lay their faults to the account of destiny. But his tolerance did not always extend to opinion. "It seems to me the worst of impiety", he said, "to doubt that the maturity of the human race will be immeasurably greater and more splendid than the blind, boisterous, blundering childhood which we are now painfully outgrowing." Such impiety, and the action it inspires, he disliked with an almost theological vehemence, and his dislike sometimes blinded him to the necessity, in the conduct of human affairs, of the opportunism he professed in criticism.

Mr. Bernard Shaw has described Archer as "the victim of an unsleeping and incorrigible sense of humour"; and a French critic, M. Augustin Filon, writing[2] of his early work, says: "L'humeur, dont il est plein, coule à torrents sur tout ce qu'il écrit." Both statements are excessive, though they are much nearer the mark than the view of him as a

the note of December 1900 to the New York *World*, and the letter written August 6, 1914, two days after the outbreak of the war, are other instances of anticipations largely justified by the event.

[1] "Burke was often right", said Charles James Fox, "only he was right too soon."

[2] *Le Théâtre Anglais*, 1896.

humourless kill-joy. His sense of humour was keen and unsleeping indeed, and it served him well both in life and in his writing. It made him, when with his intimates, the best of good company, and enabled him to take such of the buffets of life as concerned only himself with smiling philosophy. But in his work it was his servant, not his master; as we have seen, he kept it in leash, as a rule, and more and more as time went on, where it would have been inconsistent with his purpose of encouragement and stimulation to give it free play. To the last, however, humour, though it cannot be said to "inundate" his work, nearly always makes itself felt as an undercurrent, and frequently comes to the surface, often in a little eddy of apt and witty illustration; as when he says (In Praise of the Scene-painter): "As for Shakespeare, his reason for not using scenery was precisely the same as his reason for not going to Stratford by the Great Western Railway"; of a distinguished Scottish actor's Lear, "it was Ben Nevis pretending to be Etna"; or of a lecture by the Chichele Professor of Military History which "assumed the sempiternity of war": "If, in the China of Charles Lamb's fantasy, a Professor of House-burning had been appointed, he probably would not, in his inaugural lecture, have inquired whether house-burning was the only possible means of obtaining roast pig. Yet we shall all agree, probably, that an investigation of other methods of achieving the desired end would, in fact, have been more profitable."

Of pure Scottish blood, and a lover of Scotland and things Scotch,[1] Archer had his full share of Scottish clannishness. Family affection played a great

[1] "The Thames is stately, and the Severn fair; but the Tay is nobler in my memory, and the Tweed sings for ever in my heart." (Address on "World-Citizenship" to the Edinburgh Philomathic Society, 1905.)

part in his life; blood with him ran thicker than water, even to distant degrees of cousinship. But from national prejudice he was quite free. His many friendships covered not only the British Isles, but also Western Europe and the United States. His many friendships—for one of the strangest misconceptions regarding him is that he was a man of few friends. On the contrary, few men have been more dependent for their happiness on friendship, or have had more, and more devoted, friends. It is significant that when, at eight years old, he made trial, for the first and last time, of the efficacy of prayer, the boon he asked was that a school-fellow with whom he had struck up an intense friendship might be allowed to spend a week-end at his home.[1] Throughout life we find him surrounded by friends, both men and women, helping and being helped by them—for, always saving his independence, he was as ready to accept help as to give it—and his sudden death clouded the sunshine in many homes. The notion that his friends were few was probably due to his many-sidedness, and to the reticence, partly a racial and family inheritance, partly a habit evolved in the hurly-burly of life as a shield for extreme sensitiveness, which figured in the imaginations of those who did not know him as "austerity". His closest intimates would sometimes be surprised by hearing of "old friends" of his of whose existence they had been quite unaware—not that he had concealed it of set purpose, but that, the two sets of friends belonging, as it were, to different spheres of interest, it simply had not occurred to him to mention one to the other.

Many children were numbered among his friends, for love for and sympathy with childhood was one of his most marked traits. It finds characteristic

[1] *William Archer as Rationalist*, pp. 154-155.

utterance in his defence of Ibsen against the charge of having unwarrantably massacred the innocents in his plays. "It is one of the almost intolerable and unforgivable facts of life", he writes,[1] "that children do die—that innocent, and beautiful, and happy creatures are, by a greater Dramatist than Henrik Ibsen, condemned to suffering and extinction." He loved to give children presents, but did not love to receive letters of thanks from them. "I protest against the children writing", he says in a letter to a friend. "I don't see why the pleasure of receiving presents should be embittered for children by the sense of the obligatory letter looming in the future."

Stevenson, taxed with "aggressive optimism", had retorted by calling Archer a pessimist. This, in a sense, he was; but it was with what may be called a deferred and conditional pessimism, which, except as it increased his tenderness towards human-kind, had little influence on conduct; because, having relation to the ultimate constitution of things, and not to temporary and corrigible evils, it was consistent with an intense meliorism of immediate outlook and practice. Except during a brief period of shaken health in youth, and perhaps occasionally in his last days when under the shadow of public cares and personal sorrow, he rarely knew what he calls "the pessimism of mood, which is, strictly speaking, no pessimism at all"—for, he adds, "the unhappy man (whether by constitution or by circumstance) has no right to call himself a pessimist. His evidence is tainted." Speaking, in "The Origin of Good", of the people who question the ultimate triumph of good, because its "magic" works so slowly, he says: "For my part, I feel no such impatience. What are fifty centuries in the process of the ages? They are but as

[1] "Death and Mr. Bernard Shaw", *Tribune*, July 14, 1906.

the turning of an hour-glass, which may have to be turned again and again before the shout of victory can go up all along the line. But the campaign is every day being better organized, under the guidance of a more and more efficient intelligence department. And the ultimate victory was certain from the moment that the idea of good, barbed and ineradicable, embedded itself in the brain-fibre of the race. Is this extravagant optimism? Scarcely: for, behind the attainment of the highest good, there will always remain the question whether the highest good is good enough. The dice are cogged in our favour; but does it follow that the game is worth the candle?" It is clear that he was inclined to expect an answer in the negative to the question, when, if ever, it should be answered. But meanwhile, being once for all in the game, he played it with enormous zest and enjoyment, and would have had all others do likewise.

That intuition was queen in his intellect, and the reasoning powers only her efficient handmaids, is shown by the fact that there was singularly little change throughout his life in his cherished ideals or in his views on fundamental matters. His tastes might, and did, change, but these stood fast. The necessity for a National Theatre in England, as we have seen, was impressed upon his mind when he was a boy of sixteen—he was still working for it up to the end of his life. The verses on war, written in 1878, might, so far as concerns their content, have been dated 1918. His attitude towards so-called spiritualistic phenomena was essentially the same when he wrote, on the last night of his fully conscious life, his letter on the subject to Middleton Murry, as it appears in his account of the American séance which he attended at the age of twenty;

though inquiries undertaken in his later years, with, perhaps, too assured a confidence in his ability to test, singlehanded, the baffling and often tainted evidence, had slightly deflected his view towards acceptance of the spiritistic theory of the phenomena.

Above all, the chief passion of his life—his pride in the history of man and faith in his destiny—runs through it from beginning to end, only deepening as the years go on. The boy who extolled in youthful verse the Pantheon of Humanity "On Yarra's Banks", is unmistakably the father of the man who, on his death-bed, celebrated with thanks and praise the victories of his fellow-men. From this faith sprang the religion which, reinforced and spiritualized by an ever-deepening sense of the wonder and awe of the universe, was a guide to him through life. That it did not lead him astray is shown by the witness of all who knew him. "He lived 'in simpleness and gentleness and honour and clean mirth' ", wrote the oldest of all his friends at his death. "I can think of nothing which better describes him than the words of Horace:

'Integer vitæ, scelerisque purus'."

And many others, both publicly and in private, have borne a like testimony.

Let us make full allowance for the element of friendly partiality in these utterances. Let us allow, too, that, in so far as they are justified, much of the credit should be given to inherited bias and home influences. None the less, the fact that his native tendencies were never warped or deflected in a life not without its testing temptations—that "his inborn note rang true unto the end"—must be attributed in the main to the religion he had evolved for himself —"the religion of loyalty to the heroic army in which we are enrolled".

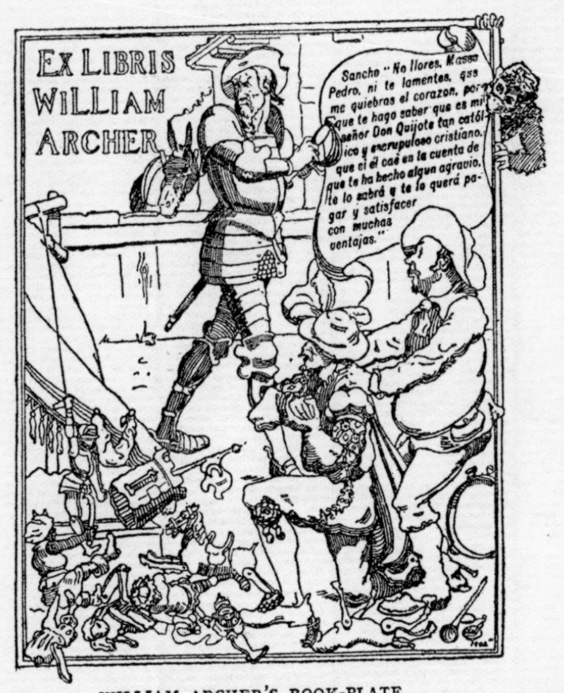

WILLIAM ARCHER'S BOOK-PLATE
(*By J. Waterston*)

BIBLIOGRAPHIC APPENDIX

A. ORIGINAL WORKS

1875

British Quarterly, April: Björnstjerne Björnson as Novelist.

1877

THE FASHIONABLE TRAGEDIAN: A CRITICISM. (With R. W. Lowe, illustrated by G. R. Halkett.) 1st edition, Thos Gray & Co., Edinburgh and Glasgow, pp. 24; 2nd edition, George Taylor, Ave Maria Lane, London, pp. 28.

1878

The Mirror of Literature, March 2: Henrik Ibsen's New Drama, "The Supports of Society".

1881

St. James's Magazine, January: Henrik Ibsen, I. February: Henrik Ibsen, II. March: Will the Drama Revive? July: Meiningen Realism. September: Is Othello a Fit Play for the Modern Stage? October: Dramatists of the Day: Mr. W. S. Gilbert, I. November: Mr. W. S. Gilbert, II.

1882

ENGLISH DRAMATISTS OF TODAY, pp. 387. Sampson Low & Co.

1883

HENRY IRVING, ACTOR AND MANAGER: A CRITICAL STUDY, pp. 108. Vellum Parchment Series, No. 3. 1st and 2nd edition, Field & Tuer, 1883. Another edition, Field & Tuer, 1884.

1884

The Theatre, March: Diderot's "Paradox of Acting". April: "Breaking a Butterfly" (criticism of).
Macmillan's Magazine. August: "Twelfth Night" at the Lyceum.
Gentleman's Magazine, November: The Local Colour of "Romeo and Juliet".
National Review, December: The Myths of "Romeo and Juliet".

1885

Time, January: Shakespeare and the Public.
Nineteenth Century, February: The Duties of Dramatic Critics.
Magazine of Art, March: The Marvellous Madonna: A Parable in Verse.
The Theatre, March: Un Monsieur de l'Orchestre. June: What Does the Public Want? July: Ophelia and Portia.
Fortnightly Review, September: Norway Today.
The Theatre, October: Miss Mary Anderson.
National Review, November: The Stage of Greater Britain.
Time, December: Robert Louis Stevenson: His Style and His Thought.
Theatre Annual, December: An Impossible Theatre.
Unwin's Annual, December: My Fascinating Friend (short story).

1886

About the Theatre: Essays and Studies, pp. 350. T. Fisher Unwin.

For *Actors and Actresses of Great Britain and the United States,* edited by Brander Matthews and Laurence Hutton, Cassell & Co., New York, 1886, etc., the following biographical sketches are by W. Archer:

Vol. I. Chas. Macklin, Tate Wilkinson.
Vol. II. Mrs. Jordan, Elliston.
Vol. III. Buckstone.
Vol. IV. Phelps.
Vol. V. Mr. and Mrs. Bancroft, Mr. and Mrs. Kendal.

Macmillan's Magazine, May: Criticism as an Inductive Science.
Fortnightly Review, June: A Plea for the Playwright.
National Review, August: A Well-graced Actress.

1887

The Drama, pp. 32 (contribution to Vol. II of *The Reign of Queen Victoria,* edited by T. Humphry Ward. Smith Elder & Co., 1887).
Time, March: Mr. and Mrs. Kendal.
Art Journal, April: The Drama in Pasteboard, I. May: The Drama in Pasteboard, II.
Nineteenth Century, October: "The Winter's Tale."
The Critic (New York)—November: Robert Louis Stevenson at "Skerryvore".

1888

Longman's Magazine, January: The Anatomy of Acting, I. February: The Anatomy of Acting, II. March: The Anatomy of Acting, III.

English Illustrated Magazine. December: *Macbeth* on the Stage. (With R. W. Lowe.)

A Sketch of the Dramatic Season in London (contributed to *The Dramatic Year, 1887–88, in the United States,* by E. Fuller. Sampson Low & Co., 1888).

MASKS OR FACES? A STUDY IN THE PSYCHOLOGY OF ACTING, pp. 232. Longmans & Co. 1888.

1889

Murray's Magazine, February: *Macbeth* and Common Sense.

Fortnightly Review, May: A Plea for an Endowed Theatre. July: Ibsen and English Criticism.

New Review, September: The Dying Drama.

1890

Time, January: Ibsen As He Is Translated.

Fortnightly Review, May: The Danish Drama of ToDay.

WILLIAM CHARLES MACREADY, pp. vii + 224 (Vol. I of *Eminent Actors.* Kegan Paul & Co., 1890–91, for which see list B, "Works Edited, etc.").

1891

Groombridge's Magazine, January: A Plea for the Unmusical.

Fortnightly Review, February: Critics "Over the Coals". September: A Pessimist Playwright (Maeterlinck). November: The Free Stage and the New Drama.

New Review, November: The Quintessence of Ibsenism: An Open Letter to George Bernard Shaw.

1892

Longman's Magazine, January: *King Henry VIII* on the Stage. (With R. W. Lowe.)

Fortnightly Review, February: The Stage and Literature.

Harper's Magazine, February: The Royal Danish Theatre.

New Review, March: The Drama. May: A Note on the Censorship.

Fortnightly Review, August: The Drama in the Doldrums.

New Review, August: The Drama.

1893

New Review, January: Webster, Lamb and Swinburne. March: The Drama.

English Illustrated Magazine, May: The Theatres.

New Review, July: The Drama.

Fortnightly Review, July: "The Mausoleum of Ibsen". August: Plays and Acting of the Season.

Die Zukunft, October: Das Ibsen-Mausoleum.

Free Review, November: The Ethics of Suicide.

Pall Mall Mazagine, December: Is the Theatre Growing Less Popular?

1894

THE THEATRICAL "WORLD" OF 1893, pp. xxxv + 307. Walter Scott, 1894.

New Review. January: French Plays and English Money. March: Hauptmann's *Hannele: A Dream Poem* (translation), I. April: Hauptmann's *Hannele: A Dream Poem* (translation), II.

Fortnightly Review, May: Some Recent Plays.

New Review, November: Maeterlinck's *Interior* (translation).

1895

THE THEATRICAL "WORLD" OF 1894, pp. xxx + 417. Walter Scott, 1895.

New Review, January: In Memoriam: R. L. S.

Contemporary Review, March: The County Council and the Music Halls.

Great Thoughts, April: The Drama.

New Review, June: The Criticism of Acting.

Fortnightly Review, August: Eleonora Duse.

1896

THE THEATRICAL "WORLD" OF 1895, pp. xxxv + 445. Walter Scott, 1896.

Cosmopolis. February: Dumas and the English Drama.

Fortnightly Review, February: George Henry Lewes and the Stage.

Magazine of Art, September: Art in the Theatre: The Limitations of Scenery.

1897

THE THEATRICAL "WORLD" OF 1896, pp. lviii + 423. Walter Scott, 1897.

Fortnightly Review, January (and *Living Age* (Boston), March): The Blight on the Drama.
Progressive Review, June: The Last Ibsen Play, *John Gabriel Borkman*: A Technical Study.
Cosmopolis, July: The Theatre in London.
Fortnightly Review, December: Shakespeare's Sonnets: The Case Against Southampton.

1898

THE THEATRICAL "WORLD" OF 1897, pp. xxvi + 452, Walter Scott, 1898.
Daily Chronicle, March 21: "To Henrik Ibsen".
Fortnightly Review, August: A Shropshire Poet.
Pall Mall Magazine, August: Recent American Verse. October, and *Living Age* (Boston), November: America and the English Language.

1899

STUDY AND STAGE: A YEAR-BOOK OF CRITICISM, pp. x + 250. Grant Richards, 1899.
Fortnightly Review, March: Pessimism and Tragedy. July: Plays of the Season.
The Bookman, July: Multiple Reviewing.
Pall Mall Magazine, August: America Today: I, North and South. September: America Today: II, The Republic and The Empire. October: The American Language. November: The American Stage, I. December: The American Stage, II.

1900

AMERICA TODAY: OBSERVATIONS AND REFLECTIONS, pp. viii + 215. Heinemann, 1900.
Pall Mall Magazine, January: The American Stage, III.
The Critic (New York), January: The Poetic Drama. February: Mr. Stephen Phillips's Play (Paolo and Francesca). May: The Celtic Drama. July: Puritanism and the Theatre. August: Quousque Tandem? (Criticism of Alfred Austin.) September: Maeterlinck and Mystery. November: "The Man That Corrupted Hadleyburg": A New Parable. December: The Scholiast on Tennyson.
Monthly Review. December: An Academy of the Dead.

1901

Pall Mall Magazine. January: The Drama: An Optimistic Survey.
The Student, January: Edinburgh Theatres Twenty-five Years Ago.
International Monthly, February: The Real Ibsen.
Monthly Review. November: A Plain Man's Politics.

1902

POETS OF THE YOUNGER GENERATION, pp. 565. John Lane, 1902.
Pall Mall Magazine. February: "Francesca da Rimini" on the Stage.
Monthly Review, July: The Case for National Theatres.
Pall Mall Magazine, November: The Theatrical Situation.

1903

Fortnightly Review. January: The Rise of Theatrical Subventions. April: A Critical Court of Honour.
Pall Mall Magazine. September: William Ernest Henley.
The Critic (New York), October: Mr. Shaw's Pom-Pom. November: England's Real Laureate.

1904

REAL CONVERSATIONS (reprinted from the *Pall Mall Magazine* for March to July, September and November, 1901; January, April, and June, 1902; February and November, 1903), pp. xi + 254. Heinemann, 1904.
Fortnightly Review, January: Ibsen's Apprenticeship.
The Critic (New York): January: Mother and Son.

1905

LET YOUTH BUT KNOW: A PLEA FOR REASON IN EDUCATION (reprinted from the *Westminster Gazette*), by "Kappa," pp. 256. Methuen & Co., 1905.
Living Age (Boston), February: The Sonnets of Shakespeare.
Cosmopolitan Review (New York), February: Henrik Ibsen: Philosopher or Poet?
Fortnightly Review, March (and *Living Age* (Boston), April): Ibsen in his Letters.
The Critic (New York), July: "The Gentle Elia."
Fortnightly Review. November: George Farquhar.

1906

The Critic (New York), January: English Estranged.
Monthly Review, June: Ibsen as I Knew Him.
The Critic (New York): July: Henrik Ibsen.
Fortnightly Review, July (and *Living Age* (Boston), September): Ibsen's Craftsmanship.
Fortnightly Review, October (and *Living Age* (Boston), November): The President's English: A Criticism and a Suggestion.

1907

A NATIONAL THEATRE: SCHEME AND ESTIMATES (with H. Granville-Barker), pp. xxxii + 177. Duckworth & Co., 1907.
Nineteenth Century. February: Ibsen's Imperialism.
Independent (New York), June: American Drama Revisited.
Albany Review, August: A Flag of Peace: A Plea for the United States of Europe.
The Tribune, October (and *Jahrbuch der Deutschen Shakespeare-Gesellschaft*, 1908): "The Fortune Theatre 1600," Reconstructed from the contract for the building preserved at Dulwich College (with W. H. Godfrey).

1908

Quarterly Review, April: THE ELIZABETHAN STAGE.
Fortnightly Review, October (and *Living Age* (Boston), November): Plays of the New Season.

1909

Pall Mall Magazine, July: The Panama Canal.
McClure's Magazine (New York), July: Black and White in the South. November: The New Drama and the New Theatre.
Fortnightly Review (and *The Forum* [New York]), December: From Ibsen's Workshop: the Genesis of his Dramas.

1910

THRO' AFRO-AMERICA: AN ENGLISH READING OF THE RACE-PROBLEM, pp. xvi + 295. Chapman & Hall, 1910.
The Forum (New York), March: The Comedies of Congreve, I April: The Comedies of Congreve, II.
Living Age (Boston), May: Björnstjerne Björnson.
Fortnightly Review, May (and *Living Age* (Boston), June): The American Cheap Magazine.

Fortnightly Review, October: The Theatrical Situation.

McClure's Magazine (New York), November: Life and Death of Ferrer, I. December : Life and Death of Ferrer, II.

1911

THE LIFE, TRIAL, AND DEATH OF FRANCISCO FERRER, pp. ix + 332. Chapman & Hall, 1911.

Living Age (Boston), January: The Theatrical Situation.

Fortnightly Review, February: The Portuguese Republic.

McClure's Magazine (New York), August: The Collapse of the Diaz Legend.

1912

ART AND THE COMMONWEAL (Conway Memorial Lecture), pp. 53. Watts & Co., 1912.

PLAYMAKING: A MANUAL OF CRAFTSMANSHIP, pp. x + 322. Chapman & Hall, 1912. Cheap edition, pp. xvi + 323, 1913. Third edition, pp. xv + 323, 1926.

THE GREAT ANALYSIS: A PLEA FOR A RATIONAL WORLD-ORDER (published anonymously, with Preface by Gilbert Murray), pp. xii + 122. Methuen & Co. 1912. Second edition (with new Preface by Gilbert Murray), pp. iv + 65. Williams & Norgate, 1931.

The Journal of English Studies. May: Some Obstacles to Spelling Reform.

1913

McClure's Magazine (New York), February: Will Japan Ever Fight the United States?

1914

McClure's Magazine (New York), January: The Making of Paris Fashions.

Fortnightly Review, July: Manners in India.

McClure's Magazine (New York), December: Can We Foretell the Future?, I.

1915

McClure's Magazine (New York), January: Can We Foretell the Future? II.

North American Review (New York), January: Fighting a Philosophy (also issued as one of the Oxford Pamphlets, pp. 26. Humphrey Milford, 1915).

Edinburgh Review, July: A German Naval Historian (Count Reventlow).

THE THIRTEEN DAYS: JULY 23–AUGUST 4, 1914: A CHRONICLE AND INTERPRETATION, pp. 244. Clarendon Press, Oxford, 1915.

1916

To Neutral Peace-Lovers: A Plea for Patience, pp. 20. Causton, 1916.

Colour-Blind Neutrality: An Open Letter to Dr. Georg Brandes, pp. 53. Hodder & Stoughton, 1916.

KNOWLEDGE AND CHARACTER: THE STRAIGHT ROAD IN EDUCATION, pp. 28. G. Allen & Unwin Ltd., 1916 (also in *Educational Review*, New York, September, 1916).

THE PLAYHOUSE (with W. J. Lawrence), pp. 28 (contribution to SHAKESPEARE'S ENGLAND, Vol. II. Clarendon Press, 1916).

Fortnightly Review, March: Fathers and Sons: Ibsen, Björnson, and the War. August (and *Living Age* (Boston), October): The Music Hall, Past and Future.

1917

INDIA AND THE FUTURE, pp. xxiv + 303. Hutchinson, 1917.

GOD AND MR. WELLS: A CRITICAL EXAMINATION OF "GOD THE INVISIBLE KING", pp. 126. Watts & Co., 1917.

501 *Gems of German Thought*, pp. xxviii + 120. T. Fisher Unwin, London; Doubleday Page & Co., New York, 1917.

Shirking the Issue: A Letter to Dr. Georg Brandes, pp. 9. Hodder & Stoughton, 1917.

Six of One and Half a Dozen of the Other: A Letter to Mr. L. Simon of The Hague, pp. 32. T. Fisher Unwin, 1917.

The Villain of the World-Tragedy: A Letter to Prof. Ulrich v. Wilamowitz-Moellendorf, pp. 40. T. Fisher Unwin, 1917.

1918

The Pirates' Progress: A Short History of the U-Boat, pp. vi + 96. Chatto & Windus, 1918.

The Peace President: A Brief Appreciation, pp. 125. Hutchinson, 1918.

Fortnightly Review, February (and *Living Age* (Boston), May): President Wilson as a Man of Letters.

Fortnightly Review, August: The Montague-Chelmsford Report. October: Obstacles to a League of Nations. December: The Two "Twelfth Nights".

1919

WAR IS WAR; or, The Germans in Belgium: A Drama of 1914, pp. x + 117. Duckworth & Co., London; Brentano's New York, 1919.

Fortnightly Review, June: On "Cutting" Shakespeare.

1920

Nineteenth Century, January: The Duchess of Malfi.

Harper's Magazine (New York), December: The Development of American Drama.

Edda (Copenhagen and Christiania): The True Greatness of Ibsen. (Lecture delivered at University College, London.)

1921

THE GREEN GODDESS: A Play in Four Acts, pp. 132. Knopf, New York, 1921. Re-issue, Heinemann, 1923.

Atlantic Monthly (Boston), June: The Great Stupidity.

Quarterly Review, July: The Germans in Belgium.

1922

Contemporary Review, June: Redistributing Shakespeare.

1923

THE OLD DRAMA AND THE NEW: An Essay in Revaluation, pp. viii + 396. Heinemann, 1923.

Norsk-Britisk Forenings Aarbok (Christiania): The Soul of Norway.

1924

Quarterly Review, April: Elizabethan Stage and Restoration Drama.

The Bookman, December (and *Living Age* (Boston), January, 1925): The Psychology of George Bernard Shaw.

POSTHUMOUS

1925

WILLIAM ARCHER AS RATIONALIST: *A Collection of his Heterodox Writings.* Edited, with Preface, by J. M. Robertson, pp. xxiii + 240. Watts & Co., 1925.

THE RELIGION OF TO-MORROW: *Correspondence between W. Archer and H. H. Powers*, pp. 72. Watts & Co., 1925.

Edda (Copenhagen): Ludvig Holberg: with special reference to *Jeppe paa Bjerget.* (Lecture delivered at Copenhagen, November, 1924.)

1927

THREE PLAYS (*Martha Washington, Beatriz-Juana, Lidia*) (with Foreword by George Bernard Shaw), pp. xl + 268. Constable, London; H. Holt, New York, 1927.

B. ENGLISH WORKS EDITED, ETC.

Anon.

Alan's Wife: A Dramatic Study. Introduction by W. Archer. Grein's Independent Theatre Series, 1893.

Congreve, W.

Plays. Introduction by W. Archer. American Book Co., New York, 1912. (Masterpieces of the English Drama.)

Dramatic Essays.

3 vols.: I, *Leigh Hunt*; II, *Wm. Hazlitt*; III, *John Forster and George Henry Lewes.* Selected and edited, with Notes and Introductions, by W. Archer and R. W. Lowe. (Introductions by W. Archer.) Walter Scott, 1894–96.

Eminent Actors.

3 vols: *Macready,* by W. Archer; *Betterton,* by R. W. Lowe; *Macklin,* by E. A. Parry. Edited by W. Archer. Kegan Paul & Co., 1890–91.

Farquhar, G.

Four Plays. Edited, with Introduction and Notes, by W. Archer. Mermaid Series. Fisher Unwin, 1906.

Gilbert, W. S.

A Stage Play. Introduction by W. Archer. New York, Columbia College Dramatic Museum Publications, 1916.

Lamb, Charles.

Essays of Elia. Introduction by W. Archer. Cassel's National Library, 1904.

Seeger, Alan.

Poems. Introduction by W. Archer. Constable & Co., 1917.

Shakespeare, W.

Works. Renaissance Edition. Vol. 34, *King Lear*, with Special Introduction by W. Archer. Harrap & Co., 1906.

Thackeray, W. M.

Works. Bedford Edition. Vol. VII, *The Newcomes*. Introduction by W. Archer. George D. Sproul, New York, 1906.

C. *FOREIGN WORKS TRANSLATED, EDITED, ETC.*

Brandes, G.

William Shakespeare: A Critical Study. Translated by W. Archer, etc. Heinemann, 1899.

Henrik Ibsen, Björnstjerne Björnson: Critical Studies. Translated and edited by W. Archer. Heinemann, 1899.

Brögger, W. C., and Rolfsen, N.

Fritjiof Nansen, 1861–1893. Translated by W. Archer. Longmans & Green, 1896.

Collin, Christen C.

The War against War and the Enforcement of Peace. Introduction by W. Archer. Macmillan & Co., 1917.

Hauptmann, Gerhart.

Hannele: A Dream Poem. Translated by W. Archer. Heinemann, 1894.

Ibsen, H.

Prose Dramas, 1 vol. (*Pillars of Society* (trans. W. Archer), *Ghosts, An Enemy of the People*). Camelot Classics Series, 1888.

A Doll's House. Translated by W. Archer. Fisher Unwin, 1889.

Prose Dramas, 1 vol. Edited by E. Gosse. (*A Doll's House, Pillars of Society, Ghosts*. Translated by W. Archer.) Lovell's Series of Foreign Literature. John W. Lovell & Co., New York, 1890.

Prose Dramas, 5 vols. Edited by W. Archer, Walter Scott, 1890–91.

Rosmersholm. Edited, with prefatory note, by W. Archer. Walter Scott, 1891.

Peer Gynt. Translated by W. and C. Archer. Walter Scott, 1892.

Ibsen, H.

The Master Builder. Translated by E. Gosse and W. Archer. Heinemann, 1893. (New Edition in the same year, with Appendix for Critics, "An Open Letter to Mr. A. B. Walkley", by W. Archer.)

Little Eyolf. Translated by W. Archer. Heinemann, London; Stone & Kimball, Chicago, 1895.

Little Eyolf. Avenue Edition. Heinemann, 1897.

John Gabriel Borkman. Translated by W. Archer. Heinemann, 1897.

When We Dead Awaken. Translated by W. Archer. Heinemann, 1900.

Prose Dramas. New and Revised Edition, 5 vols (*The League of Youth, Pillars of Society, A Doll's House, Ghosts, An Enemy of the People*). Edited by W. Archer. Walter Scott, 1900–01.

The Wild Duck. Edited by W. Archer. Walter Scott Publishing Co., 1905.

Rosmersholm. Edited, with Introduction, by W. Archer. Walter Scott Publishing Co., 1906.

The Lady from the Sea. Edited, with Introduction, by W. Archer. Walter Scott Publishing Co., 1906.

Collected Works. Copyright Edition (with Introductions), by W. Archer. 12 vols. Heinemann, London; Scribner's Sons, New York, 1906, etc.

Peer Gynt. Translated by W. and C. Archer. Chas. Scribner's Sons, New York, 1907.

The Pretenders. Translated by W. Archer, Heinemann, 1913.

Peer Gynt. Theatre Guild Edition. Charles Scribner's Sons, New York, 1923.

Ghosts. Translated by W. Archer. Eleanora Duse Series of Plays. Brentano's Ltd., 1924.

Kjelland, A. L.

Tales of Two Countries. Translated by W. Archer. Red Letter Stories. Osgood & Co., London; Harper & Bros., New York, 1891.

Maeterlinck, M.

Interior. Translated by W. Archer. (Modern Plays edition Johnson and Erichsen.) Duckworth & Co., 1899. Reissue in Cowan's International Library, 1908, and Cowan's Copyright Series, 1911.

Mantzius, K.

History of Theatrical Art, 6 vols. Introduction by W. Archer. Duckworth & Co., 1903, etc.

Nansen, F.

Eskimo Life. Translated by W. Archer. Longmans & Co., 1893.

Farthest North, 2 vols. Translation revised by W. Archer. A. Constable & Co., 1897.

INDEX

INDEX

[*N.B.—William Archer's principal works have been indexed under his name.*

Only plays with which W. A. was specially concerned, or which were of importance to his development or to the dramatic movement, have been indexed—see section "Plays."]